LITERARY PATRONAGE IN THE ENGLISH RENAISSANCE:
The Pembroke Family

Literary Patronage in the English Renaissance:
The Pembroke Family

MICHAEL BRENNAN

ROUTLEDGE
London and New York

First published in 1988 by
Routledge
11 New Fetter Lane, London EC4P 4EE

Published in the USA by
Routledge
in association with Routledge, Chapman & Hall, Inc.
29 West 35th Street, New York NY 10001

Printed in Great Britain
by Billing & Sons Limited, Worcester.

British Library Cataloguing in Publication Data

Brennan, Michael
    Literary patronage in the English
    Renaissance: the Pembroke family.
    1. Herbert. Family 2. English literature
    — Early modern, 1500–1700 3. Authors
    and patrons — England — History
    I. Title
    820'.79   PR428.P37

ISBN 0-415-00327-X

Library of Congress Cataloging-in-Publication Data

ISBN 0-415-00327-X

Contents

For My Parents

Tables

Acknowledgements

I have incurred many debts during the composition of this
book. The Earl of Pembroke generously allowed me access
to his archive room and private library at Wilton House. I
appreciated the assistance offered to me by his agent, Robin
Mellish, and by Penelope Rundle of the Wiltshire Records
Office. I am particularly indebted to the staff of the
Bodleian Library, Oxford; the Brotherton Library, Leeds; the
Folger Shakespeare Library, Washington; and the Huntington
Library, California.

I received much valuable advice and criticism during
the early stages of my research for this book from my
D.Phil. supervisors, Katherine Duncan-Jones and Penry
Williams; and from Professor Gerald Aylmer, Jean Bromley
(Jean Robertson), Martin Butler, Lord Dacre of Glanton
(Hugh Trevor-Roper), Professor Richard Griffiths, Margot
Heinemann, Lisa Jardine, David Maskell, David Norbrook,
Veronica Ortenberg, John Pitcher, John Rathmell and Kevin
Sharpe. Angela Archdale saved me much labour by entering
the final version of the typescript onto a word processor.
Further acknowledgements are contained in the notes. Any
errors which remain are mine alone.

1. Family Tree of the Herbert Family (simplified)

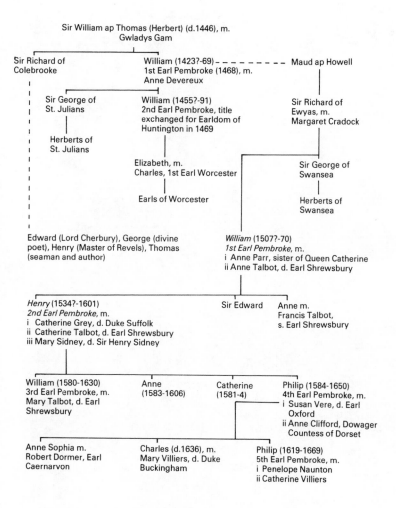

Sir William ap Thomas (Herbert) (d.1446), m. Gwladys Gam

Sir Richard of Colebrooke

William (1423?-69) – – – – – – – – – Maud ap Howell
1st Earl Pembroke (1468), m. Anne Devereux

Sir George of St. Julians

William (1455?-91) 2nd Earl Pembroke, title exchanged for Earldom of Huntington in 1469

Sir Richard of Ewyas, m. Margaret Cradock

Herberts of St. Julians

Elizabeth, m. Charles, 1st Earl Worcester

Sir George of Swansea

Earls of Worcester

Herberts of Swansea

Edward (Lord Cherbury), George (divine poet), Henry (Master of Revels), Thomas (seaman and author)

William (1507?-70) *1st Earl Pembroke*, m.
i Anne Parr, sister of Queen Catherine
ii Anne Talbot, d. Earl Shrewsbury

Henry (1534?-1601) *2nd Earl Pembroke*, m.
i Catherine Grey, d. Duke Suffolk
ii Catherine Talbot, d. Earl Shrewsbury
iii Mary Sidney, d. Sir Henry Sidney

Sir Edward

Anne m. Francis Talbot, s. Earl Shrewsbury

William (1580-1630) 3rd Earl Pembroke, m. Mary Talbot, d. Earl Shrewsbury

Anne (1583-1606)

Catherine (1581-4)

Philip (1584-1650) 4th Earl Pembroke, m.
i Susan Vere, d. Earl Oxford
ii Anne Clifford, Dowager Countess of Dorset

Anne Sophia m. Robert Dormer, Earl Caernarvon

Charles (d.1636), m. Mary Villiers, d. Duke Buckingham

Philip (1619-1669) 5th Earl Pembroke, m.
i Penelope Naunton
ii Catherine Villiers

Preface

The functioning and efficacy of literary patronage in most cultures owes much to tradition and the prevailing social and political conditions. Of no less importance are the characters and tastes of the patrons themselves, particularly how they choose to interpret their obligations of patronage. A state may make provision for the fostering of literature through sponsorship, cash grants or legislation, but it cannot readily bring forth influential men and women who are willing to give freely of their time, money and expertise in order to support literary talent. Such patrons must be allowed to develop and mature alongside the culture which they patronise.

This book traces the literary and artistic involvements of one specific group of noble patrons, the Herbert family, Earls of Pembroke, between 1550 and 1650. William Herbert (1507?-70), raised to the peerage as the first Earl of Pembroke in 1551, was a shrewd and calculating courtier who founded the family's fortunes and held important court positions under four successive monarchs. His son, Henry (1534?-1601), the second Earl, was a hard-working President of the Council in the Marches of Wales but is now remembered by literary historians chiefly because he took as his third wife in 1577 the most renowned Elizabethan patroness of literature, Mary Sidney (1561-1621), the sister of Sir Philip. Her two talented sons, William (1580-1630), the third Earl, and Philip (1584-1650), the fourth Earl, are best known as the 'incomparable pair of brethren' to whom the Shakespeare First Folio (1623) was dedicated.

The literary and personal relationship between Mary, Countess of Pembroke, and her brother, Philip, lies at the centre of this book. The Countess's commitment to literary endeavour provides an outstanding example of the contribution made by Tudor and Stuart aristocratic women to the development of English vernacular literature. In his turn, the popularity of Philip's writings played a major part in establishing the credibility of the vernacular among his contemporary writers. Much of Sidney's reputation as both a writer and patron was carefully formulated by his relatives and friends. Although after his death, the legend of Philip Sidney rapidly caught the imagination of the reading public, the leadership of English writers was a distinction which he had never really sought for himself while alive. In assessing Sidney's importance to the late-Elizabethan literary Renaissance, we must begin by recognising that his constant awareness of the tensions between the active and contemplative life - more specifically, the pursuit of political responsibility at court or pastoral retreat to his sister's country residence - was a vital factor in the formulation of his literary ambitions. During some of his most productive periods as a writer, Philip derived great support from his sister's sustained hospitality at Wilton House and her enthusiastic participation in his literary schemes. She also played a major role in fostering and preserving his posthumous literary reputation. It is, therefore, by viewing him as, to a great extent, a carefully groomed product of aristocratic family patronage, dispensed by the Dudleys and the Herberts, that we may effectively differentiate between the myth and the reality of his remarkable fame as a patron of letters.

In all, nearly 250 writers regaled the Herberts with an impressive array of dedications and literary tributes. Apart from immediate members of the royal family, only the Dudleys, Cecils and Howards received a comparable range of dedications. The Herberts attracted the attention of a host of minor authors as well as numerous writers of the first rank, including Sir Thomas Browne, George Chapman, Samuel Daniel, Michael Drayton, John Ford, Ben Jonson, Philip Massinger, Thomas Nashe, Edmund Spenser and many others. Members of a wide range of professions - stationers, academics, lawyers, churchmen, actors, civil servants, medical practitioners, soldiers and explorers - presented the Herberts with samples of their literary wares. There seem to have been few limits to the kinds of literature which might be addressed to them, as volumes on such diverse subjects as statecraft, natural and local history, mathematics, emblems, agriculture, needlework, astronomy, horsemanship and New World exploration came their way.

The sources used in this study of the Herbert family's literary patronage also require brief comment. As far as I have been able to ascertain, no senior member of the family before Sidney, sixteenth Earl of Pembroke (d.1969), made any systematic attempt to establish a family archive. Inevitably, time and indifference have worked their insidious effects. During the sixteenth and seventeenth centuries, the Earls of Pembroke lived at various times of the year in London, Wales and Wiltshire, an arrangement which served to disperse further the family's papers. Major losses from their libraries and picture collections have also been occasioned by the extravagance of various later Earls; and by two sales of books, pictures, furnishings and other collections after the deaths of Philip, the fourth Earl, in 1650, and Thomas, the eighth Earl, in 1733. More recently, the English system of estate duties has further ravaged the family's collections. Some of the most serious losses for this study were probably caused by a disastrous fire in the south wing of Wilton House in 1647 or 1648. Although the whole range was probably not gutted, a considerable amount of the contents was presumably lost. Valuable evidence was thereby almost certainly destroyed concerning the design of the house and its fittings, books, paintings and sculptures during the time of the first four Earls of Pembroke.

Yet, despite these losses, by drawing on material from a wide range of other sources, and recording the gaps which inevitably remain, it has proved possible to demonstrate the remarkable range of the Herberts' literary patronage before 1650. It has also become clear from these researches that a reconsideration of the characters and political skills of the first, third and fourth Earls of Pembroke is long overdue. William, the first Earl, has often been depicted as a violent opportunist who was perhaps the last illiterate privy councillor in England. In reality, he was one of the most able and successful of the Henrician courtiers who rose to prominence in the 1540s above the ruins of the English Church. His grandson, William, the third Earl, sometimes dismissed as a charming but ineffectual individual, the Hamlet of James's court according to one historian, has been no less misrepresented. Certainly, he was much loved and greatly respected by many of his contemporaries; but he was also a far more determined and effective politician than has generally been credited. His cultural tastes were wide-ranging. He penned amusing courtly verses, collected paintings and received an impressive array of literary dedications and tributes. As Lord Chamberlain (1615-26), he was in overall charge of court dramatics and, as Chancellor of Oxford University (1617-30), the friend of many academics and students. He was also an accomplished performer in court masques and tilts, and knew personally several of the most prominent poets, dramatists and actors of his generation, including almost certainly Shakespeare. Whether he was the mysterious young friend and/or 'Mr. W.H.' of the <u>Sonnets</u> is much less clear.

Preface

William's younger brother, Philip, the fourth Earl, was an erratic but fascinating individual. His character and public career encompassed a series of stark contradictions. He began James's reign as a royal favourite with great expectations, but by the time of Charles I's execution, he was one of the most reviled of all court figures. In conversation, as the mood took him, he could be charming and ingratiating, or, according to contemporary commentators, a violent and foul-mouthed boor. James, however, evidently rated him as a shrewd assessor of men; and he became a close personal friend of Charles, although he eventually chose to support the parliamentary cause in the mid-1640s. Philip Herbert's name prefaced many notable literary works, but he reputedly took pleasure in vaunting his preference for horses and dogs over poets and scholars. In sharp contrast to this apparent indifference towards books and learning, he was a prominent performer in court masques, a frequenter of plays, a discriminating collector of paintings, an employer of talented artists and the sponsor of ambitious architectural schemes. Of the first four Earls of Pembroke, Philip is the most intriguing, both as a patron and a personality. When placed within their political as well as their literary contexts, it becomes clear that the Herberts and their closest associates formed one of the most influential family groupings in terms of aristocratic patronage of the arts during the English Renaissance.

1 The Pursuit of Patronage

THE PURSUIT

Between 1550 and 1650, aristocratic literary patronage in England was a system invested with high hopes and golden images but, at the same time, expected to deliver practical benefits. The majority of writers who endeavoured to engage the sympathetic interest of noble patrons were seeking some form of protection, preferment or reward. The patron 'could give the poet not only money', Patricia Thomson explains, 'but a home, an education, work, protection against calumny or piracy and above all, the genuine encouragement which could only arise from a shared interest in literature.'[1] The key to success frequently lay in securing the personal support of an individual who was willing to act as a sponsor, employer, defender, literary critic or even as a friend, thus enabling the writer to rise above the shoals of other aspiring courtiers who could also deftly wield a pen. By way of introduction to the Herberts' literary patronage, this chapter investigates more generally how and why writers went about seeking patronage from members of the English nobility, and with what results, during the time of the first four Earls of Pembroke.

When Francis Davison, the ambitious son of Queen Elizabeth's Principal Secretary, William Davison, edited the printed verse miscellany, A Poetical Rhapsody (1602), a court commentator, John Chamberlain, remarked drily: 'It seems young Davison means to take another course and turn poet, for he hath lately set out certain sonnets and epigrams.'[2] His edition was regarded by those familiar with the ways of the court as a bold attempt to use literature to attract the interest of influential patrons. In the days before standardised school examinations, civil service entrance

procedures and systems of paper qualifications, achievements in poetry, prose, languages and rhetoric could provide
visible evidence of imaginative talents and analytic skills;
qualities of distinct advantage to those who sought employment in either a literary or courtly capacity.

Certain kinds of literary skills were regarded as
recognised currency at court. Plays and poems were an
essential ingredient of many forms of courtly ceremonials,
such as accession-day celebrations, entertainments in
honour of visiting dignitaries and seasonal revels. Young
men, fresh from the universities, tried their hand at translating important works from the classics. More experienced
courtiers penned tracts on political and religious problems,
educational principles and provincial issues. Clergymen
sought out stationers to print the texts of edifying sermons
delivered before members of the royal family and aristocracy. Soldiers put their manuals of military tactics into
circulation at court and doctors dedicated medical treatises
to their noble patients. Even those who were devoted more
to Mammon than the Muses, such as merchant-venturers,
found time to use the linguistic skills which they had
acquired through business to translate popular literary works
from continental languages. Numerous other pen-pushers,
mindful of court fashions, imitated the example of Sir
Thomas Wyatt, the Earl of Surrey, Sir Philip Sidney and
other high-ranking courtiers who regarded literary effusions
as one of their most favoured forms of private and
communal relaxation.

Like any other aspiring courtier, the ambitious writer
was expected to keep a sharp eye out for prospective
patrons, calculating from whom he might gain the most
advantage. He needed to be able to form a rapid assessment
of a great noble's wealth, influence and possible response to
an unsolicited approach. The young John Donne, already
weary of court life, savagely mocked this kind of blatant
opportunism:

> Oh monstrous, superstitious puritan,
> Of refined manners, yet ceremonial man,
> That when thou meet'st one, with inquiring eyes
> Dost search, and like a needy broker prize
> The silk, and gold he wears, and to that rate
> So high or low, dost raise thy formal hat.[3]

There was a skill, however, in seeking literary patronage

which went far beyond the mere cultivation of exaggerated courtesy or the scribbling of a flattering dedication. The role of the patronage-hunter at court required patience, persistence and determination. It was also beneficial, before offering a dedication, for a writer to form an estimation of his patron's literary interests. Francis Bacon made the obvious but crucial point that he always took great care when addressing dedications, 'to choose those that I hold most fit for the argument'.[4] Time and occasion, of course, did not always allow a writer to gain a detailed knowledge of a prospective patron's tastes. But it was imperative, in such a frenetic and unpredictable environment as the court, for a writer to find for himself openings which might be exploited and patrons whose sympathies might be aroused.

Once a writer had set his sights upon a patron, one of the most convenient means of introducing himself was the dedicatory or panegyric address, frequently used to preface literary works in both manuscript and print. Such tributes, designed as graceful and attractive literary artefacts in themselves, were open to a variety of interpretations. They could be read as personal compliments to the recipient or as advertisements of their authors' literary skills and career ambitions. In printed works, multiple dedications were common and generalised panegyrics were sometimes printed with a blank space left for a suitable name to be entered at a later stage.[5] Many dedications were couched in a markedly stylised language of extreme devotion. Indeed, in dedicating the First Folio of Shakespeare's plays to William and Philip Herbert, the actors John Heminge and Henry Condell remarked: 'we have justly observed, no man to come near your L.L. but with a kind of religious address.' There is still perhaps a tendency for a modern reader's eyes to glaze over when faced with these kinds of dedicatory tributes; and it is tempting to dismiss them as little more than sycophantic ephemera. No doubt, a fawning Uriah Heep figure sometimes did lurk, pen in hand, behind a dedicatory façade of carefully chosen insincerities. But more frequently, the lavish vocabulary and archly-rhetorical formulation of dedicatory paneygrics were regarded as a form of ritualised tribute in which the author was expected to cultivate a deliberately heightened style.

Despite this desire to endow a patron's reputation with images of excellence, writers were also practical, calculating creatures who tended to categorise patrons according to their influence and utility. If a noble's

3

fortunes were seen to be taking a downward turn, few writers felt any compunction in abandoning him, in the hope that a more profitable connection might be found. When in 1615 Robert Carr (or Ker), Earl of Somerset (c. 1587-1645), fell from favour on account of his indirect involvement in the murder of Sir Thomas Overbury, his appeal to the majority of writers at court evaporated almost overnight. In less fraught circumstances, changes of patron were commonplace. Francis Bacon dedicated the 1597 edition of his Essays to his brother Anthony; the 1612 edition to his friend, Sir John Constable; and that of 1625 to the Duke of Buckingham.[6] Thomas Hastler, clearly no great diplomat, did not hesitate to inform his Baronet patron, Sir Francis Wortley, that if his book had been more important, he would have addressed it to the third Earl of Pembroke.[7] Inevitably, even a courtier of Pembroke's distinction occasionally lost out in this relentless pursuit of pre-eminence. In 1621 William Slatyer dismissed the attractions of 'Pembroke's ancient style', in favour of addressing his history of Britain to the Duke of Buckingham, whom he thought could more readily give his muse, 'free access' unto King James's 'good grace'.[8] Within the continually changing hierarchies of the royal court, the patron-client relationship was rarely a permanent or exclusive one. Ever hopeful of advancement or favour, suitors frequently paid their respects to several important personages at once. Taking this approach even further, Henry Lok addressed sixty individuals in as many commendatory sonnets at the end of his collection of divine poetry, Ecclesiastes (1597). Geoffrey Whitney's A Choice of Emblems (1586) contained over ninety different dedicatory addresses.[9]

THE PATRONS

Writers tended in their compositions to envisage the whole environment of court life as a heightened and intoxicating world: 'At court the spring already advanced is', Donne quipped, 'The sun stays longer up.'[10] The attendance of a large number of wealthy and influential patrons at court, including aristocrats, leading churchmen, military commanders and distinguished members of the professions, ensured that it became the goal of a host of lesser mortals who hoped to engage their interest and favour. Although the disconcerting thought that, 'courtiers as the tide do rise and fall', gnawed at the minds of many writers, few would have denied that the court still managed to retain an almost hypnotic quality:

> Where all the bravery that eye may see,
> And all the happiness that heart desire,
> Is to be found.[11]

The King or Queen was envisaged as the focus of court life and the ultimate source of all beneficence and rewards dispensed by court patrons. Writers sought to reassure themselves that the arts were esteemed at court by praising the sovereign's own cultural achievements: Henry VIII's enthusiasm for music and poetry, Edward VI's boyish erudition, Elizabeth's facility with languages, James's theological scholarship, and Charles's exquisite tastes in the visual arts. Although the sovereign was of considerable importance as a figurehead, court writers held few expectations of personal rewards from the King or Queen, in return for their dedicatory panegyrics. In 1635, after nearly twenty-five years of publication, George Wither lamented:

> So, I myself, (although not out of pride,
> As many think it) have so much relied
> Upon the royal gift, neglecting so
> To fortify the same, as other do
> By making friends.[12]

The direct recipients of royal patronage were mainly the aristocracy and court office-holders, who received, at the discretion of their sovereign, cash rewards, land or property, grants of monopolies and preferment to lucrative positions. As far as common courtiers and writers were concerned, there was usually little chance of gaining any direct benefits from a well-turned royal panegyric. Besides, it was exceptionally difficult, even for a favoured courtier, to catch his sovereign's eye. Determined to impress Queen Elizabeth, Sir John Harington was reduced to such stratagems as leaving a copy of his epigram, 'in praise of her reading', 'behind her cushion at my departing from her presence'.[13]

The best a writer could usually hope for by way of royal reward was some kind of pension in recognition of services to the court. Spenser was awarded £50 a year after the publication of <u>The Faerie Queene</u>, and Jonson received a pension of 100 marks a year (about £30). However, the fact that the abysmal versifier Thomas Churchyard was another recipient of a royal pension suggests that such rewards were sometimes granted simply to acknowledge sheer length of court service, rather than only as a tribute to outstanding literary achievement. Generally, royal patrons considered themselves neither obliged nor expected to dispense rewards to writers out of their own funds.[14] There was one notable exception - King James's precocious eldest son, Prince Henry - but the primary obligation of a sovereign to the literary patronage system was to act not as a dispenser of rewards but as an example of personal excellence and a pattern of liberality. Donne carefully explained this divinely-ordained duty of the sovereign:

> Princes animate,
> Not only all their house, but all their State.
> Let no man think, because he is full, he hath all.
> Kings (as their pattern, God) are liberal
> Not only in fullness, but capacity,
> Enlarging narrow men, to feel and see,
> And comprehend the blessings they bestow.[15]

The ideal royal patron of literature, as in so many other matters of courtier-management, was Queen Elizabeth. A well educated and intelligent woman, she kept a tight hold on her own purse-strings and sensibly left the administration of the literary patronage system to her appointed delegates, the aristocracy and court office-holders.

Eleanor Rosenberg's book, Leicester Patron of Letters (1955), was the first detailed study of Elizabethan literary patronage to set out clearly the theory that the Queen, 'delegated to her nobles the responsibility for encouraging authors and scholars'. Rosenberg emphasised Elizabeth's political intentions in formulating close links between power and patronage in the minds of her aristocracy:

> In thus assigning the patron's responsibility almost entirely to the men of wealth and power who formed her privy council and her court, as in the delegation of governmental functions, Elizabeth was merely carrying to a logical conclusion the policy of centralization and delegation of authority which she had inherited from her father.[16]

Adopting such a policy, she argued, became for the Queen

an effective means of controlling her court office holders. However, Rosenberg's use of the word 'delegation' in this context is misleading. As in all other forms of clientage, the crucial bond between the sovereign and a high-ranking patron was primarily one of 'dependence' rather than 'delegation'. Patronage was thereby envisaged as a means of unifying the whole nation. 'Functioning informally within the constitutional elements of the state', Linda Levy Peck explains, 'patronage provided both the essential means by which Renaissance rulers gained the allegiance of the politically important and the primary method by which they integrated regional governments and elites into the state.'[17]

At court, where so much intense concentration was brought to bear upon the personality of the sovereign, royal tastes could exercise a marked influence over the cultural pursuits of the aristocracy. When, for example, it became clear in the mid-1560s that Queen Elizabeth wished to foster high educational standards among the ruling classes, scholarly clients hastened to dedicate suitably learned texts to their aristocratic patrons. Similarly, when Charles I was building up his extensive royal picture collection, members of the aristocracy followed suit, finances permitting (or, in several cases, even when they did not). The court was a place, 'where all affections do assent/Unto the King's'; and it was thought advantageous for the fashionable aristocratic patron to be seen keeping in step with royal preferences.[18]

In addition to acting as mirrors of monarchic taste, some members of the nobility fostered their own scholarly interests through personal dealings with men of letters. William Blount, Lord Mountjoy (d. 1534); William Cecil, Lord Burghley (1520-98); Sir Francis Walsingham (1536-90); and Thomas Howard, Earl of Arundel (1585-1646), took great pleasure in the company of scholars and writers. Another breed of noble patron, represented by Thomas Sackville, Lord Buckhurst (c. 1527/36-1608); Edward de Vere, Earl of Oxford (1550-1604); Robert Devereux, Earl of Essex (1566-1601); and Sir Philip Sidney (1554-86), were, to varying levels, endowed with the spark of literary creativity, thereby earning the intense admiration of other authors for practising the skills which they patronised. In sharp contrast, numerous prominent courtiers, including Sir Christopher Hatton (1540-91), and George Villiers, Duke of Buckingham (1592-1628), were generously praised by writers in dedicatory tributes but appear to have been either unable or unwilling to develop any significant interest in literature.

7

The Pursuit of Patronage

Of no less importance were the high-ranking literary patronesses of the period. Social and educational conditions dictated that all the major works of the English literary Renaissance were written by men. But these same authors were frequently heavily dependent upon women for their literary motivation and encouragement. Many Tudor and Stuart poets - and this will be a recurrent theme in later pages - would have been bereft of much of their inspiration and support if women had not been ready to assume for them the various identities of patroness, sponsor, literary adviser, wife, friend and mistress. The pattern for this extensive female involvement in literature and scholarship was firmly set by members of the royal family. During the early Tudor period, Henry VII's mother, Margaret Beaufort, Dowager Countess of Richmond and Derby (c. 1443-1509), and two of Henry VIII's Queens, Catherine of Aragon (d. 1536) and Catherine Parr (1512-48), had been firmly committed to the furtherance of classical and scriptural learning. Queen Elizabeth (1533-1603), an able scholar and linguist in her own right, built upon their example to revitalise the whole mythology of the royal court as a source of inspiration for writers. In the seventeenth century, Queen Anne (1574-1619) was an enthusiastic sponsor of court masques, and Queen Henrietta Maria (1609-69) immersed herself in drama, recusant literature and works written in her native French tongue.

This prolonged royal example of female patronage of literature was eagerly imitated by several generations of aristocratic women. William Cecil's formidably erudite second wife, Mildred Cooke (d. 1589), was easily a match in learning for her spouse and the distinguished scholars who frequented Cecil House in Westminster. Motivated by political designs, Anne Seymour, Duchess of Somerset (d. 1587), collaborated in her husband's sponsorship of Protestant polemic. Many more, such as Lucy Russell, Countess of Bedford (d. 1627), and Christiana Cavendish, Countess of Devonshire (d. 1675), were prized by writers for their genuine appreciation of literary talent. Others, such as Lady Mary Wroth (c. 1587-1651), and Lady Elizabeth Carey (fl. 1602-5), the wife of Henry, Viscount Falkland, earned for themselves considerable contemporary reputations as writers. Throughout the Tudor and Stuart periods, a significant number of high-ranking women possessed the inclination, education, taste and time to cultivate the literary arts in ways which were often beyond the ability of their male relatives.

Although aristocratic patrons and patronesses had many motives for involving themselves in literature, it is possible to identify two distinct attitudes which frequently guided their dealings with writers. The first was dependent upon the medieval and renaissance tradition of 'noblesse oblige', in which a healthy relationship between the arts and the nobility was both expected and widely admired. Edmund Spenser explained how the court poet could both nourish and preserve nobility:

> The sacred Muses have made always claim
> To be the nurses of nobility,
> And registers of everlasting fame,
> To all that arms profess and chivalry.

This relationship between poets and patrons was envisaged as a central tenet of the courtly code. Poets, Spenser suggested, were able to endow great figures with fame and immortality through the priceless gift of literary praise. In return for this glorification, members of the nobility were expected to support generously those who thus enabled them to transcend time and death:

> Then by like right the noble progeny,
> Which them succeed in fame and worth, are tied
> T'embrace the service of sweet Poetry
> By whose endeavours they are glorified,
> And eke from all, of whom it is envied,
> To patronise the author of their praise,
> Which gives them life, that else would soon have died,
> And crowns their ashes with immortal bays.[19]

In conjunction with this courtly interpretation of the aristocracy's role in literature, a second distinct approach to patronage was established in England during the 1530s, virtually single-handedly, by Henry VIII's Vice-Gerent of the Church, Thomas Cromwell (d. 1540). Cromwell sought, with considerable success, to harness scholarship to religious policy by manipulating the skills of writers in a polemical justification of his reorganisation of the English Church. This form of patronage attracted men of letters who either possessed an ardent commitment to the causes which their tracts supported, or those who simply sought to use this opportunity of sponsorship as a means of ingratiating themselves with a powerful patron. Cromwell was most concerned with the rapid and effective production of literary propaganda. At the same time, however, this kind of utilitarian approach to literature helped to foster among the aristocracy a heightened awareness of the ability of the scholar, the historian, the antiquary, and even the poet, to occupy the roles of moral commentator and governmental adviser.

More often than not, Tudor and Stuart patrons brought a blend of these two approaches to their involvements with literature. In addition to his undoubted skills as a manipulator of propagandists, Thomas Cromwell was a largely self-taught scholar, widely read and an able linguist. Conversely, some of those who combined the roles of patron and poet, such as Sir Philip Sidney and the Earl of Oxford, were prepared, if so required, to use literature for personal ends. Sidney wrote and circulated at court a Discourse on Irish Affairs (1577), vindicating his father's administration of land taxes in Ireland; and in 1585 compiled a spirited defence of the reputation of his uncle, the Earl of Leicester. After incurring the displeasure of the Queen during the early-1580s for marrying without her permission, Oxford proved himself adept at exploiting court plays performed by his own actors as a means of easing himself back into royal favour.[20] Other members of the aristocracy with genuine literary interests, such as Robert Dudley, Earl of Leicester (c. 1532-88), and his brother Ambrose, Earl of Warwick (c. 1528-90), took it for granted that their patronage of letters would include the sponsorship of polemical writings.

To soften this sharp division between the courtly and the utilitarian approach to literary patronage, Tudor and Stuart writers sought to depict the act of literary dedication as an expression of a reciprocal relationship between a client and his patron. The translator and soldier, William Blandie, reminded the Earl of Leicester:

> neither Princes may live clear and known to posterity without the pen and helping hand of learneds' Art: neither men excelling in learning, would be either in life reputed or spoken of after death, without the countenance, defence, and patronage of noble Peers.[21]

Such a view tactfully left unspoken the realisation that for many noble patrons, Leicester included, the call of posterity was often a distinctly secondary consideration, as compared with their appreciation of literary skills as a powerful tool through which to influence public opinion.

REWARDS AND DISAPPOINTMENTS

Clearly, it is often difficult to sift out the purely literary influences from other factors which may have contributed to the advancement of any particular court writer. Nevertheless, there is little reason to doubt that literature played some part in helping Edmund Spenser to become a secretary and civil servant, Christopher Marlowe a political agent, Sir John Davies and Abraham Fraunce court lawyers, Josuah Sylvester a Groom of the Chamber, and Giles Fletcher an Ambassador to Moscow. Appointments gained through court patronage provided writers with a welcome source of relatively regular income, enabling them either to substitute their literary interests with more remunerative pursuits or, if their commitment to letters was genuine, to dedicate more time to their compositions. Another select group were honoured with posts or titles at court which did not necessarily provide them with an ample living but publicly acknowledged the esteem in which their literary talents were held: Samuel Daniel became licenser to Queen Anne's Revels, James Howell was appointed Historiographer Royal and Ben Jonson was recognised as the King's Poet.[22]

There were also numerous positions in a nobleman's household, such as those of chaplain, physician, secretary, tutor and man-servant, which could be held by men with literary interests. These posts were highly prized as status symbols, even though their occupants had no guarantee of tenure. An attachment to a nobleman's establishment supplied the basic necessities of accommodation and daily sustenance but, in other respects, the terms of employment were often drawn up informally. Clearly, such a system lay wide-open to abuse; and there are several instances of retainers and personal servants complaining to influential figures about the behaviour of their aristocratic employers.[23] Many of the writers who dedicated literary works to the Herberts had extensive experience of aristocratic service, although not always in Herbert family households. John Caius (or Keys), John Jones, Thomas Moffet and Alexander Read were family physicians, treating various noblemen who sometimes acted as their literary patrons. Michael Florio, Samuel Daniel, Michael Drayton and Henry Peacham all held appointments as family tutors. Gervase Babington and Henry Parry served as chaplains at the Countess of Pembroke's country residence, Wilton House; while many other clergymen-authors, such as Robert Bruen and John Thornborough, occupied Herbert family livings.

The stability and continuity of aristocratic family patronage, compared to that of the court, was clearly demonstrated by the lasting relationships which sometimes developed between respective generations of retainers and their employers. Philip Massinger, the son of the second Earl of Pembroke's secretary, proudly dedicated his play, The Bond-man (1624), to the fourth Earl, in order to 'make tender of all duties, and service, to the noble family of the Herberts, descended to me as an inheritance from my dead father, Arthur Massinger. Many years he happily spent in the service of your honourable house, and died a servant to it.' Similarly, the Markham brothers dedicated some of their compositions to the Herberts because of the intimacy which had long existed between the two families. When he addressed the sixth book of his Cavelarice (1607) to Philip Herbert, Gervase gratefully recalled the generosity which the first and second Earls of Pembroke had shown to his family. His brother, Francis was content simply to mention in The Book of Honour (1625) that he was, 'at this present one of the oldest servants of the House of Wilton'. Several other writers, unable to point to fathers or grandfathers who had enjoyed Pembroke patronage, took refuge in claiming that their respective ancestors had once been associated in the dim and distant past. Rowland Vaughan and John Dowle both resorted to this tactic in their dedications; and it was a popular belief in John Donne's family that one of his ancestors had battled alongside one of the Herberts' ancestors.[24] These writers may have been firmly convinced of the truth of such links which had the added charm of being very difficult, if not impossible, to check.

In addition to preferment, dedications frequently solicited from their recipients various kinds of protection. In the most extreme cases, the sympathetic interest of a powerful patron could determine matters of personal safety. The poets William Hunnis and George Wither, for example, were probably reprieved from imprisonment by the respective efforts of the first and third Earls of Pembroke. When Ben Jonson was incarcerated in 1605 for his part in the composition of Eastward Ho!, he wrote letters to the third Earl and his brother, Philip, eloquently pleading for their assistance in obtaining his release. Requests also abounded in dedications for protection from the barbs of literary criticism, delivered by 'curious censurers' and the 'tongues and pens of calumniators'. It is difficult to imagine, however, how a patron could have been expected to silence such critics; and it is probable that these requests were intended not to be interpreted literally but rather taken as tokens of allegiance.

Most writers also hoped that a dedication to a prominent individual would elicit some form of monetary reward. There is little possibility, however, of providing an overall analysis of financial benefits gained from literary patronage since only fragmentary records have survived. Very occasionally, a considerable sum seems to have been involved. George Chapman claimed to have been promised £300 by Prince Henry on the completion of his Homer translations, but failed to receive anything from the Prince's executors after his death. Bitterly lamenting that, 'Homer, no patron found; nor Chapman friend', he resentfully pointed out:

> Not thy thrice sacred will
> Sign'd with thy death; moves any to fulfil
> Thy just bequests to me.

More commonly, much lesser amounts were offered, and £2 to £3 has generally been regarded as the upper limits of what an author might expect to gain from a well-aimed dedication.[25]

The only known document providing specific figures of earnings from literary dedications during this period is a manuscript entitled, 'Eupolemia or good warfare against Satan the Devil', by Richard Robinson, a minor court writer and freedman of the Leathersellers' Company.[26] The 'Eupolemia' includes a list of 'all his printed works', published between 1576 and 1599, along with licensing details and a record of the responses elicited by his dedications. Robinson made clear that the 'Eupolemia' did not contain a fully comprehensive account of his earnings from literary patronage. Nevertheless, it still provides an informative guide to the kinds of patron a court writer might approach; ranging from members of the aristocracy, court office holders and churchmen, to City of London dignitaries, the Master and Wardens of Robinson's own company, the Leathersellers', and provincial gentry. Robinson appears to have considered 10s or 6s.8d as a reasonably generous return but, occasionally, the receipt of 6 Angels (about £3) produced an ecstatic response. Among his most liberal patrons were the Uvedales of Dorsetshire who gave him 50s for the second edition of a collection of devotional extracts, The Vineyard of Virtue (1591), (Table, no 6). Other dedicatees were less open-handed. When in 1602 he dedicated the third edition of a work to the Bishop of Chichester, Robinson indignantly recorded that he: '(not so thankful as I deserved) gave me but 2s for my book dedicatory' (no 3).

It was also customary for Robinson to receive from the printer, in exchange for his manuscript, about 25 copies of the printed version, which he could then sell privately. During the late 1570s, he was able to ask 12d for an octavo volume of 10 sheets, and between 1582 and 1592 made up to 40s from selling extra copies of his quarto publications. Sometimes, Robinson produced a book for which there was a clearly identifiable market. In 1583 he addressed to Mr Thomas Smith a volume entitled, 'The laudable society, order & unity of Prince Arthur and his knights of ye round table in London.' Smith, the chief customs officer at the port of London, was the leader of this Arthurian Order and rewarded Robinson's efforts with 5s (no 14). Furthermore, 56 'knights' of the society also each bought a copy of the book for 18d, and an unspecified number of esquires paid 8d for theirs; bringing Robinson's receipts from this single volume to over £4.9s. Similarly, his translation of Leland's Life of Prince Arthur (1582) (no 12), brought him £2.2.8d from dedications, and 'at least 40s' from the sale of 25 extra copies; a combined total of £3.2s.8d. The sale of extra copies by the author was an essential procedure unless the dedicatee of the volume proved exceptionally generous. When in 1590, for example, Sir Christopher Hatton gave no less than 6 Angels (about 60s) for his dedication (no 15), Robinson praised 'his noble patronage and benevolence', explaining: 'So that I bestowed very few of these books abroad by reason of his liberality which kept me from troubling my friends abroad for one whole year's space afterwards.' However, when the Earl of Warwick ignored a dedication to him in 1582 (no 13), Robinson complained bitterly: 'I was therefore driven to make benefit of 100 books within 2 years space afterwards to the value of £10.'

Although it is impossible to determine how represent-

2. Richard Robinson's <u>Eupolemia</u> (1603): Benefactors and Rewards

[1 Angel — about 10s   **1 French Crown — about 6s]**

A		Books in Octavo	
1)	1576 i)	Mr Simon Roe, Master of the Leathersellers' Company	2s.6d
	ii)	The members of the Leathersellers'	7s.6d
2)	1577	Sir William Winter, Surveyor of the Queen's Navy	2 French Crowns
3)	1577	Margaret, Countess of Lyneux	13s.4d
	1601 (rpt)	The Wardens of the Leathersellers'	20s.0d
	1602 (rpt)	Dr Watson, Bishop of Chichester	2s.0d
4)	1578	Dr Nowell, Dean of St Paul's	10s.0d
5)	1579 i)	Philip Sidney	4 Angels
	ii)	Sir Henry Sidney	10s.0d
6)	1579	Mr Edmund Uvedale of Dorsetshire	4 Angels
	1591 (rpt)	Mr Edmund and his parents, Mr Henry and Mrs Elizabeth Uvedale	50s.0d
7)	1580	Edward, Earl of Rutland	6 Angels
8)	1580	Mr David Lewys, Judge of the Admiralty	20s.0d
9)	1583	Dr Goodman, Dean of Westminster	8s.0d
	1590 (rpt)	Dr Goodman, Dean of Westminster	2s.0d
	1593 (rpt)	Dr Goodman, Dean of Westminster	2s.0d
10)	1587	Sir George Barne, Lord Mayor of London	10s.0d
	1590 (rpt)	Sir George Barne, Lord Mayor of London	5s.0d
	1594 (rpt)	Sir Cuthbert Buckle, Lord Mayor of London	5s.0d

B		Books in Quarto	
11)	1576	Sir William Allyn, Alderman of London	40s.0d
12)	1582 i)	Lord Arthur Grey, Baron of Wilton	10s.0d
	ii)	Sir Henry Sidney	6s.8d
	iii)	Mr Thomas Smith, Chief Customs Officer for the Port of London	6s.0d
13)	1582	Ambrose, Earl of Warwick; but after his death, the Dowager Countess gave Robinson, for two books	no reward 13s.4d
14)	1583	Mr Thomas Smith	5s.0d
15)	1590	Sir Christopher Hatton, Lord Chancellor	6 Angels
16)	1592 i)	Sir John Puckering, Lord Keeper of the Great Seal	2 Angels
	ii)	Lady Puckering	6s.8d

ative Robinson's receipts were in terms of those received by court writers in general, his 'Eupolemia' spells out the difficulties an author faced in trying to earn even a meagre living from literary pursuits alone. Between 1595 and August 1602, when the 'Eupolemia' abruptly ends, Robinson recorded further rejections of his literary works without reward by Queen Elizabeth herself, Sir Thomas Egerton, Lord Keeper of the Great Seal, and the Bishop of Lincoln. By then, he was homeless, mourning the recent death of his only child, and reduced to pawning 'diverse good books out of my chest', along with 'my very gown from my back' - Robinson's fate after 1602 is unknown.

The dismal progress of Robinson's career makes it all the more understandable why the prospect of frustration and failure at court prompted numerous expressions of weary depression and angry cynicism from successive generations of English writers. Spenser became preoccupied with the ways in which the court patronage system laid itself wide open to exploitation by unprincipled manipulators. His 'Mother Hubberd's Tale' (1591), relentlessly probed the weakness of the Elizabethan patronage system, and catalogued, in agonising detail, the experiences which awaited the expectant courtier:

> Most miserable man, whom wicked fate
> Hath brought to court, to sue for had ywist,
> That few have found, and many one hath mist;
> Full little knowest thou that hast not tried,
> What hell it is, in suing long to bide:
> To lose good days, that might be better spent;
> To waste long nights in pensive discontent;
> To speed today, to be put back tomorrow;
> To feed on hope, to pine with fear and sorrow;
> To have thy prince's grace, yet want her peers;
> To have thy asking, yet wait many years;
> To fret thy soul with crosses and with cares;
> To eat thy heart through comfortless despairs;
> To fawn, to crouch, to wait, to ride, to run,
> To spend, to give, to want, to be undone,
> Unhappy wight, born to disastrous end,
> That doth his life in so long tendance spend.

Several years later, little had changed. In his 'Satire 5', Donne created a relentless downward spiral of depression as he described the vicissitudes and degradation of preferment-hunting at the royal court:

> Then man is a world; in which, officers
> Are the vast ravishing seas; and suitors,
> Springs; now full, now shallow, now dry; which, to
> That which drowns them, run: these self reasons do
> Prove the world a man, in which, officers
> Are the devouring stomach, and suitors
> The excrements, which they void. All men are dust,
> How much worse are suitors, who to men's lust
> Are made preys. O worst than dust, or worm's meat,
> For they do eat you now, whose selves worms shall eat.

It was disturbing enough for men of letters to perceive a sharp disparity between the ideal and the reality of court patronage. However, the writer's greatest dilemma lay in the pressing need to become a courtier himself in order to promote his own work and career. It is easy to detect the tone of wounded pride in Donne's desperate lament:

> Oh, let me not serve so, as those men serve
> Whom honours' smokes at once fatten and starve;
> Poorly enriched with great men's words or looks.

Elsewhere, he bitterly concludes: 'And they who write to lords, rewards to get, / Are they not like singers at doors for meat?' The adoption of the role of the courtier was frequently regarded by writers as an irksome and demeaning necessity which formed an unhappy contrast to their self-appointed and more dignified identity as court commentators. Time and time again, we find in the works of talented and ambitious men of letters, lavish panegyrics uneasily rubbing shoulders with satiric condemnations of the court patronage system. The vehement bitterness of 'Mother Hubberd's Tale', for example, is preceded by a graceful dedication to the 'most fair and virtuous' Lady Compton and Mountegle. Most Tudor and Stuart writers were struck (along with modern readers of their dedications) by the marked disparity between their glorious images of an ideal patronage system and the stark, depressing reality of a court life in which too many writers competed for too few rewards. Richard Robinson and countless other pursuers of literary patronage at court would have nodded silently in agreement with the doleful lament, attributed to Sir Walter Raleigh: 'Say to the court it glows, / And shines like rotten wood.'[27]

Inevitably, writers learned to regard court patronage as simply one potential source of reward for literary endeavour. As Robinson's 'Eupolemia' reveals, the Church, particularly its deaneries and the episcopate, was viewed as another important institution in the patronage of learning. The City of London also offered rich pickings to writers, prompting an unending stream of dedications to its Mayors and civic holders. Other popular targets for literary solicitations included the membership of the Inns of Court; City companies, ranging from the Stationers' and Barber Surgeons' to the Fishmongers' and Saddlers'; and wealthy investors in the Merchant Venturers, East India, Virginia and other companies. Similarly, members of city corporations in the provinces, along with their church communities, landed gentry, justices of the peace and militia chiefs, often found themselves the recipients of dedicatory addresses. Writers might also approach acquaintances, friends and relatives, not only as possible purchasers of extra copies of their books but also as their dedicatees. The seeking of all forms of patronage was, to a certain extent, a lottery but the wise - and generally far more successful - patronage-hunter was he who realised from the outset that the possibility of aristocratic sponsorship or favour was to be viewed as no more than an unpredictable source of occasional support, rather than as a reliable route to a secure and profitable livelihood.

'ONE THAT FASHIONED HIS OWN FORTUNE'

Through a combination of natural talent, determination and good fortune, William Herbert (c.1507-70), later first Earl of Pembroke, laid firm foundations at the court of Henry VIII for his own advancement and the future prosperity of his family. Little is known about Herbert's early years - it is not even certain when he was born - but a legend has developed which depicts him as an ill-educated soldier of fortune, ruthlessly thrusting himself upward through the Tudor patronage system. This impression is due largely to Aubrey's memorable sketch of Herbert in his fascinating, but notoriously unreliable, Brief Lives:

> He was (as I take it) a younger brother, a mad fighting young fellow. 'Tis certain he was a servant to the house of Worcester, and wore their blue coat and badge. My cousin Whitney's great aunt gave him a golden angel when he went to London. One time, being at Bristol, he was arrested, and killed one of the Sheriffs of the city. He made his escape through Backstreet, through the (then great) Gate, into the Marsh, and got into France.[1]

Herbert was also long remembered for his highly developed instinct for political survival which enabled him to remain in high office through four successive reigns. As late as 1670, the centenary of his death, he was still celebrated as, 'one that fashioned his own fortune: his disposition got favour, and his prudence wealth (the first to grace the second, and the second to support the first).'[2]

There was, however, rather more to Herbert than the

homicidal opportunist suggested by these portraits. In addition to his own entrepreneurial skills, Herbert possessed the distinct advantage, to a courtier seeking favour, of a long family tradition of distinguished royal service. His grandfather, William ap Gwilym (known at the English court as William Herbert) had received in 1468 the Earldom of Pembroke, of the first creation, as a reward for assisting Edward IV against the Lancastrian threat to his throne.[3] Gwilym was an immensely ambitious man. In 1466 he had seen his eldest son and heir, William, betrothed to Edward IV's future sister-in-law, Mary Woodville, and he was also keen to engineer a marriage between his daughter Maud and the young Henry Tudor, later King Henry VII. However, less than a year after becoming Earl of Pembroke, Gwilym was beheaded, on the order of the Earl of Warwick, after his capture at the battle of Banbury where he had commanded forces loyal to Edward IV. Following Edward's restoration in April 1471, the first Earl's eldest son, William, succeeded to the title (although he was obliged to exchange it for the Earldom of Huntingdon in July 1479, at the command of the King, who wished to bestow the title of Pembroke upon his own son, Edward). The Earl also had an illegitimate son, Richard, who attended the English court, attaining the position of Gentleman Usher in the household of Henry VII. Richard's son, William, our present subject, was therefore maintaining a family tradition of royal service by attending the court of Henry VIII, rather than being, as Aubrey suggests, merely 'a stranger in our country (a Welshman), and an upstart'.[4]

An attachment to an aristocratic household was regarded as a valuable form of training for any youth who harboured ambitions to advance himself at the English court. Aubrey asserts that William Herbert became a liveried servant, probably a page or valet, in the entourage of his kinsman and guardian, Charles Somerset, Earl of Worcester (c. 1460-1526). An accomplished soldier and diplomat, Worcester was a prominent figure at the early-Henrician court, and could claim personal acquaintance with at least three of the greatest patron-princes of Europe. He attended on official business the court of the Habsburg Emperor Maximilian I (d. 1519); and also met his grandson, the Emperor Charles V (d. 1558), at Windsor. In his capacity as Lord Chamberlain of the royal household, he played a prominent role in the arrangements for Henry VIII's renowned encounter with Francis I in 1520 at 'the Field of the Cloth of Gold'. The young William Herbert could not have hoped to find a more illustrious aristocratic household than Somerset's for his early courtly and chivalric training.

From these auspicious beginnings, Herbert progressed smoothly into royal service and by 1526 was listed among the Gentleman Pensioners to the King.[5] This post carried with it few specific duties and was designed to continue his courtly grooming as a soldier and servant of the sovereign. Herbert's future looked distinctly promising but, suddenly, his name disappears from English court records. One possible solution to this mystery is provided by Aubrey's account, already quoted, of Herbert murdering a man in Bristol and being obliged to save his own skin by fleeing to France:

> In France he betook himself into the army, where he showed so much courage, and readiness of wit in conduct, that in short time he became eminent, and was favoured by the king (Francis I), who afterwards recommended him to Henry the VIII of England, who much valued him, and heaped favours and honours upon him.[6]

If there is any truth in this colourful story, then Herbert, like his guardian the Earl of Worcester, would have enjoyed a first-hand experience of the magnificent court of Francis I. The French King, upheld by Castiglione as the epitome of the ideal royal patron, was a skilled horseman, a lover of ceremonial and pageant, and a generous patron of painters, sculptors and scholars. He was a prolific sponsor of grand architectural schemes, building the Italianate Châteaux of Chambord and Madrid, and extensively renovating the Palaces of the Louvre and Fontainebleau. This remarkable young man somehow also found the time to listen to the poet Alamanni's readings of Dante, to correspond with Erasmus and to employ the skills of Leonardo da Vinci and Benvenuto Cellini.[7]

Although there can be no certainty in the matter, the possibility remains that William Herbert was the product of a sophisticated courtly training rather than being, as is usually suggested, an upstart soldier of fortune. The splendour of his lifestyle after he became an Earl in 1551, ostentatious even by Tudor standards, coupled with his assiduous and highly effective cultivation of royal favour during four successive reigns, both point to this conclusion.

Whatever the truth of William Herbert's early exploits, by the mid-1530s he was once more engaged in the furtherance of his own career. In 1535 one William Herbert, described as an Esquire of the King's Body and almost certainly our man, was appointed to the post of Attorney-General of Glamorgan.[8]

At some stage during the mid-1530s, William Herbert married Anne, the younger daughter of Sir Thomas Parr (d. 1518), who had been Master of the Wards and Comptroller of the household during the early years of Henry VIII's reign. Although the Parrs were an ancient family, Anne had been only moderately provided for at her father's death and William Herbert would not have gained any great material or social advantage through such a union. However, this rather unremarkable marriage was endowed with a whole new significance, when on 12 July 1543, Anne's elder sister, Catherine, became the sixth Queen of Henry VIII. Herbert soon began to reap a rich harvest of royal favour. Between 1543 and 1546 he was knighted, appointed Captain of the town and castle of Aberystwyth, and became a Gentleman of the Privy Chamber. The King also appointed him Steward of extensive royal properties in the west of England and granted him the manor of Hendon in Middlesex and the crown lands and castle of Cardiff in Glamorganshire. In 1546 the importance attached to Herbert's presence at court was recognised by Henry's grant of the Keepership of Baynard's Castle, on the banks of the Thames, which became the main London residence of his family.[9]

Such a prominent courtier also required a rural retreat. In a series of royal grants made between 1541 and 1544, Herbert received the estate and buildings of the dissolved Abbey of Wilton, about three miles west of Salisbury. The last Abbess, Cecily Bodenham, had been forced to leave in 1539 and, by the time the Wilton estate came into Herbert's hands, the buildings and land were in a sadly neglected state. He immediately instigated schemes for the re-development of the site along lines which would adequately reflect his status at court. At a cost of over £10,000, a large, quadrangular house was erected, fronted by a court-yard and surrounded by a high wall. The main entrance was through an imposing archway set in the centre of the east front which led to the inner quadrangle.[10] Nothing is known about the architects and craftsmen employed by William Herbert, but a tradition has persisted that he took advice from the court painter and designer, Hans Holbein, the younger. Holbein, however, died in 1543 and there is no evidence that he was ever involved in the plans for Wilton House.[11] Of the rest of the original buildings, only the east front remains, much altered.

Although it seems probable that Wilton House was not completed in time for Henry VIII to visit it, William Herbert's continuing favour with the King and his wife's intimacy with Queen Catherine drew the Herbert family ever closer into royal circles. Lady Anne Herbert shared her sister's high educational ideals, and may have discussed with her the organisation of a royal nursery for Prince Edward and the two Princesses, Mary and Elizabeth, for which John Cheke and Roger Ascham were engaged as tutors. Not everyone at court, however, was favourably impressed by the Parr sisters' intellectual pursuits. The Queen was accustomed each afternoon to meet with a circle of friends, including Lady Anne Herbert, and to discuss passages from the scriptures. These periods of study were interspersed with sermons from, 'divers well learned and godly persons', who did not hesitate to expose and examine various abuses in the Protestant Church. It was even rumoured that the Queen - a mere woman - took it upon herself to raise such issues with the King. This potential influence over Henry VIII's attitudes soon prompted the concern of the more conservative elements at court, led by Stephen Gardiner, Bishop of Winchester (c. 1483-1555), and Sir Thomas Wriothesley (1505-50), the Lord Chancellor. According to John Foxe, Gardiner persuaded the King to allow articles to be drawn against the Queen, by suggesting that 'the religion by the queen so stiffly maintained, did not only disallow and dissolve the policy and politic government of princes but also taught the people that all things ought to be in common.' Her closet was searched for seditious books and charges were also drawn against those ladies closest to her, including Lady Anne Herbert. Although nothing incriminating appears to have been located, the matter was eventually resolved only by the Queen and her ladies assuring the King in person that they fully respected his wisdom and authority in all religious matters.[12]

Once Henry had satisfied himself of his Queen's personal loyalty and obedience, the Parr sisters were able to extricate themselves from this potentially dangerous predicament. Nor did Gardiner's accusations do any great harm to the Herberts' highly favourable position at court. In 1546 William Herbert was named as one of the executors of the King's will, in which he was bequeathed £300; he was also chosen as one of the twelve privy councillors to advise the future Edward VI. Henry VIII died on 28 January 1547 and at his funeral Herbert rode in the chariot carrying the King's coffin.

1547-58

Within three days of Edward VI's accession, Edward Seymour (created Duke of Somerset on 16 February), with the assistance of Sir William Paget, one of Henry VIII's most trusted advisers, had firmly grasped power as Governor of the King and Protector of the realm. William Herbert was an important cog in Somerset's political machine. The Duke's brother, Thomas, who had previously aspired to the hands of the Princesses Mary and Elizabeth, became Herbert's brother-in-law by marrying the widowed Queen Catherine in 1547. Herbert had keenly supported the election of Somerset as Protector and in 1548 was rewarded by becoming a Knight of the Garter and Master of the Horse. In the following year, William Thomas's 'contemptu mundi' treatise, The Vanity of this World, the first literary work known to have been addressed to a member of the Herbert family in the sixteenth century, was dedicated to Lady Anne Herbert. Its political and religious alignment in favour of Somerset's regime was forcefully asserted by the dedication which assured Lady Anne that 'at this present the light of truth does more flourish here amongst us in England, than elsewhere throughout the whole world.'[13] However, despite the close personal and political ties between Herbert and Seymour, their relationship became seriously strained in 1549. In that year there were disturbances in several of the western counties. Herbert raised large forces from his Wiltshire estates and combined with John Russell, soon to be Earl of Bedford, in an attempt to combat them. When Herbert was away in the west, the enmity which had been simmering between Protector Somerset and his rival, John Dudley, Earl of Warwick, came to a head. The forces of Herbert and Russell, then gathered at Andover, were considered to be the decisive factor. Somerset believed that their loyalty would enable him to defeat his rivals and totally control the Council. After apparently temporising, Russell and Herbert clarified their position with a message from Wilton on 9 October 1549, announcing support for the Council which was then dominated by Warwick. A few days later, the Duke of Somerset was arrested and placed, for a short period, in the Tower.[14]

Two years after these events, Warwick was able to instigate Somerset's arrest, trial and execution. Herbert deftly negotiated this transition and gained rich rewards by siding with John Dudley. He was appointed President of the Welsh Council in April 1550, and raised to the peerage on 10 October 1551 as Baron Herbert of Cardiff; on the following day he was created Earl of Pembroke. Herbert's prestige at court was now high. In November the Queen Dowager of Scotland, Mary of Guise (the mother of Mary Queen of Scots), paid a state visit to Edward VI and was provided with accommodation at Baynard's Castle. By the end of 1551, he was regarded as one of the three most powerful men in England. The Spanish ambassador, Jehan Scheyfve, noted that the Earl of Warwick, along with the Earl of Pembroke and William Parr, Marquis of Northampton (Herbert's brother-in-law), now ruled, 'in such sort that no one in the Council dares to oppose him'.[15]

Pembroke's promotion at court prompted a rapid literary response. On 1 April 1552 John Caius, a distinguished Greek scholar, medical practitioner and refounder of Gonville and Caius College, Cambridge (1557), dedicated to Pembroke a treatise on The Disease Commonly Called ... Sweating Sickness. This notorious affliction, the cause of numerous fatalities during the Tudor period, was of immediate concern to members of Edward VI's entourage. In 1551 an epidemic had swept London, killing the young Henry Brandon, who had been one of the King's companions in Queen Catherine Parr's royal nursery. Caius, according to his dedicatory address, had been persuaded by various 'friends and acquaintances', to pen this vernacular tract for the instruction of all courtiers and, he added pointedly, other 'English men not learned'.[16] There followed a more authoritative version in Latin, De Ephemera Britannica, aimed specifically at the medical profession. The prominence which Caius attained at court from these publications presumably played a significant part in his subsequent appointment as personal physician to Edward VI.

Soon afterwards, William Barker (or Bercher) dedicated to Pembroke the first edition of his translation of Xenophon's Cyropaedia, a biographical panegyric of the Persian prince, Cyrus the Great. Barker was a protégé of Queen Anne Boleyn who had sent him to St John's College, Cambridge, at her own expense. Between 1549 and 1553 he lived and worked in Italy, although he claimed to have completed the translation before his departure.[17] Xenophon's Cyropaedia became one of the most widely read handbooks of courtly, civil and military behaviour during the second half of the sixteenth century. Puttenham compared it to Plato's Republic, Homer's Odyssey and Thomas More's Utopia. Sidney also held Xenophon in the highest regard, placing his work alongside that of Homer and Virgil in providing a pattern of virtue to princes. The choice of Pembroke's name to preface this translation of the Cyropaedia became in itself a long-lived testimony to his prominence at the late-Edwardian court since Barker's version (reprinted, in expanded form, in 1567) remained the only one available to English courtiers in their native tongue until 1632.

In view of the importance within court circles of both Caius's Sweating Sickness and Barker's Cyropaedia, it becomes all the more difficult to lend credence to the snippets of court gossip which have earned Pembroke the notoriety of being possibly the last illiterate Privy Councillor in England.[18] In 1550 it was asserted that he could neither 'read nor write', nor knew any other language but his 'native English'. Twenty years later, the poet Thomas Churchyard remarked that Pembroke, 'no school point knew'. William Camden corroborated these comments by reporting that the Earl was unable to provide Cecil and Queen Elizabeth with a written account of his dealings with Mary Queen of Scots during the late 1560s, 'in regard he could not write himself'. Many years later, John Aubrey endowed these reports with a ring of finality by insisting that Pembroke, 'could neither write, nor read, but had a stamp for his name', presumably to spare him the indignity of making a mark.[19] This evidence, however, is far from conclusive. Several examples of Pembroke's signature have survived, consisting of a mixture of unconnected capitals and lower case letters. Although they do not suggest a great familiarity with the pen, I have not come across a single example which appears to have been made with a stamp. It is even possible that Welsh may have been William Herbert's first language and that he never acquired anything more than a rudimentary knowledge of written English. Whatever the truth of the matter, the sheer prominence of an aristocratic patron could provide court writers with a more than adequate compensation for any inability to appreciate the literary quality of their compositions.

Although he owed his earldom to John Dudley, William Herbert was an unpredictable ally. As early as December 1551, it was becoming evident at court that the relationship between the two men was far from harmonious. Dudley, however, remained heavily dependent upon Pembroke's support, particularly in May 1553, when suspicions grew that Edward VI was close to death. Scheyfve, the Spanish ambassador, warned: 'On every side ... plans and preparations are being made to strengthen and consolidate the position.' He noted on 12 May that, 'by means of the Duke of Northumberland's intercession, the Earl of Pembroke's eldest son, who is at present very ill, is to marry the ... Duke of Suffolk's second daughter.' These marriages were duly solemnised on 25 May at Durham Place, Northumberland's London mansion. Lord Guildford Dudley was married to Lady Jane Grey; Lady Catherine Dudley to Lord Henry Hastings, the son of the Earl of Huntingdon; and Lord Henry Herbert to Lady Catherine Grey. Pembroke was, thereby, publicly allied to Northumberland's apparent 'designs to deprive the Lady Mary of the succession to the crown'.[20]

The brief reign of Lady Jane Grey and the failure of Northumberland's schemes need no recounting here. However, Pembroke's behaviour at this time, illustrating his skill in siding with the winning party, is less well known. Almost as soon as Northumberland's forces had left London to oppose Mary's in the Eastern counties, Pembroke was reported to have brandished his sword before his fellow privy councillors, uttering the cry: 'either this sword shall make Mary queen, or I'll lose my life'.[21] A meeting was held at his London house, Baynard's Castle, on the pretext of consulting with the French ambassador, but really to consolidate the Earl's plans for denouncing John Dudley. When the Lord Mayor of London read out Mary's triumphant proclamation in Cheapside on 19 July, Pembroke was spotted alongside him, ostentatiously celebrating her victory by throwing his cap full of coins to the crowd.

Mary's advisers regarded Pembroke with justifiable suspicion; and she soon replaced him with the Bishop of Worcester as President of the Council in the Marches of Wales. But he was too powerful to be totally disregarded. On 8 August he was one of the chief mourners at Edward VI's funeral and five days later was appointed as a privy councillor. He attended Mary's coronation on 29 September, at which his eldest son and heir, Henry, was created a Knight of the Bath. Little by little, a mutually suspicious but working relationship was established between Pembroke and the Queen.

During August 1553, Pembroke would have desired to play down his embarrassing association with Northumberland. It was, therefore, unfortunate that on 21 of that month, the day before John Dudley's execution, a Florentine Protestant, Michael Angelo Florio, addressed to Henry Lord Herbert, Lady Jane's brother-in-law, a manuscript treatise on Italian grammar, 'Regole de la lingua Thoscana'.[22] Florio described the Earl of Pembroke as, 'extremely kind to foreigners', but by August 1553 Michael Angelo possessed all the wrong associations. He had been employed as tutor to Lady Jane Grey and had been treated by her father, the Duke of Suffolk, as though he was, 'one of his dearest and nearest relations'. Florio had also recently addressed a catechism to King Edward which lavished praise and expressions of personal loyalty on the Duke of Northumberland. When we remember that the Duke had desperately tried, just before his execution, to avoid Mary's retribution by insisting that the whole scheme of usurpation had been Pembroke's, it seems certain that Florio would have found little welcome at Wilton House or Baynard's Castle. Frances Yates remarked that, 'if the duke's plan had succeeded, Michael Angelo's fortune would have been made'. However, by March 1554, Florio was virtually destitute and felt himself threatened by the new Catholic regime. He fled to the continent where he continued to vituperate against, 'that impious, cruel, brazen Jezabel the Queen'.[23]

Queen Mary's marriage treaty with Philip of Spain in January 1554 prompted almost immediately a popular rebellion led by Sir Thomas Wyatt, the son of the Henrician poet. This uprising provided Pembroke with a golden opportunity to earn his Queen's genuine gratitude. An army was hastily raised in London and, under the Earl's command, efficiently routed the remnants of Wyatt's forces in Fleet Street. Wyatt and about 100 other individuals were executed, including Lady Jane Grey and her husband, even though neither had been involved personally in the conspiracy. One of those hanged, drawn and quartered was the Protestant propagandist, William Thomas, whose The Vanity of this World had been dedicated to William Herbert's wife in 1549.

Pembroke appears to have adapted himself readily to the expectations of a Catholic court. Along with other prominent aristocrats, he had been given a pension of £500 by Charles V's envoy, Egmont, to persuade him to agree to Mary's wedding with Philip. In June 1554, he laid on a spectacular welcoming party at Wilton for Philip's ambassador, the Marquis de las Novas. At the wedding ceremony in Winchester Cathedral, Pembroke, along with the Marquis of Winchester and the Earls of Bedford and Derby, gave away the bride in the name of the realm. As Mary and Philip moved away from the High Altar at the end of the ceremony, Pembroke bore before the bridegroom the Sword of State. On 29 July Pembroke and the pro-Catholic Earl of Arundel dined intimately with Philip and the Queen; according to Spanish reports, they were 'the greatest men of the realm at present'.[24]

Mary's ardent desire to reverse the processes of the dissolution found few supporters among the Protestant aristocracy who had made considerable gains from the dispersal of Church lands. Pembroke was one of those most threatened by this proposed policy. As early as July 1553, in the wake of Northumberland's fall, the Bishop of Winchester had intimated to the Earl that he would soon be obliged to hand over the revenues 'from the Cathedral Church of Winchester'. Soon afterwards, it was reported that Mary proposed to revoke all grants of Church lands, much to the indignation of, 'the whole Council, and particularly the Earl of Pembroke'. Although such a radical reversal of policy would have been virtually impossible to carry out, Pembroke was wily enough to make the occasional gesture to placate the Queen. In 1557, for example, it was rumoured that one of his Church properties, the former priory of the Observant Friars at Southampton, was to be restored, 'to its ancient estate' - needless to say, nothing ever came of this scheme.[25]

There has also survived an illuminated manuscript which may exemplify Pembroke's flexibility in accommodating the rise and fall of specific religious cults. Prior to Mary's accession, the Earl had personally supervised the removal of a statue of the Virgin Mary at Penrhys in the diocese of Llandaff.[26] Naturally, the discredited cult of the Virgin was triumphantly reasserted with the return of Catholicism to England. At this period, William Herbert had in his possession a valuable heirloom, now in the Philadelphia Museum of Art, known as the 'Pembroke Hours' or Horae Pembrochianae. This outstanding Book of the Hours of the Blessed Virgin Mary had been commissioned in about 1440 by William ap Gwilym, Earl of Pembroke of the first creation, and then handed down through the family. It was probably during Mary's reign that several interesting additions were made. Twenty leaves of vellum were inserted at the beginning, on the first of which was emblazoned the Pembroke coat of arms. On the following leaf was a full-length portrait of the Earl, kneeling at a prie-dieu, clad in armour and, presumably, praying to the Virgin. At the end of the volume was inserted, 'A prayer for men to say entering into battle', by Pembroke's sister-in-law, Queen Catherine Parr.[27] The Horae Pembrochianae thereby reminded its readers of the Earl's royal connections and, at the same time, demonstrated his conveniently rediscovered devotion to the cult of the Virgin.

Philip, an intelligent and cultivated man, made considerable efforts to treat affably his wife and members of the English nobility. However, the political and religious anxieties which his presence occasioned in the minds of English courtiers overshadowed any ideas which they might have had of forging closer links between the cultures of England and Spain. In September 1555 Philip departed for the Netherlands, leaving the government of the realm in the hands of seven councillors, including Pembroke. This transference of authority was greeted by an outburst of Protestant propaganda which sought to weaken Mary's religious position in England. One of these anti-Catholic tracts, A New Book of Spiritual Physic (1555), was published with an address to Pembroke and nine other prominent aristocrats. Its author, William Turner, had been chaplain and physician to the Duke of Somerset but fled the country on Mary's accession. His text comprised a series of intricate arguments designed to vilify the Catholic influence in England but, at the same time, to confound an outright charge of anti-Catholicism. Initially, he professed to be concerned with offering a true definition of nobility and with lamenting the paucity of learning among courtiers. Only in the last two-thirds of the volume did he introduce his real subject. Recalling the 'true religion that was exercised in King Edward's days', he launched a sustained attack on the 'Romish Church', 'which hath erred shamefully many hundred years'.[28] Turner had been a prominent leader of the reform movement during Henry VIII's reign and his works had been banned under the Act of Six Articles. In view of the sentiments expressed in A New Book of Spiritual Physic, it is not surprising to find that this tract was also rapidly banned in 1555 by a Council

Proclamation.[29]

In the following year, Pembroke's name, along with Arundel's, Derby's and Shrewsbury's, was prefixed to another attack on the Queen's religious policies, entitled <u>The Copy of a Letter</u>. Its author, John Bradford - to be distinguished from the Protestant martyr of the same name - had been associated with the Dudley conspiracy of March 1556 which sought to depose Philip and Mary in favour of Elizabeth; and he was executed for his involvement in Thomas Stafford's ill-fated raid on Scarborough in the following year. In May 1556, Mary had sought approval from Derby, Shrewsbury and Pembroke to have Philip crowned King of England. Rumours circulated that Pembroke was going 'to fetch the crown from the Earl of Shrewsbury to crown the king withal'.[30] Bradford's letter had probably been written shortly afterwards as an attempt to consolidate opposition to the scheme. But it is unlikely that Pembroke would have compromised his own position by offering overt support to anti-Marian propagandists. In fact, I have located only a single instance in which the Earl appears to have actively sought to protect one of Mary's opponents. In 1556 he was reported as having intervened to save the life of one of the conspirators in the Dudley plot, William Hunnis, who had been, and perhaps still was, in his service.[31] Generally, however, during Mary's reign Pembroke was careful neither to antagonise nor overtly befriend the two rival factions at court, led by the Protestant William Paget and the Catholic Stephen Gardiner.

Doubts over the Earl's religious allegiances were counterbalanced by his usefulness as a soldier. His appointment in 1551 as Lord Lieutenant of Wales had placed him in overall military command of the Welsh shires. Pembroke also kept himself well-informed over continental conflicts; and his role in the suppression of the Wyatt rebellion did much to enhance his reputation with the Queen.[32] In March 1556 the French were intent upon expelling the English from what both sides regarded as their own territories. At Philip's command, Pembroke organised the fortifications of Guisnes and was appointed Governor of Calais. In the following year, the Earl and his son, Henry, were present at the storming of St Quentin, when Duke Anne de Montmorency (1492-1567), Constable of France and a renowned patron of the arts, was captured.

In about 1556 Nicholas Smyth translated into English Politian's Latin version of the <u>History</u> of the Roman empire by the Greek author, Herodian. He selected Pembroke as his patron, 'whom not only fame, but also experience, doeth apparently prove, to be the perfect patron of knightly prowess, and virtue', reminding him how the Emperor Alexander Severus and other renowned generals had been 'accustomed to consult with such as were expert in histories', before engaging the enemy in battle. Similarly, William Barker's translation of the Cyropaedia provided Pembroke with ancient but still respected advice on, 'the shifts and escapes from the enemies, the foresight of dangers and avoiding of perils'.

The Earl of Pembroke was responsible for the education of his own two sons, Henry and Edward, along with Henry Compton, the son of his second wife, Anne (d. 1588). Barker's translation of the Cyropaedia had been specifically dedicated to the Earl as an educational exercise for his charges, 'whom ye love and bring ... up in learning'. Barker explained that he had translated this work to encourage them, 'to learn to turn Latin out of English', and praised Pembroke's efforts in finding them a 'good school-master'. This individual was almost certainly one H[enry?] Iden, whom Barker had known personally during his stay in Italy. In 1557 Iden dedicated to these three young men his translation of Giovanni Gelli's immensely popular Circes, a series of dialogues between Ulysses and eleven people who had been transformed into beasts by Circes; all of whom, apart from the elephant, found their animal life preferable to human existence. This choice of a text by Gelli (1498-1563), a founder of the Florentine Academy and the authoritative Italian commentator on Dante, is of especial significance. Gelli, originally a shoemaker, was a resolute advocate of the use of the vernacular, writing most easily in colloquial Italian. For mid-Tudor translators such as Iden and Barker (who published his own translation of Gelli's I Capricci in 1569), Gelli's works were visible proof of the triumphal assertion of a vernacular tongue over the deadening authority of Latin.

THE QUEEN'S SERVANT

Princess Elizabeth was at Hatfield when news reached her of Queen Mary's death on 17 November 1558. On the journey to London she was accompanied by a group of prominent lords, including the Earl of Pembroke who ceremonially carried her sword. During the coronation, he was observed supporting her 'by the arms' in the procession to the Abbey. By mid-December he was so well established in the royal entourage that the Spanish Ambassador, the Count de Feria, advised Philip II to settle immediately the arrears in his pension: 'He is one of the best servants your Majesty has here and is a man of authority ... since the new queen succeeded he has always been about the palace and does not leave her side.'[33]

This confidence in Pembroke's loyalty to a Catholic ruler, however, runs contrary to the evidence offered by an anonymous tract, 'The device for alteration of religion at the first year of Queen Elizabeth', which urged the Earl and three other privy councillors (the Earl of Bedford, the Marquis of Northampton and Lord Grey de Wilton) to support the Queen in her plans for Protestant re-alignment and changes in the liturgy. In fact, Pembroke was appointed in 1559 as one of the commissioners in charge of the administration of the Oath of Supremacy. But a curious twist to the already complex issue of the Earl's religious allegiance is provided by the account in Camden's Britannia (1586) of Elizabeth's preparations for the change of religion. Almost certainly working with a copy of 'The device' in front of him, Camden reproduced exactly its list of privy councillors advising the Queen on religious matters, except for Pembroke, whose name was silently replaced by that of William Cecil.[34] Camden's reasons for making this substitution are unknown; although it may perhaps be taken as an indication of the considerable doubts which lingered over Pembroke's religious loyalties right up to his death in 1570.

On a personal level, William Herbert carefully courted the new Queen's favour through a variety of social engagements. Elizabeth honoured his London household by dining at Baynard's Castle on St George's Day, 1559. During the afternoon of 28 April 1560 Pembroke was in her company at court, judging a series of jousts held between Lord Sussex, Lord Robert Dudley, Lord Hunsdon and others. On new Year's Day 1562, as usual, gifts were exchanged between the Queen and her leading courtiers. Pembroke presented her with a purse containing £30 in new angels, and his wife gave her £15 in a 'cherry bag of crimson satin'. On 15 January, Elizabeth came again to dine at Baynard's Castle. One observer reported that 'at night there was great cheer and a great banquet and after a mask, and her Grace stayed the night'. Similar festivities, including 'great mummeries and masques', were held at Baynard's Castle on 17 February 1563 to celebrate the double wedding of Pembroke's daughter, Lady Anne Herbert, to Lord Talbot, and Henry Lord Herbert to Lady Catherine Talbot, the children of the sixth Earl of Shrewsbury.[35]

In addition to these courtly pursuits, Pembroke played his part in supporting the early-Elizabethan campaign to promote a wider appreciation of the need for an educated court élite. After leaving Henry Iden and their other private tutors, the Earl's eldest son, Henry Lord Herbert, was sent to New College, Oxford, and his brother, Edward, to Peterhouse, Cambridge.[36] Although he did not know the Earl personally, Jasper Heywood took advantage of this connection to dedicate his translation of Seneca's Hercules Furens to Pembroke in 1561. Heywood belonged to a group of young university men, including Alexander Neville, Thomas Nuce, John Studley and Thomas Newton, who, soon after Elizabeth's accession, undertook the translation into English of various plays attributed to Seneca. To gain maximum publicity for this scheme, the completed volumes were dedicated to figures of national importance. Prior to 1561, Heywood had already addressed translations to Queen Elizabeth and Sir John Mason, the Chancellor of Oxford University. In his dedication to Pembroke, he explained that he wished to demonstrate, 'myself so loving to my country', by furthering, 'the knowledge of the unripened scholars of this realm'.[37] His country, however, was not willing to harbour his active commitment to Catholicism; and on 21 May 1562 he was enrolled in the Society of Jesus at Rome.

Before Elizabeth's accession, Pembroke had served two separate terms as President of the Welsh Council (1550-3; 1555-8), and was a native Welsh speaker. His entourage contained a nucleus of his fellow nationals, and the Welsh divine, Gruffydd Robert, in his dedication of Drych Cristionogawl, noted that Pembroke, 'insisted even at court in addressing his fellow-countrymen in their native tongue'. Naturally, Herbert became something of a focus for Welsh writers. Sir John Prise of Brecon, the noted historian and collector of monastic manuscripts, paid generous tribute to his patronage.[38] Another native of Wales, the poet Arthur Kelton, dedicated to him a 'Book of Poetry in Praise of the Welshmen'.[39] Some of Pembroke's employees in the Welsh Marches considered the mere mentioning of his name as an effective means of drawing attention to themselves at the English court. One such individual, John Gwynne, presented to William Cecil, probably during the 1560s, an historical and topographical study of Wales, proudly announcing himself as 'Surveyor of North Wales, and servant to the right honourable the Earl of Pembroke.'[40]

In 1567 the Earl's name was once again associated with Catholicism through the dedication to him of a short course on Welsh grammar by Gruffydd Robert, penned to supply the needs of Roman Catholics in Wales, particularly missionary priests. Later in the same year, the Spanish ambassador, Guzman de Silva, considered Pembroke a Catholic and feared that this allegiance might be jeopardised by his closeness to the Protestant Earl of Leicester. Herbert, however, was careful to make the occasional overt gesture in support of the Protestant faith. The effective surrender of Calais, by the Treaty of Câteau-Cambrésis in 1559, occasioned considerable problems for the merchant staplers there, who petitioned Pembroke for assistance. He responded promptly by inviting some of them, along with a number of oppressed Protestant weavers from the Low Countries, to settle on his Wilton estate.[41]

By nature Pembroke was a 'politique', placing political and family considerations above any form of sectarian religious commitment. However, his desire to steer a middle course between Protestantism and Catholicism appears to have caused him considerable problems during the last few years of his life. Pembroke's health began to fail from 1564 onwards and, although he was appointed Lord Steward of the Royal Household in 1568, he played thereafter a much less prominent role in court politics. Nevertheless, during this period, the Earl seems to have fostered a friendly association with Thomas Howard, Duke of Norfolk, the head of England's leading Catholic family. On one memorable occasion in November 1566 the Queen voiced doubts at court over Norfolk's loyalty to her. When Pembroke spoke up in Howard's defence, she angrily dismissed Herbert, according to a Spanish report, as a 'swaggering soldier'.[42] In 1567 a second edition of William Barker's translation of Xenophon was published. Its prefatory material laid great emphasis upon the bonds of intimacy which had developed between the Howards and the Herberts. By this time Barker had found employment in Norfolk's household. In addition to reprinting the original dedication to Pembroke, he added another to the Duke's eldest son, Philip, reminding him of the 'friendship' his father shared with William Herbert. 'I dare say', Barker concluded, that Pembroke 'will be both a father and a grandfather to you, if excuse should require.'

Barker wrote these words on 8 January 1567. In May of the following year, Mary, Queen of Scots, arrived as a refugee in England, having been deposed in favour of her infant son, James VI. By October rumours were circulating that the Duke of Norfolk aspired to marry Mary, whom he hoped would then be officially recognised as Elizabeth's successor. In the spring of 1569, it became clear that Norfolk had gathered a considerable body of support at court, including Pembroke, Leicester and Arundel. The Queen, however, soon announced her firm opposition to any such scheme, and towards the end of September, Pembroke and Arundel were forbidden to come into her presence. Contrary to Elizabeth's orders, Norfolk had left court on 21 September. He tried to return early in October but was intercepted and placed in the Tower. Pembroke, Arundel and others were first confined to their lodgings, and then arrested for interrogation. Sir Thomas Smith, who was in charge of questioning some suspects of lesser rank, stated that William Barker had been 'the most doer betwixt the Duke and other foreign practisers', extracting his information from Norfolk's secretary, Bannister, 'with the rack', and from Barker, 'with the extreme fear of it'.[43] The evidence supplied by these two men eventually helped to send the Duke to the block in 1572.

In directing the Queen's response to the Norfolk marriage plans, Cecil was almost certainly taking advantage of the situation to resolve a serious threat to his own authority at court which had come to a head in February 1569. Camden later recalled:

> Certain Lords of England, amongst whom were the Marquess of Winchester, the Duke of Norfolk, the earls of Arundel, Northumberland, Westmorland, Pembroke, Leicester and others, sought causes against Cecil ... for that they repined at his power with the Queen, suspecting him to favour the House of Suffolk in the succession to the crown and feared lest he would stop the course of their designs. They conspired therefore secretly to cast him into the Tower.[44]

Although Pembroke was soon released after interrogation in November 1569, Cecil had effectively neutralised the personal threat which the Earl and his associates had posed. Pembroke's court career was all but finished. Rumours circulated that he was to be deprived of the Stewardship, and it was not until mid-December that the Queen publicly forgave him. She then accepted his offer of assistance in the suppression of the Northern Rising although, as it turned out, his services were never required. Just over three months later, on 17 March 1570, Pembroke died at Hampton Court. His martial exploits and outstanding success as a courtier were celebrated in Holinshed's Chronicles, and in verse elegies by Thomas Churchyard and George Coryat.[45]

As a politician and public servant, Pembroke belonged to that talented group of sixteenth-century courtiers, including the Marquis of Winchester and the Lords Hunsdon, Burghley and Paget, who were first generation in the peerage. His significance as a literary patron is less clear-cut. Suspected of illiteracy and perhaps able to read and write (if at all) only in his native Welsh, William Herbert appears at first sight as an unlikely patron of English writers. Nor can we hope to discover the full extent of his artistic involvements since very few of his family papers have survived. A brief reference in court records, for example, to his purchase in 1567 of 'certain works of marble jasper' from abroad, may be merely an isolated transaction or, alternatively, a clue that Pembroke collected such artefacts extensively. Similarly, the noted Elizabethan scientist and astrologer, John Dee, left a tantalisingly obscure reference to a possible period of employment in the Earl's service, by jotting down on the 'errata' page of one of his books: '"Veni in servitiu" comitis W. Pembrok, 1552, fine februarii die 28.'[46] But, ultimately, Pembroke's reputation as a patron of letters owed little to his personal dealings with writers. They addressed tributes to him primarily because he was seen to wield great power and influence. He was represented in literary tributes as an outstanding warrior-courtier, acclaimed on the battlefield and celebrated as an upholder of the concept of courtly magnificence in his own lifestyle. Literary skills were to him a functional tool, to be used in the education of a court élite or as a means of influencing religious and political opinion. Above all, they provided an effective medium for the celebration and assertion of the Herbert family name.

'THE COMMON RENDEZVOUS OF WORTH IN HIS TIME'

The legendary reputation of Philip Sidney is one of the most closely studied phenomena of sixteenth-century English literature. John Buxton's conclusion was emphatic: 'inspiration from Sidney set the English Renaissance on its course'. Jan van Dorsten went further, describing Sidney's impact on literature in terms of its international significance: 'Against all odds and almost single-handedly, he provided the ambience and inspiration that was to initiate one of the greatest periods in European literary history.'[1] Nor does such praise seem out of keeping with the views of Sidney's own contemporaries. They considered that his prodigious personal talents had naturally led him to encourage the efforts of others. One of his closest friends, Fulke Greville, later summarised the essential details of Sidney's idealised reputation as a courtier and patron:

> Indeed, he was a true model of worth ... such a lover of mankind and goodness that whosoever had any real parts in him found comfort, participation and protection to the uttermost of his power ... The universities abroad and at home accounted him a general Maecenas of learning, dedicated their books to him, and communicated every invention or improvement of knowledge with him ... Men of affairs in most parts of Christendom entertained correspondency with him ... his heart and capacity were so large that there was not a cunning painter, a skilful engineer, an excellent musician or any other artificer of extraordinary fame that made not himself known to this famous spirit and found

him his true friend without hire, and the common
rendezvous of worth in his time.[2]

The development of this myth of patronage is all the
more remarkable in that Sidney never held high office under
Elizabeth and, from the early-1580s onward, grew
increasingly disillusioned with his career as a courtier.
Furthermore, Sidney's own intemperate generosity,
combined with his family's perennial financial difficulties,
ensured that he was rarely in a position to make any
substantial rewards to deserving writers. Yet it was the life
of the real man, with all its limitations and disappointments,
that formed much of the foundation for his later reputation.
In particular, his family contacts were of crucial and lasting
significance to his public life. They provided him not only
with the basic principles of his academic and courtly
education but also with the roots of his political ambitions
and allegiances. The main purpose of this chapter is to
trace, within the context of the development of Sidney's
literary reputation during his lifetime, how the various
family links between the Sidneys and the Herberts served to
confirm his commitment to learning and, in no small
measure, fostered his remarkable literary productivity after
1577.

One of the strongest influences brought to bear on
Philip as a child was the need for him to develop a firm
sense of duty towards his family. When he was about eleven
years old, his father, Sir Henry, advised him: 'Remember,
my son, the noble blood you are descended of, by your
mother's side; and think that only, by virtuous life and good
action, you may be an ornament to that illustr[ious]
family.'[3] Philip's mother, Mary Dudley, was the sister of the
Earl of Leicester. In his Defence of Leicester (c. 1585), a
retort to a savage attack made on his uncle in a tract known
as Leicester's Commonwealth, Sidney was proud to assert: 'I
am a Dudley in blood ... my chiefest honour is to be a
Dudley, and truly am glad to have cause to set forth the
nobility of that blood whereof I am descended.' His father's
ancestors were no less a source of honour to him and in the
same paragraph Sidney insisted: 'I may justly affirm that I
am by my father's side of ancient and always well esteemed
and well matched gentry.'[4]

Sir Henry Sidney served Elizabeth as both her Lord
Deputy in Ireland and President of the Welsh Council. It is
clear that he envisaged for his eldest son an active career in

public service. He advised Philip: 'exercise that practice of learning often; for that will stand you in most stead in that profession of life that you are born to live in.'[5] Sir Henry also regarded scholarship as an integral aspect of his own private pursuits. He was a keen book collector, purchasing printed works from the London stationer, Richard Tottel, and exchanged rare volumes with his friend Matthew Parker, Archbishop of Canterbury, a founder member of the Society of Antiquaries. It has even been suggested that Sir Henry's zeal as a bibliophile may have led him to obtain some of Bale's collection of books and manuscripts which disappeared under suspicious circumstances in Ireland.[6]

Although Sir Henry was an accomplished scholar in his own right, he was careful to impress upon Philip that literary pursuits were to be regarded only as a diversion from, or more properly, a servant to an active career in public service. By enrolling Philip at Shrewsbury School on 16 November 1564, Sir Henry selected an educational institution where, under the direction of its master, Thomas Ashton, the students' studies were geared to the intellectual demands of their intended careers in court and public service rather than to the pursuit of knowledge for its own sake. The school's curriculum was centred upon the works of Livy, Caesar, Sallust, Cicero, Isocrates and Xenophon, all of whom had been not only authors but also politicians.[7] Greville explained that even Philip's own compositions were to be regarded as the product of a similar attitude: 'his end was not writing even while he wrote, nor his knowledge moulded for tables or schools, but both his wit and understanding bent upon his heart to make himself and others, not in words or opinion, but in life and action, good and great.'[8]

One proven route to power and influence at court for a talented young man was to be found through the diplomatic service. Sir Francis Walsingham, who eventually became Sidney's father-in-law and political mentor, was for several highly successful years Queen Elizabeth's envoy to the French court before becoming her Principal Secretary in England. F.J. Levy has suggested that Philip's family may have been intending for him to follow in Walsingham's footsteps. Consequently, measures were taken to ensure that he possessed a first-hand knowledge of continental courts and European politics. At a time when grand tours were still comparatively rare, Philip travelled to Paris in summer 1572, Frankfurt in the following winter, then

Vienna, Venice, Padua, the Rhineland and the Netherlands. Honoured with the grandiose title, 'son of the Viceroy of Ireland', and presumed to be the heir to the Earls of Leicester and Warwick, Sidney visited foreign courts, observed their ways of diplomacy and absorbed their attitudes to the arts.[9]

The express purpose of Sidney's travels was to attain 'the knowledge of foreign languages', but it is clear that an ambassadorial role was already being envisaged for him. His tutor, Hubert Languet, constantly emphasised this objective, insisting that Philip corresponded with him in the international language of Latin; as well as advising him to ply diligently his studies of history, a subject of obvious importance to an ambassador. Furthermore, although Philip was as yet devoid of any significant military or political experience, Languet had already marked him out as a potential leader of European Protestants, uniting the Lutherans, Calvinists and English Anglicans against the increasing threat of militant Catholicism.[10]

Sidney returned to England at the end of May 1575, a credit to his family and acclaimed by the Protestant intelligentsia of Europe. In 1577 the Queen appointed Philip as ambassador to Germany, officially to offer her condolences to the Emperor Rudolph on the death of his father but also, according to Greville, who travelled with Sidney on the mission, 'to salute such German princes as were interested in the cause of our religion or their own native liberty'. After completing his duties, Sidney was able to meet the man he most admired in European politics, William of Orange. Their encounter was a great success and turned out to be one of the peaks of Philip's brief political career. Orange informed Greville 'that, if he could judge, her Majesty had one of the ripest and greatest counsellors of state, in Sir Philip Sidney, that at this day lived in Europe'.[11] He crowned their meeting by suggesting that a scheme which amounted to a proposed union of Holland and Zeeland with England should be celebrated by the marriage of his daughter to Philip. Although Elizabeth's characteristic caution ensured that nothing ever came of these plans, Sidney's role in the affair was regarded as a signal success by his family. By the time of his return to England in June 1577, Philip Sidney had every reason to believe that he was at the beginning of a long and distinguished career in public service.

THE HERBERTS, SIDNEYS AND DUDLEYS

The marriage on 21 April 1577 of Sir Henry Sidney's eldest surviving daughter, Mary, to Henry, second Earl of Pembroke, marked an increased intimacy between the two families.[12] The second Earl's father had been regarded from the early-1560s as a close associate of Robert Dudley, Earl of Leicester. Mary's marriage bore all the signs of being primarily a political alliance, engineered by Leicester who even assisted her impecunious father in raising the dowry.[13] Wilton House soon became a regular meeting ground for the Herberts, Sidneys and Dudleys. In June 1577 the Earl of Leicester and his brother Ambrose, Earl of Warwick, visited Pembroke and his new Countess at Wilton. Leicester subsequently went privately with Pembroke to the spa at Buxton. There was another family congregation at the Herberts' home in August, which included Philip and Robert Sidney. Philip returned to his sister at Wilton only a month later. By December 1577, a court commentator, scenting more than family friendship, noted that Leicester had yet again slipped off to Wilton, 'to sport there awhile', reappearing at court just before Christmas, after 'making merry with his nephew, the Earl of Pembroke'.[14]

There is little doubt that most of these and subsequent visits were motivated primarily by family events. In November 1578, for example, the Herberts, Sidneys and Dudleys all assembled at Wilton for a protracted celebration to mark the Countess of Pembroke's seventeenth birthday.[15] Other meetings, however, were rather less innocent in intent. Pembroke's main London residence, Baynard's Castle, was used as a base for Leicester's discussions with the Herberts and Sidneys over the proposal for Elizabeth to marry the Duke of Alençon, the younger brother of a previous prospective spouse, the Duke of Anjou. Hostility towards this alliance came to a head in August 1579 with the publication of John Stubbs's attack on the marriage, The Discovery of a Gaping Gulf. On the 25th of that month, it was reported by Mendoza, the Spanish Ambassador, that Leicester, 'Lord Sidney and other friends and relatives', met at 'the Earl of Pembroke's house'. His report continued: 'They no doubt discussed the matter, and some of them afterwards remarked that Parliament would have something to say as to whether the Queen married or not. The people in general seem to threaten revolution about it.'[16]

The possibility of a civil uprising over the affair, in

fact, was extremely remote. Nor was there much likelihood of the Queen being cajoled by parliamentary pressure. A third and more viable alternative, the production by Leicester's allies of a written statement on these proposals, was probably discussed in detail during the meeting at Pembroke's residence. Philip Sidney, who had already ably defended his father's administration of land tax in a Discourse on Irish Affairs, was a natural choice for the authorship of such a document. Hubert Languet was later to remind Sidney that he had been 'ordered to write as you did by those whom you were bound to obey' - almost certainly the Earls of Leicester and Pembroke, and perhaps Sir Francis Walsingham. Sidney's tract, A Letter ... to Queen Elizabeth, achieved a wide manuscript circulation. It avoided making any direct criticism of the marriage, unlike Stubbs's more sensational printed diatribe, which depicted Alençon as a notorious debauchee: 'the old serpent himself in the form of a man come a second time to seduce the English Eve and to ruin the English paradise'. In contrast, Sidney guardedly solicited the Queen to consider very carefully how this foreign influence could effect England, particularly its Protestants, 'your chief, if not your sole, strength'.[17]

Stubbs's intemperate words earned for him and his stationer the barbaric response of having their right hands struck off. Sidney ran little risk of such a severe punishment but it soon became apparent that his absence from court for a while would be advisable. He withdrew to his sister's home at Wilton from March to August 1580. The prospect of such a visit was made all the more attractive by the imminent arrival of the Countess's first child. Her son, William, was born on 8 April and Sidney represented Leicester at the christening the following month. Sidney almost certainly took no further part in the marriage debate but his retreat into Wiltshire may have revived court suspicions that the Herberts' country residence, like their London home, was becoming a centre for intrigue. Even when Sir Henry Sidney visited Wilton in May 1580 for the apparently innocuous purpose of attending the christening of Pembroke's son, Walsingham was obliged to warn him a few weeks later that the Queen, 'hath commanded me to recommend unto your Lordship the more earnestly, for that she is given to understand, that your Lordship doth sometime resort to Wilton; which ... she somewhat misliketh', In April 1581, the Earls of Pembroke and Leicester were publicly brought into line by being ordered, along with others, to meet Alençon on his arrival in England. The clearest gesture of submission to the royal will came from Philip Sidney himself who, on New Year's Day 1581, presented the Queen with a 'whip garnished with small diamonds' as a token of his deference to her absolute authority over the marriage question.[18]

'DONE ONLY FOR YOU, ONLY TO YOU'

The ambitious Elizabethan courtier generally envisaged creative literary composition as a pursuit most suited to times of relaxation or when employment in court service was not available. Much of Sidney's Old Arcadia appears to have been penned in response to just such circumstances. Some preliminary drafts were probably begun soon after his embassy to Germany in June 1577, which coincided with his several visits to see his sister in that year. His subsequent withdrawal to Wilton from March to August 1580 would have then provided him with an extended and relatively uninterrupted period of writing. It becomes tempting, therefore, to imagine that Sidney's literary career was first stimulated, in no small measure, by his sister's company and the congenial family environment which he found at Wilton. A.C. Hamilton speculated that Philip and Mary could have whiled away their 'idle times' together by reading romances. 'Since these would have been chiefly foreign', he continued, 'a concern for English letters may have led her to suggest that he write a romance in English.'[19] Whatever the Countess's role in the composition of the Arcadia, Sidney himself insisted that he had written it chiefly to please her: 'you desired me to do it, and your desire to my heart is an absolute commandment. Now it is done only for you, only to you.' Furthermore, Philip described in his dedicatory address how he had sent to the Countess his rough drafts whenever it had not been possible for him to write in her presence.

Although Philip appears to have regarded the Countess as his closest literary associate during the composition of the Old Arcadia, their familiarity was not of any long standing. They had spent only the briefest of periods together as children and Philip left for the continent in the summer of 1572 when his sister was ten years old. In February 1575, the Queen wrote to Sir Henry Sidney to offer her condolences on the death of his daughter, Ambrosia. At the same time, she extended an invitation for Mary to join her entourage of ladies at court. Such an advantageous opportunity was readily accepted and, in the following June, Mary and her parents accompanied the Queen's mid-summer progress to Leicester's country estate at Kenilworth. Philip Sidney, recently returned from his triumphant European travels, was also in the party, thereby enjoying his first extended period of time in Mary's company. He may also have been with the court at Woodstock in September 1575 when his sister received her earliest known poetic tribute, amidst a garland of complimentary verses addressed to the ladies of the royal entourage:

Tho young in years, yet old in wit
A gest due to your race,
If you hold on as you begin,
Who ist you'll not deface? [20]

In subsequent years a deep and lasting affection developed between Philip and Mary. Exactly how intimate this relationship became has long fascinated the idly curious. Although in the Old Arcadia Philip described himself as, 'the writer who doth exceedingly love you', these words are firmly rooted in the traditionally fulsome language of dedicatory panegyrics. Interest, however, has been fuelled by Aubrey's recounting of a scandalous rumour about Philip: 'there was so great love between him and his fair sister that I have heard old gentlemen say that they lay together, and it was thought the first Philip Earl of Pembroke [ie. the fourth Earl] was begot by him.'[21] Clearly, with only this kind of gossip to go on, it is impossible to clarify the exact nature of their intimacy. Nevertheless, there is little reason to doubt that the affectionate bonds which many later writers envisaged between Philip and Mary were firmly based in reality.

Wilton House provided Sidney with one of his main centres of activity as a writer, an importance which was occasionally reflected in his poems and correspondence. Certain Sonnets 22, 'The 7. Wonders of England', opens with a description of Stonehenge, situated within easy reach of the Pembrokes' country residence: 'Near Wilton sweet, huge heaps of stones are found.' Another poem, printed in the 1613 edition of the Arcadia, entitled 'A Dialogue between two shepherds, utter'd in a pastoral show, at Wilton', is possibly by Sidney since he is known to have involved himself there in such entertainments. Also of interest is a letter which Sidney wrote from Wilton on Whitsunday, 22

May 1580, to his young friend, Edward Denny, recommending him to study the works of Aristotle, Cicero, Plutarch, Xenophon, Livy, Tacitus, Machiavelli, Froissart, Guiccardini, Holinshed and numerous other writers. Of course, Philip may have compiled this particular list from memory. But it is difficult to imagine how he could have been so heavily engaged in literary pursuits at Wilton between 1577 and 1580 without making at least occasional reference to his sister's library.[22]

The growth of Sidney's preoccupation with the related themes of courtly disillusion and rural retreat coincided with his several withdrawals to Wilton House from 1577 onward. His lack of success in securing royal employment at court was beginning to cause him acute anxiety and the thought of burying himself in rural obscurity periodically occupied his mind. In October 1578 Languet wrote to him with some disquiet: 'I am especially sorry to hear you say that you are weary of the life to which I have no doubt God has called you, and desire to fly from the light of your court and betake yourself to the privacy of secluded places to escape the tempest of affairs by which statesmen are generally harassed.'[23] We must, of course, be careful to avoid falling into the trap of reading Sidney's fictions as straight autobiography. But in The Lady of May, or in the tensions between political responsibility and pastoral retreat facing Basilius and the melancholy knight, Philisides, in the Old Arcadia, it is possible to detect reflections of Sidney's own ponderings over the choice between the active or the contemplative life. In other words, Wilton House provided an environment - perhaps the major one - where Sidney was able to find the peace and leisure to contemplate the difficulties of transforming his reputation as a gilded youth with great expectations into that of a statesman-like leader of European Protestantism.

In addition to these personal considerations, Philip's letter to Denny indicates that his political philosophy may also have been taking a more sceptical turn during his enforced rustication at Wilton. He strongly recommended to his friend the works of Guiccardini, the meticulous and incisive analyst of Florentine government; and Machiavelli, whose purpose Alberico Gentili informed Sidney, was not 'to instruct the tyrant, but by revealing his secret counsels to strip him bare'. Most significantly, Sidney's admiration for Tacitus, whose editio princeps had appeared as recently as 1575, placed him in the vanguard of a growing group of

English Taciteans who sought to apply his understanding of statecraft and probings into the hidden workings of courts to late-Elizabethan and early-Jacobean governments.[24]

Although, in his own opinion, Sidney was both inactive and frustrated as a courtier between 1577 and 1580, all the evidence suggests that the time he spent at Wilton marked for him a period of intense literary and intellectual development. Through the company of his sister and the pleasures of her home, 'an Arcadian place and a Paradise', according to Aubrey, Sidney was able to enhance the contemplative side of his nature as a creative writer and political thinker. But if the active life of a courtier was still to be pursued, Wilton House could also be seen as a refuge from personal responsibility and public duty. In September 1580 Languet warned Sidney that his long retirement at Wilton was beginning to make his friends, both in England and abroad, think 'that you are tired of that toilsome path which leads to virtue, which you formerly pursued with so much earnestness'. Not wishing to become a Basilius, Sidney wrote to his brother, Robert, in October 1580, remarking that he had 'given over the delight in the world'; a phrase which has been interpreted as indicating that his residence at Wilton had by then come to an end.[25]

'TO MY BIRTH I OWE / NOBLER DESIRES'

The late 1570s and early 1580s were a period of growing discontent for Philip Sidney. In addition to his own lack of preferment at court, he considered his father, Sir Henry, to be both under-funded and unappreciated in Ireland by the Queen. Furthermore, her procrastination over offering military or financial help for the support of European Protestantism led Philip to confess to Languet in March 1578: 'unless God powerfully counteract it, I seem to myself to see our cause withering away'.[26] Much of Sidney's prestige during his travels through Europe had derived from his being the Earl of Leicester's heir, but the latter's marriage to the Earl of Essex's widow, and the birth of their son in 1581, dashed Philip's hopes of inheriting the Dudley fortune. At court tournaments, Sidney had borne the emblem, 'SPERO' (I hope) but, according to Camden, after being displaced as Leicester's heir, he adopted the impresa SPERAVI (I have hoped), with the word dashed through to indicate his loss. His predicament also appears to have found expression in the semi-autobiographical sonnet, Astrophil and Stella 21:

> to my birth I owe
> Nobler desires, least else that friendly foe,
> Great expectation, wear a train of shame.
> For since mad March great promise made of me,
> If now the May of my years much decline,
> What can be hoped my harvest time will be?

It is perhaps of significance to note at this point that in November 1581, when Penelope Devereux married Lord Rich, Philip was staying at the Pembroke's London house, Baynard's Castle. In the previous month Penelope's guardian, the Countess of Huntingdon, had visited Wilton for the christening of the Countess of Pembroke's eldest daughter, Catherine. The match with Robert Rich had been finally confirmed only in mid-September and there is little doubt that this forthcoming marriage - of a young woman once proposed as a spouse for her still unwed brother - would have been of considerable interest to Mary Herbert. The topic must surely have occupied much of Mary's conversation with the Countess of Huntingdon during her stay at Wilton. Philip himself returned to Wilton in December for the duration of the Christmas season, during which he may well have first considered, perhaps with his sister's encouragement, putting down on paper his clearly mixed feelings towards Penelope's marriage. If - and this is purely hypothetical - he went so far as to attempt early versions of some of the Astrophil and Stella sonnets, then it is possible that, as with the Arcadia, the Countess of Pembroke was sometimes with him as he wrote or read through drafts which he later brought to her.[27]

Sidney probably lingered at Wilton well into January before once again seeking to immerse himself in public affairs. He served as a member of parliament, busying himself on various committees which considered such issues as seditious attacks on the Queen, the curriers of London and Raleigh's receipt of letters patent for overseas discovery. Meanwhile, Sir Henry attempted to find some appointment for his son in Ireland and Philip himself solicited, unsuccessfully, for preferment in Wales. In matters of diplomacy, Sidney played a prominent part in various court tournaments, staged for distinguished visitors, including the well-known 'Foster Children of Desire' before the French commissioners at Whitsun, 1581. He also explored the possibility of establishing in the Azores a piracy base against the Spanish treasure fleets, which was to be led by Drake and to sail under the flag of Don Antonio, the pretender to the Portuguese throne. Closer to home, he entered negotiations with the Earl of Angus, the leader of the pro-English faction at the Scottish court, and showed a keen interest in the Catholic threat of Mary, Queen of Scots, and the necessity of providing James with an English subsidy. On the continent, he maintained close contacts with friends in Germany and the Low Countries and continued to support the latter's appeals to Elizabeth for help.

Despite the diversity of these involvements, Sidney was still not employed by the Queen in any really important state business. With a considerable amount of time on his hands, the Herberts were again able to provide Philip with a congenial family environment and a rural retreat away from the pressures of the court. When, for example, de Ségur, Henry of Navarre's secretary and an active reformer, arrived in England in July 1583, Sidney took him off to Wilton to visit the Herberts and, no doubt, to discuss European affairs in relative privacy. It was, however, probably the pleasure which Philip derived from his sister's company which most often lured him back to rural Wiltshire, even after his marriage in September 1583 to Walsingham's daughter, Frances. In the following year, for example, they both came to stay at Wilton when the Countess was expecting another child.[28]

Although genuine friendship should be regarded as the prime motivation for this intimacy between the two families, the Sidneys were fortunately placed in having such powerful relatives. In 1584 the Earl of Pembroke played a significant role in the introduction of Philip's brother, Robert, to personal wealth and public affairs. To bolster their family's precarious financial position, the Sidneys sought for Robert the hand of Barbara Gamage, a rich Welsh heiress. There were rival suitors but Pembroke had persuasive words by letter with her guardian, Sir Edward Stradling. The subsequent marriage of Robert to Barbara has been described as, 'a triumph for the influence of Pembroke and for the credit of the Sidneys'. The Earl continued to further Robert's career by urging Stradling to support his election as a knight of the shire of Glamorgan; an objective which was also successfully achieved. In response to this family association, Simon Robson, the compiler of The Choice of Change (1585), a popular miscellany of adages and proverbs, dedicated this work jointly to the Earl of Pembroke, Philip and Robert Sidney, describing them as, 'linked & united together in an indissoluble band of amity & fraternity.'[29]

In his <u>Defence of Poetry</u>, penned in the early 1580s, Sidney noted: '(I know not by what mischance) in these my not old years and idlest times [I have] ... slipped into the title of a poet.' This apparently off-hand remark provides a key to an understanding of the developments which were taking place at this period in Sidney's view of himself as a writer. Frequently inactive as a courtier, he increasingly found in literary pursuits a source of intellectual activity and ambition. The <u>Old Arcadia</u> had begun as little more than a means of private relaxation, to be shared only with his sister, but the <u>Defence</u> marks Sidney's 'emergence as a public poet, a role which he fulfils by revising and recasting the <u>Old Arcadia</u> into ... the <u>New Arcadia</u>'.[30]

At the same time, Sidney's public reputation as a patron was steadily growing. His involvement with poetry had been first mentioned after his visit to Heidelberg in 1577 by the German scholar, Paul Schede (also known as Melissus), who addressed him as, '<u>Sydnee</u> <u>Musarum</u> <u>inclite</u> <u>cultibus</u>'. Until then, the literary tributes paid to him by Henri Estienne, Thomas Drant, Théophile de Banos and Lambert Daneau had been offered primarily as tokens of friendship and in admiration of his youthful promise rather than in recognition of any acknowledged importance as a writer or patron.[31] Edmund Spenser and Gabriel Harvey appear to have been the individuals most responsible for the formulation, in its earliest stages, of Sidney's public reputation in England as a man of letters. In <u>Gratulationes Valdinenses</u> (1578), a collection of poetic panegyrics, Harvey addressed him as one, '<u>In</u> <u>quibus</u> <u>ipsae</u> <u>habitent</u> <u>Musae</u>, <u>dominetur</u> <u>Apollo</u>'; Spenser dedicated <u>The Shepherd's Calendar</u> in 1579 to 'the noble and virtuous gentleman most worthy of all titles both of learning and chivalry M. Philip Sidney'; and in the following year, the <u>Familiar Letters</u> of Spenser and Harvey again referred to Sidney's literary pursuits.

Strangely, these determined efforts to publicise Sidney's commitment to literature did not stimulate any widespread appreciation during the 1580s of his poetic skills. A sprinkling of authors - Thomas Howell (one of the Countess of Pembroke's servants), Du Bartas, Geoffrey Whitney and Edmund Molyneux - made isolated references to Sidney's own literary pursuits but the majority of writers were more concerned to promote his image as an ideal courtier. Consequently, works were dedicated to him on such diverse topics as horsemanship, military tactics, Ireland, Latin pronunciation, Ramist logic, ancient history, geography and international law. It seems unlikely, in fact, that Sidney would have desired to cultivate for himself any great public reputation as a man of letters. Although he brought a growing intellectual commitment to his literary endeavours during the early 1580s, an involvement in the commercial world of print would have been both compromising and demeaning for a courtier of Sidney's social status.[32]

It was the public realm of politics which exerted the strongest hold over Sidney's ambitions during the last two years of his life. In July 1585 he was appointed as joint Master of the Ordnance, to serve alongside his uncle, the Earl of Warwick, in the organisation of the nation's defences. Despite these duties, a desire for action remained with him and, in the following month, he was prevented from joining Drake's expedition to the West Indies only by the Queen's direct intervention. Events in Europe, however, were taking a decided turn for the worse from an English point of view. The assassination in July 1584 of the leader of the Dutch rebels, William of Orange, had left Elizabeth with little choice but to send a military force to the Low Countries. If the Spanish army were to quell the Dutch, as it increasingly threatened to do under its redoubtable commander, the Prince of Parma, then there was nothing to stop Philip II from turning his attentions towards England. The interventionist policy advocated by Leicester and Sidney in the late 1570s, for so long shunned by the Queen, was rapidly becoming a necessity. Following the publication, in five languages, of A Declaration of the Causes Moving the Queen to Give Aid to the ... Low Countries, Sidney's appointment as Governor of Flushing was confirmed on 9 November 1585.[33] At last, tha active life of a soldier, statesman and Protestant hero was about to begin.

'THE HONOURABLEST DEATH THAT COULD BE DESIRED'

The news of Sidney's death on 17 October 1586 from wounds received on the battlefield at Zutphen evoked an international response. He was lamented by King James of

Scotland; Ortel, the Dutch envoy in London; Louise de Coligny, widow of William the Silent; her friend the lawyer, Jean Hotman; and numerous scholars, including Justus Lipsius and Duplessis-Mornay. The States of Zeeland in the Low Countries wished to undertake his burial and promised to erect a magnificent memorial in his honour. King Philip II inscribed a brief but evocative note on the dispatch announcing Sidney's death: 'He was my godson'. At home, Greville was stunned with grief. 'The only question I now study,' he wrote to the Scottish ambassador, 'is whether weeping sorrow, or speaking sorrow, may most honour his memory, that I think death is sorry for.'

In his biography of Sidney, Roger Howell remarked that the 'central event of his career had been his death'. His youth and reputed bravado on the battlefield accentuated a national sense of loss. His state funeral at St. Paul's on 16 February 1587 was built up into an intensely dramatic expression of national mourning. Verse elegies by Thomas Churchyard, George Whetstone and other minor court poets were hastily printed, lamenting the loss of an outstanding chivalric hero. A flurry of popular ballads in his memory, none of which has survived, were entered in the Stationers' Register throughout 1587. Commemorative volumes of elegiac tributes were also produced by the universities of Cambridge, Oxford and Leiden. One of the Oxford collections, Peplus (1587), was compiled by members of New College and dedicated to Sidney's brother-in-law, the second Earl of Pembroke, who had studied there.[34]

During his life, Sidney's powers of patronage had been severely restricted by his lack of high office and persistent shortage of finance; in death, such limitations became irrelevant. The elegists were free to represent him not only as the perfect Protestant knight but also as the ideal patron - generous, discriminating and a source of inspiration for other writers. Thomas Lant made reference to his liberality; Angel Day celebrated him as a poet; and John Phillips recalled how Sidney had 'scaled Parnassus and sat ... amongst the Muses'. Predictably, the university elegists made great play of his devotion to letters. In the Oxford Exequiae volume, Richard Latewar and Francis Mason appear to have already known about the Arcadia and Astrophil and Stella; Richard Eedes described Sidney as his 'first author of my writing poetry'; and George Carleton was even able to note that the Arcadia had been written at Wilton, 'Pembrochia in aula'. The Peplus collection contained a memorable pastoral elegy, 'Lycidas', by John Gifford, which was devoted to the theme of Sidney's patronage of English poetry. The elegists derived consolation from the thought that Sidney understood and sympathised with the dilemmas of seeking literary patronage. He was envisaged as that most rare of patrons - one who genuinely cared about his clients. In John Phillips's words, he was 'to the learned liberal, to suitors a great comfort'. It was perhaps Thomas Nashe who best expressed the idea that Sidney's personality had been perfectly suited to the role of a literary patron:

> Gentle Sir Philip Sidney, thou knew'st what belonged to a scholar, thou knew'st what pains, what toil, what travail, conduct to perfection: well could'st thou give every virtue his encouragement, every art his due, every writer his desert.[35]

In view of his high social status, literary talents and heroic death, it is unsurprising that Sidney rapidly became the most widely acclaimed Elizabethan patron of letters. Yet there is a much less impressive side to his activities as a courtier which serves to emphasise how his contemporaries and later generations chose to concentrate upon the myth rather than the realities of his life. As regards his political involvements, Sidney was a failure in his own terms. The cause of European Protestantism, which he had so resolutely espoused, neither fired the Queen's imagination nor attracted her financial support. On a personal level, Sidney's social and political aspirations never received the all important stimulus of prolonged royal favour. Watching his father being gradually worn down by an unrewarding Governorship of Ireland, and kicking his own heels at court and Wilton, Philip began to believe, with some justification, that the Queen's attitude towards his family was more one of suspicion than favour. Even the awarding of his knighthood in January 1584 had proved a hollow source of honour. Prince Casimir of the Palatinate had named Sidney as his proxy when he was unable to attend his installation as a Knight of the Garter. However, court regulations decreed that only someone already of equivalent rank could perform such a duty. Sidney was hastily knighted, a beneficiary not of his own worth but of ceremonial necessity.[36] Four years later, his funeral united the nation in communal grief but doubts still linger over the exact

motives behind such a lavish commemoration. Even though
Sidney's body had arrived in London on 5 November 1586, his
funeral did not take place until 16 February 1587; a delay
which is usually explained by the complications involved in
the execution of his will. It should not be overlooked,
however, that Sidney's funeral was scheduled just eight days
after the execution of Mary, Queen of Scots. Such an
ostentatious public spectacle would have provided Elizabeth
with a convenient means of distracting the minds of the
London populace from the controversial beheading of a
Catholic queen.

During the 1580s, Elizabethan writers were looking for
a hero: in Sidney they had at last found their man. His lack
of royal favour, his empty knighthood and even the possible
manipulation of his funeral for political ends could not
tarnish the dazzling image of perfection with which poets
were determined to endow him. Through his death, Sidney
became, virtually overnight, a Protestant martyr and the
embodiment of nationalistic chivalry. Arthur Golding, who
completed his translation of Duplessis-Mornay, concluded in
its dedication:

> He died ... of manly wounds received in service of
> his Prince, in defence of persons oppressed, in
> maintenance of the only true Catholic & Christian
> religion, among the noble, valiant, and wise, in the
> open field, in martial manner, the honourablest
> death that could be desired, and best beseeming a
> Christian knight, whereby he hath worthily won to
> himself immortal fame among the godly, and left
> example worthy of imitation to others of his
> calling.[37]

Printed in 1587, Golding's words illustrate how Philip's long-
lived image as a perfect knight and English hero was already
in a remarkably advanced state of formulation within a year
of his death.

PRIVATE WORKS MADE PUBLIC

In his dedication of the Old Arcadia to the Countess of Pembroke, Sidney warned her to 'keep it to yourself, or to such friends who will weigh errors in the balance of good will', concluding that its 'chief safety shall be the not walking abroad'. According to Greville, Sidney had wished to have all the manuscripts of the Arcadia destroyed after his death: 'he bequeathed no other legacy but the fire to this unpolished embryo'.[1] However, towards the end of 1586, Greville unexpectedly received notification from the London stationer, William Ponsonby, that another unnamed member of the book-trade had already gone so far as to submit an unauthorised manuscript of the Arcadia for licensing. Although this illegal act was rapidly suppressed, Greville made it clear in a letter to Sir Francis Walsingham that Sidney's relatives and friends could no longer hold any real hopes of preserving his literary remains in a state of inaccessible manuscript respectability. Taking a sensible view of the situation, Greville realised that an authorised edition of Sidney's compositions would be a useful means of ensuring that he received 'all those religious honours which are worthily due to his life and death.' Once Sidney's executors had decided that they could trust him, Ponsonby would have been regarded as a useful intermediary, providing a necessary link with the commercial side of publishing. No doubt much consideration was given to the matter until 23 August 1588 when Ponsonby not only obtained the licence for the Arcadia, but was also granted the rights to 'A translation of Salust de Bartas. Done by the same Sir P. in the English.'[2]

Greville had been first encouraged into poetic

composition by Sidney who bequeathed to him, along with Edward Dyer, all his books including a now lost manuscript of the revised Arcadia. This intimacy, combined with the fact that Ponsonby had gone to him rather than to anyone else, made him the most obvious choice as the first editor of Sidney's literary remains. Using his own manuscript of the revised Arcadia, Greville acted as 'the over-seer of the print', assisted by one of his close friends, the Oxford scholar, Dr Matthew Gwinne, and almost certainly by the translator and lexicographer, John Florio, the son of the Florentine Protestant, Michael Angelo. There is no evidence that the Countess chose to involve herself personally in the editorial process for this edition although, presumably, Sidney's dedicatory address, 'To My Dear Lady and Sister', could only have been included with her permission. Greville's editorial labours appear to have met with the Herberts' approval and in 1590 the Earl of Pembroke appointed him as secretary to the Council in Wales. He continued to be regarded with favour and by 1593 was in the uniquely privileged and highly lucrative position of being not only Pembroke's secretary but also a councillor, clerk of the Council and sole keeper of the Signet.[3]

The publication of the Arcadia in 1590 confirmed Sidney's already acclaimed leadership of vernacular writers; and its dedication drew attention to the Countess of Pembroke's close involvement in his literary activities. Her importance was clearly recognised in 1591 by the stationer, Thomas Newman, who included in his unauthorised quarto of Astrophil and Stella an address by Thomas Nashe, praising her patronage of poetry: 'whom Arts do adore as a second Minerva, and our Poets extol as the patroness of their invention'. As is well known, this bold ploy did not work, and Newman's edition was rapidly suppressed. It is possible that he was made to reprint, at his own expense, a revised text of the sonnets with his own and Nashe's address removed.[4] Despite this rigorous censorship, it is apparent that in the early 1590s, the popularity of the Arcadia was stimulating a ready market for works associated not just with Sidney but also with the Countess herself. Between 1590 and 1592, Ponsonby published Spenser's The Faerie Queene and his Complaints volume, six works by Abraham Fraunce and one by Thomas Watson, all prefaced by fulsome dedicatory panegyrics of the Countess.[5] But, without doubt, Ponsonby's greatest coup was in 1592 to publish in one volume, Mary Herbert's own translations from the French of Robert

Garnier's Roman tragedy, <u>Antonius</u>, and Duplessis-Mornay's philosophical treatise, <u>A Discourse of Life and Death</u>. This publication confirmed Ponsonby's acceptance as the Sidney group's recognised publisher and, at the same time, provided a remarkable indication of the Countess's own growing commitment to the medium of print. Henceforth, she becomes the most important figure in the editing and publication of Sidney's compositions.

Desirous of doing full justice to her brother's literary talents, Mary set about producing a superior text of the <u>Arcadia</u> to that of the 1590 edition. She was assisted in this endeavour by Hugh Sanford, a talented and versatile man who had previously been engaged at Wilton House as a tutor to her eldest son, William. The 1590 edition, based upon Sidney's own revisions, had broken off in the middle of a sentence in the third book and contained only two sets of eclogues. This incompleteness, combined perhaps with Greville's division of the books into chapters and his ordering of the eclogues, appears to have been at the root of the Countess's dissatisfaction. She directed Sanford in 'correcting the faults' and supplied the 'defects' of the 1590 edition from her own copy of the <u>Old Arcadia</u>. The end result was 'most by her doing, all by her directing' but, overall, she probably attempted little more than a dutiful interpretation of her brother's notes and manuscript revisions.

Sanford promised the readers of the 1593 <u>Arcadia</u>: 'Neither shall these pains be the last ... which the ever-lasting love of her excellent brother will make her consecrate to his memory.' The next step in this process was the publication of an authoritative version of the <u>Defence of Poetry</u> which Ponsonby duly entered in the <u>Stationers' Register</u> on 29 November 1594. A few months later, another stationer, Henry Olney, also obtained a manuscript of the work from an unauthorised source and decided to risk publication. By changing the title to an 'Apology for Poetry' and omitting the author's name, he too obtained a licence on 12 April 1595. Like Newman, Olney claimed to have been motivated only by a desire to propagate Sidney's literary reputation and to be 'the first public bewrayer of poesy's Messias'. Predictably, this explanation did little to assuage the family's disapproval and his edition was suppressed in favour of Ponsonby's authorised text.[6]

The 1598 <u>Arcadia</u> volume formed effectively the first collected edition of Sidney's writings. Calculated to curtail any more unauthorised publishing, it included four other compositions by Sidney and was assembled with the full approval of his family. The Arcadia was reprinted from the 1593 edition and the Defence followed Ponsonby's 1595 version. Texts were also supplied, almost certainly by the Countess, of Certain Sonnets, Astrophil and Stella and The Lady of May. This volume marked the culmination of both the Countess of Pembroke's and Ponsonby's involvement with Sidney's literary remains. Only a year later, a pirated version of the Arcadia was printed in Edinburgh by Robert Waldegrave and sold for 3s less than Ponsonby's edition. Ponsonby succeeded in claiming damages for this breach of his licence, although he published no further editions of Sidney's works and died in 1604. Other stationers took over his titles but there is no evidence that the Countess played any part in their subsequent editions before her death in 1621.[7]

Spenser's compositions were the only ones by a living Englishman worthy of being ranked alongside Sidney's during the 1590s. That at least was the opinion of many of their contemporaries, who could not have failed to recognise the signal service which Ponsonby had performed in making readily available most of the printed works of both men.[8] Samuel Daniel in the 1594 dedication to the Countess of Pembroke of his play, Cleopatra, triumphantly celebrated their respective achievements in proving the English tongue to be worthy of comparison with other European languages:

> ... great Sidney and our Spenser might,
> With those Po-singers being equalled,
> Enchant the world with such a sweet delight,
> That their eternal songs for ever read,
> May show what great Eliza's reign hath bred.
> What music in the kingdom of her peace
> Hath now been made to her, and by her might,
> Whereby her glorious fame shall never cease.[9]

Few late-Elizabethan poets would have disputed the pre-eminence which Daniel awarded to Sidney and Spenser as the leaders of English writers. It is debatable, however, whether Sidney would have achieved such a ranking so quickly without the combined efforts of the Countess of Pembroke and William Ponsonby in ensuring the transmission of his compositions through print to a national and ultimately international audience.

'THE DEAREST SISTER OF THE DEAREST BROTHER'

The Countess of Pembroke's father died in May 1586, her
mother in August and her eldest brother, Philip, in October.
A surge of public sympathy was evoked for the surviving
members of the Sidney family. In Holinshed's Chronicles it
was interpreted as an exemplum of 'the variableness of
fickle fortune' that 'father, mother, and son ... should come
to their fatal ends and fall of name and family, within the
compass of less than six months'.[10] In view of these events,
it is understandable that the Countess should have sought
consolation in literary pursuits, translating by May 1590
Duplessis-Mornay's A Discourse of Life and Death. Known as
the 'Pope of the Huguenots', Mornay had been one of
Sidney's closest continental friends. Philip began, just before
his death, to translate his most ambitious work, a defence of
Christianity against paganism, entitled a Treatise of the
Truth of the Christian Religion. This was a long and
cumbersome volume, worthy in motive but weighed down by
Mornay's excessively zealous tone. In contrast, the
Countess's material possessed a far more personal and
informal quality, having been composed for Mornay's wife,
at her request, as a wedding present. The Discourse had first
appeared in print as a preface to Mornay's selected translations from the letters and essays of Seneca, and was a
variation on the literary tradition of ars moriendi.[11]
Reflecting Mornay's own religious commitments, it also
owed much to Calvin's Institutes and Meditations on the
Future Life. Overall, the Discourse concerned itself more
with the futility of courtly ambition than with death itself.
The courtier's life was envisaged as one of pathetic self-
delusion and great emphasis was placed upon the need to
escape periodically, 'out of the corruption of the world, into
some country place from infected towns'.[12] Published in
1575, the sentiments expressed in the Discourse would have
been in keeping with Sidney's own disillusionment with court
life during his various visits to Wilton between 1577 and
1580. By translating it, the Countess may even have been
carrying out a scheme which she had discussed with her
brother.

A similar contemplation of the futility of human
ambition lay at the centre of another work translated by the
Countess, Petrarch's 'Triumph of Death', a disturbing poem,
indulging in a series of macabre images of the power of
death: 'Popes, emperors, and kings, but strangely grown,/ All

naked now, all needy, beggars all', (80-1). The Trionfi, written soon after Petrarch's Laura died in 1348, comprise six vernacular poems in 'terza rima', depicting the allegorical triumphs of love, chastity, death, fame, time and eternity. The poet's sense of inconsolable bereavement in the 'Triumph of Death', mingled with a desire to be reunited with Laura by shaking off the shackles of mortality, bears a strong resemblance to the sentiments expressed in the Countess's own elegy, 'To the Angel Spirit of ... Sir Philip Sidney', penned as a preface to their collaborative meta-phrase of the Psalms of David:

> I can no more: dear soul I take my leave;
> Sorrow still strives, would mount thy highest sphere
> Presuming so just cause might meet thee there,
> Oh happy change! could I so take my leave. (88-91)[13]

The Countess's own sense of loss, however, was never explicitly stated in her translations of Duplessis-Mornay or Petrarch; nor was 'To the Angel Spirit' published during her lifetime. Once again, it was Spenser who led the way, commending to his contemporaries the Countess's close and loving relationship with her brother. He had been, to a great extent, responsible for the initial formulation of Sidney's public reputation in England as a man of letters, and he saw Mary Herbert as his worthy successor. In a dedicatory sonnet appended to the 1590 edition of The Faerie Queene, he fondly recalled his personal allegiance to Sidney, 'who first my Muse did lift out of the floor', and explained how this loyalty:

> Bids me most noble lady to adore
> His goodly image living evermore,
> In the divine resemblance of your face.

Similarly, Spenser's dedication to the Countess of 'The Ruins of Time' in the Complaints volume insisted upon his personal love for 'that most brave knight your noble brother deceased', and honoured him as 'the hope of all learned men'. The implication contained in these lines is not difficult to interpret. Writers who had admired Sidney's patriotism, 'life exchanging for his country's good', and had drawn inspiration from his enthusiasm for learning, could now hope that the Countess of Pembroke would seek to emulate her brother's example.

Four years later, with her edition of the <u>Arcadia</u> and some of her own translations in print, Spenser could describe the Countess unambiguously as her brother's intellectual and spiritual heir. In <u>Colin Clouts Come Home Again</u> (1595), Spenser celebrated the intimate bonds between Sidney, in his familiar guise as Astrophel, and Mary Herbert, whom he chose to represent as Urania, the Muse of Christian poetry:

> ... in the highest place,
> <u>Urania</u>, sister unto <u>Astrofell</u>
> In whose brave mind, as in a golden coffer,
> All heavenly gifts and richs locked are:
> More rich than pearls of <u>Inde</u>, or gold of <u>Opher</u>,
> And in her sex more wonderful and rare. (486-91)

Appended to this volume was an interesting collection of elegiac verses in Sidney's honour, headed by Spenser's own pastoral lament, 'Astrophel', and dedicated to Philip's widow, Frances, now married to the Earl of Essex.[14] Spenser presents himself as a kind of literary 'master of ceremonies', offering a poem of his own by way of introduction to a series of personal tributes from a group of Sidney's friends and admirers, including Lodowick Bryskett, Walter Raleigh, Matthew Roydon and Greville or Dyer. Their poems exude a tone of social and intellectual familiarity with Sidney and concentrate attention upon his three distinct public roles as ideal courtier, national leader and man of letters.

The question of the Countess's personal involvement in the <u>Astrophel</u> collection centres upon the disputed authorship of a poem appended to Spenser's 'Astrophel' elegy, known as 'The Doleful Lay of Clorinda'. In introducing these lines, Spenser remarked:

> But first his sister that <u>Clorinda</u> hight,
> The gentlest shepherdess that lives this day:
> And most resembling both in shape and spright
> Her brother dear, began this doleful lay.
> Which lest I mar the sweetness of the verse,
> In sort as she it sung, I will rehearse. (211-16)

It has sometimes been either argued, or simply assumed, that the ninety-six line lament which followed was actually written by the Countess.[15] In 'The Ruins of Time' Spenser implied that by 1591 she had already composed some form of elegiac tribute to her brother:

> Then will I sing: but who can better sing,
> Than thine own sister, peerless lady bright,
> Which to thee sings with deep heart's sorrowing.
> (316-18)

However, it is doubtful that Spenser was referring here to 'The Doleful Lay.' It is in stark contrast to the Countess's other known poetry and, in fact, closely follows the structure of the elegiac form employed in the November eclogue of The Shepherd's Calendar, as well as that in Daphnaida which consisted of framework, narrative and complaint. Since the framework and narrative of the Spenserian elegy was embodied in the 'Astrophel' poem, it appears that 'The Doleful Lay' was being used as the complaint and to demonstrate the consolation that Astrophel was now enthroned in paradise. In elegiac verse, it was common for poets to subsume their personality into the fame of a great figure. Spenser, for example, had previously attributed the complaint of Daphnaida to Arthur Gorges, in the role of Alcyon; in 'The Ruins' the woman representing Verlame had uttered the complaint.[16] On balance, it seems that 'The Doleful Lay' was probably from Spenser's rather than the Countess's pen.

In response to Spenser's lead, along with Philip's dedicatory address to her in the Arcadia, the Countess came to be regarded by many late-Elizabethan writers as, first and foremost, a 'principal ornament to the family of the Sidneys'. Poets viewed her as a vital link in a family chain. Thomas Churchyard suggested that this kinship doubled her perfection as a patron, describing her as, 'Pembroke a pearl, that orient is of kind, /a Sidney right'. Imitating Spenser's image, Abraham Fraunce celebrated her as 'morientis imago Philippi'; Thomas Moffet deemed her the 'inheritor of his wit and genius'; while the literary critic, Francis Meres, denoted her as 'the noble sister of immortal Sir Philip Sidney'.[17] It was perhaps the pastoral poet, Michael Drayton, who made the most effective use of this theme. The efficacy of family patronage, and its continuation through inheritance, was of particular importance to Drayton, who was himself a long-term client of the Gooderes. In his Idea the Shepherd's Garland (1593), he provided a mythologised panegyric of the Countess's kinship: 'Apollo was thy sire, Pallas herself thy mother, /Pandora thou, our Phoebus was thy brother'; and elsewhere suggested that Philip, 'on his death-bed by his latest will, /To her bequeath'd the secrets of his skill.' Having lost its most outstanding leader, Drayton continued, the poetic fraternity in England ardently hoped that the Countess would assume responsibility for 'erecting learning's long decayed fame'.[18]

TRUTH IS HER STUDY AND MEDITATION IS HER EXERCISE

Deemed to be the living sister of a Protestant saint, the Countess of Pembroke was regarded not only as a potential leader of poets but also as a focus for pietistic and meditative religious writings. Once again, the development of this aspect of her literary identity owed much to Spenser's imagination. In 'L'Envoy' to 'The Ruins of Time', the poet first addressed the 'immortal spirit of Philisides', now 'the heaven's ornament', and then explained to the Countess how she might also reach out towards this state of perfection through meditation:

> And as ye be of heavenly off spring born,
> So unto heaven let your high mind aspire,
> And loath this dross of sinful world's desire. (684-6)

Later poets interpreted this attractive image in one of two ways. Some, like Barnabe Barnes, offered the Christian consolation that, through death, the Countess would eventually attain eternal life with her beloved brother:

> After thy mortal pilgrimage dispatch'd
> Unto those planets where thou shal't have place
> With thy late sainted brother to give light:
> And with harmonious spheres to turn in race.

This sentiment also found expression in the lines, previously quoted, from the Countess's own poem, 'To the Angel Spirit'. Other writers were more ambitious, imagining Mary Herbert, while still on earth, as being capable of reflecting an image of her brother's sanctity to those mere mortals who venerated her. The divine poet, Henry Lok, enthusiastically adopted such an approach, comparing her:

> To that extinguish'd lamp of heavenly light,
> Who now no doubt doth shine midst angels bright:

> While your fair star, makes clear our dark'ned sky
> He heaven's; earth's comfort you are and delight,
> Whose - more than mortal - gifts you do apply.[19]

The Countess herself appears to have been pleased by the thought of being deemed a source of celestial inspiration, and she endeavoured to represent her completion of Philip's metaphrase of the Psalms as a humble expression of this gift. Dedicating the completed work to her brother's memory, she explained in 'To the Angel Spirit':

> To thee pure sprite, to thee alone's address'd
> This coupled work, by double int'rest thine:
> First raised by thy blest hand, and what is mine
> Inspir'd by thee, thy secret power imprest. (1-4)

The translation of the Psalms into English verse was a popular literary and devotional exercise. Between 1500 and 1640 over 100 different versifications are known to have been produced. The most commonly used version by Sternhold and Hopkins went through 500 editions and issues within a century of its publication. Sidney, however, had chosen to follow continental rather than native precedents, in particular, the French metrical psalter, commenced in the 1540s by Clement Marot, and later completed by the French theologian, Théodore Beza, one of Calvin's staunchest supporters in Geneva. During the sixteenth century, psalmody and Protestantism went increasingly hand in hand. Calvin himself penned a preface for the Marot/Beza version; oppressed French Protestants adopted some of them as their 'songs of freedom'; and Sidney, along with other serious-minded courtiers, regarded the Psalms as 'the chief [kind of poetry] both in antiquity and excellency'. In this respect, the Countess's completion of Philip's metaphrase may be regarded as an extended eulogy of her brother's reputation as a leader of English Protestantism.[20]

On a more personal level, the Psalms provided the meditative Christian with a means of contemplating three basic issues of Christianity: love, death and the promise of everlasting life. In mourning her brother, it would have been natural for the Countess to turn to the Psalms for both consolation and understanding. She may have recalled, for example, how St Augustine had sought to come to terms with his own mortality by having copies of various Penitential Psalms hung around his death-bed. Fear of death can ultimately be quelled in the Christian mind only through faith in God's love; and Marot pointed out in a metrical preface to his own versifications, addressed to the ladies of France, that the Psalms should be regarded as the most elevating kind of love lyrics. Their primary focus, of course, was the efficacy of divine love. But it is easy to appreciate the Countess's desire to offer her poetic labours in completing her brother's metaphrase as an expression of her deep, personal love for Philip. Although their collaborative version of the Psalms did not reach print until as late as 1823, at least sixteen manuscripts have survived and there seems to have been a considerable contemporary awareness of her labours. The Countess's completion of her brother's work was regarded as the ultimate proof of her personal, intellectual and, above all, spiritual 'oneness' with Philip; as Donne put it:

> Two, by their bloods, and by thy spirit one;
> A brother and a sister, made by thee [ie God]
> The organ, where thou art the harmony. [21]

The late-Elizabethan period saw a flourishing of the Tudor tradition, descending from Lady Margaret Beaufort, Queen Catherine of Aragon and Queen Catherine Parr, of pietistic works of literature dedicated to royal and aristocratic women. The Countess of Pembroke, in her identity as Urania, the Muse of Christian poetry, received the dedications of a significant number of devotional works. Abraham Fraunce's The Countess of Pembroke's Emanuel (1591), offered her an account, in English hexameters, of Christ's early life and resurrection, along with a selection of Fraunce's own versifications of the Psalms. Nicholas Breton dedicated no less than five of his pietistic compositions to Mary Herbert and, although none was of any great literary merit, they provide a convenient illustration of the range of subject matter and tone adopted in such works. The Pilgrimage to Paradise was published with The Countess of Pembroke's Love in 1592; the former comprising a poetic allegory of the five senses and a castigation of city life, and the latter, a representation of the Countess as an ecstatic Christian. The Countess of Pembroke's Passion, which may be regarded as a continuation of the Love, was addressed to her only in manuscript and was later dedicated to another patroness, Mary Houghton, under a new name, The Passions of the Spirit. The next work Auspicante Jehova or Mary's

Exercise (1597), was a collection of prayers in prose compiled for her personal use. Finally in 1601, The Ravish't Soul and the Blessed Weeper provided the Countess with a rather long-winded poetic hymn, celebrating God's glories and including an account of Christ's love for the three Marys, especially Mary Magdalene, with whom Breton compared the Countess at every conceivable opportunity.[22] Little point would be served in extending this catalogue, except to note that veneration continued to be paid to the Countess's piety right up to her death in 1621, through lavish tributes in Aemilia Lanyer's Salve Deus Rex Judaeorum (1611), John Davies of Hereford's Muses's Sacrifice (1612) and Robert Newton's The Countess of Montgomery's Eusebia (1620).

A considerable number of aristocratic women were addressed in pietistic works at this period. Henry Lok, part of whose sonnet to the Countess has already been quoted, addressed similar verses in his Ecclesiastes (1597) to twenty court ladies, including the Marchioness of Northampton, and the Countesses of Derby, Cumberland, Warwick and Essex. Similarly, Aemilia Lanyer, describing her 1611 volume of devotional verses as 'that which is seldom seen, /A woman's writing of divinest things', praised a broad cross-section of female court society, beginning with Queen Anne and her daughter, Princess Elizabeth, and including the Dowager Countesses of Cumberland and Kent, along with the Countesses of Pembroke, Bedford, Suffolk and Dorset. The patronage of devotional literature became for these ladies not just a literary function but, on account of their sex, virtually a spiritual obligation. After all, in Lanyer's eyes, the justification for such a view was emphatically spelled out in the New Testament:

> it pleased our Lord and Saviour Jesus Christ, without the assistance of man, being free from original and all other sins, from the time of his conception, till the hour of his death, to be begotten of a woman, born of a woman, nourished of a woman, obedient to a woman; and that he healed women, pardoned women, comforted women: yea, even when he was in his greatest agony and bloody sweat, going to be crucified, and also in the last hour of his death, took care to dispose of a woman: after his resurrection, appeared first to a woman, sent a woman to

declare his most glorious resurrection to the rest of his disciples. [23]

'FOR SHE ENJOYS THE WISE MINERVA'S WIT'

Aristocratic patrons who were known to indulge in literary composition were all the more admired for so doing. Although there is no certainty over how much of the Countess's work remains unidentified or has been lost, she appears to have enjoyed the respect awarded to an established literary figure. Thomas Churchyard, for example, insisted:

> For she enjoys the wise Minerva's wit,
> And sets to school, our poets ev'rywhere:
> That doth presume, the laurel crown to wear,
> The Muses nine, and all the Graces three:
> In Pembroke's books, and verses shall you see.

For modern readers, the Countess's reputation as a writer must rest upon the following works which have been, more or less, conclusively attributed to her: translations of Garnier's Antonius, Duplessis-Mornay's A Discourse of Life and Death and a translation of Petrarch's 'Triumph of Death'; a short pastoral poem, 'A Dialogue Between Two Shepherds', first published in Francis Davison's A Poetical Rhapsody (1602); and metaphrases of Psalms 44-150, along with, in one manuscript, her dedicatory poem to Queen Elizabeth, 'Even now that care ...', and another to her brother, 'To the Angel Spirit ...'

As a translator of prose, the Countess's most notable quality was her diligence. Apart from a few minor mistranslations, her version of A Discourse of Life and Death sought to render Mornay's sombre French prose almost literally and, in places, word for word. There is a sense of ease and fluency in her translation which may indicate that she had perused the original French version many times and, as seems likely, sympathised deeply with its subject matter. [24]

In poetry, her skills as a metrician merit the attention of modern readers. Her version of Antonius was a generally accurate and literal translation of the 1585 French edition and was remarkably successful in the difficult exercise of converting Garnier's alexandrines into English blank verse. No less impressive was her response to the challenge posed by Petrarch's 'Triumph of Death'. The Trionfi were well known in England through adaptations and borrowings by Hawes, More, Skelton, Surrey and even Queen Elizabeth.[25] Henry Parker, Lord Morley, had compiled the first complete English translation in the mid-1550s, and William Fowler, Queen Anne's Scottish Secretary, made another translation in about 1587. Parker's version, however, was composed in stumbling iambic couplets, making his laboured and metrically erratic version as uneven as it was inaccurate; while Fowler's energies had been dissipated in the virtually impossible task of reconciling the flowing 'terza rima' of the Italian with the cumbersome 'fourteener' form of his translation. In contrast to these uninspired renderings, the Countess's version of 'The Triumph of Death' was both clear and accurate. She chose to retain Petrarch's 'terza rima' structure and compressed, with considerable ingenuity, his eleven syllable lines into English iambic decasyllables. Occasionally, her determination to reflect the Italian metrical structure and word order led to the convolution typical of many Elizabethan translations. But, overall, the proficiency of her translation makes it an impressive tribute to the diligence with which she tackled the challenge of metrical experimentation in English verse.

The culmination of her metrical endeavours is to be found in the Sidney versions of the Psalms of David. Strictly speaking, these poems were not translations but rather a complex series of versifications in which she 'devised a quite extraordinary variety of forms, each conformable to the emotional tenor of the individual psalm'. The Countess evidently detected in her brother's versions a desire to create a different stanzaic structure or rhyme scheme for each psalm and dutifully followed his example. Overall, her reworkings of Psalms 44-150 reveal a remarkable technical virtuosity and convey the impression that the Countess was putting herself through a rigorous process of metrical self-education. Once again, her diligence is unmistakable, and the surviving manuscripts of the Psalms record a constant process of alteration and experimentation, earning her the title of an 'inveterate tinkerer' from William Ringler.[26] Although the Countess's versions were more artificial in effect than her brother's, they were also more elaborate and more elegant. There seems ample justification for the view that in her versifications, along with Philip's, we find a 'definitive attempt to bring the art of the Elizabethan lyric into the service of psalmody'.[27]

When considering the Countess's compositions, it is

important to avoid falling into the trap of attempting to elevate her literary talents to complement her exalted social position. Mary Herbert was, without doubt, of considerably greater importance to her contemporaries as a patron than she ever was as a poet. She satisfied herself, as far as we can tell, with a derivative rather than an innovative role as a writer. Instead of producing her own prose romance - as her niece, Lady Mary Wroth, was to do in the early seventeenth century - she edited her brother's Arcadia. In her own literary pursuits, original lyric verse appears to have played a distinctly secondary role to the translation of other men's thoughts.

Referring to the period of Shakespeare's lifetime, Virginia Woolf remarked: 'It is a perennial puzzle why no woman wrote a word of that extraordinary literature, when every other man, it seemed, was capable of a song or sonnet.'[28] A short answer to this observation is that, in fact, a handful of women did put pen to paper during the Tudor period. Queen Mary and Queen Elizabeth led the way in performing those kinds of exercises in translation recommended by Vives and other educationalists, a practice imitated by a considerable number of aristocratic families. In the household of Henry Fitzalan, twelfth Earl of Arundel (1511-80), his daughters, Mary and Jane, were proficient translators of Greek works into Latin; and the learned daughters of Sir Anthony Cooke were similarly well grounded in such academic pursuits.[29] In his Description of England (1577), William Harrison commended the number of women who knew Greek, Latin, Spanish, Italian and French, and was impressed by others who occupied themselves, 'in writing volumes of their own, or translating of other men's into our English and Latin tongue'.[30] Between the early 1570s and the end of Elizabeth's reign, Isabella Whitney composed love ballads derived from mythological stories, Margaret Tyler translated Spanish romances into English, and pietistic works were translated from the French by Anne Prowse and Ann Dowriche.

Original composition by women was far less common - and even rarer in the vernacular. Katherine Killigrew (b.1530), one of Anthony Cooke's daughters, wrote her own Latin epitaph. The three daughters of Protector Somerset, Anne, Margaret and Jane, penned 400 Latin distichs to mark the death of Margaret of Valois, which were published at Paris in 1550. The Latin poems of Elizabeth Jane Weston (1582-1612), who spent most of her life abroad, reached print at Frankfurt in 1602. One of the few aristocratic women, apart from the Countess of Pembroke, to see her own compositions published was Anne Cecil (1556-1587/8), who had once been considered as a spouse for Philip Sidney but instead married the Earl of Oxford in 1571. She wrote four epitaphs on her son which were published, although it is not known if this was done with her permission, in John Soowthern's Pandora (1584). Far more frequently, original compositions in the vernacular by women circulated only in manuscript and have long since become impossible to identify positively.

Some women, then, did regard translating and creative writing as a worthwhile private pursuit; and a minority even allowed their works to reach the presses. But, in principle, Woolf's question remains a valid one. The names of Isabella Whitney, Margaret Tyler and Ann Dowriche are familiar to few modern readers and it appears that not a single major work of literature was produced by a woman between 1500 and 1600. Why was this so? The first and most important reason relates to the social position occupied by most Tudor women. It has been calculated that over 770 different women received literary dedications during the period of this study.[31] Yet, despite this impressive statistic, women were more often than not regarded by writers as simply less important and influential than men. Spenser, for example, observed a strict hierarchy in the ordering of his dedicatory sonnets printed with The Faerie Queene (1590), praising first the great officers of state, then Earls, Barons and Knights, followed by two outstanding women, the Countess of Pembroke and Lady Carey, and, bringing up the rear, 'all the gracious and beautiful ladies in the court'. Of course, aristocratic women were accorded a great deal of respect by writers, but within their own world - that of the family circle and the royal court - they occupied, as compared with their fathers, husbands and sons, a position of dependence. Inevitably, there were some rare exceptions, notably Bess of Hardwick and Lucy, Countess of Bedford, both of whom appear to have gained, through a combination of their own forceful personalities and marriage, an independence remarkable among noble women before 1650. However, all aristocratic women, Bess and Lucy included, were, at various times, totally dependent upon the advantages derived from the wealth of a father or a husband. And it hardly needs to be noted that, although a position of dependence and social inferiority can engender a great deal of respect and affection, it is not the best means of endowing its occupant with either a sense of authority or importance.

Two other factors contributed significantly to the Elizabethan woman's apparent hesitancy over adopting publicly the role of a writer. First, the courtly disinclination towards print was accentuated in the case of women. In his preface to Newman's edition of Astrophil and Stella, Thomas Nashe remarked that poems 'be oftentimes imprisoned in ladies' casks'. Other writers were also aware of this feminine tendency to protect both their own work and that of their friends from public gaze. The poet and writing-master, John Davies of Hereford, drew attention to this problem in The Muses' Sacrifice (1612) when he politely complained in a joint dedication to the Countesses of Pembroke and Bedford and Lady Carey: 'you press the press with little you have made'.

Secondly, the early-Henrician movement, stimulated by More, Vives and later educationalists such as Mulcaster, which encouraged noble women to acquire a classical training, gradually fizzled out during the mid-sixteenth century and was replaced by a much less academic code. In 1561 Sir Thomas Hoby's translation of Castiglione's The Courtier was published, which commended the concept of women and men sharing a common culture, sitting alternately in the ducal salon and exchanging views on the court, religion, morality and the arts. But in reality, Castiglione was intent upon promulgating a totally different ideal of aristocratic womanhood, insisting still upon some literary interests while placing much more emphasis upon the acquisition of social graces and skills in music, dancing, painting and pleasing conversation.[32] The cult of the literary amateur, which pervaded late-Elizabethan court society, was in keeping with the spirit of The Courtier and did much to prompt young men, who had enjoyed the benefits of private tutors, first-rate schools and the universities, to try their hand at verse and prose composition. The position for women, who were entirely dependent upon the familial household for their education, was very different. As the ideals of Vives were replaced in their fathers' minds by those of Castiglione, a familiarity with the pen was regarded as an increasingly less important acquirement for young girls of aristocratic status.

'AND SETS TO SCHOOL OUR POETS EVERYWHERE'

In comparing Wilton House to 'an Arcadian place and a paradise', Aubrey described Mary Herbert's home as 'like a College, there were so many learned and ingeniose persons. She was the greatest patroness of wit and learning of any lady in her time.'[33] Even after her death, men of letters fondly recalled how her country house had been 'like a little university' and an 'excellent nursery for learning and piety'.[34] Long before Ben Jonson immortalised Robert Sidney's Penshurst, his sister's house at Wilton had been celebrated as a centre of civilised life and hospitable patronage. Nicholas Breton was almost certainly referring to Wilton when he praised the homelife of an unnamed but noble patroness in his Wit's Trenchmour (1597):

> Her house being in a manner a kind of little court
> ... where first, God daily served, religion truly
> preached, all quarrels avoided, peace carefully
> preserved, swearing not heard of, where truth was
> easily believed, a table fully furnished, a house
> richly garnished, honour kindly entertained, virtue
> highly esteemed, service well rewarded and the
> poor blessedly relieved.[35]

Although the Countess frequently resided at other Herbert residences in London, Ludlow, Ivychurch and Ramsbury, the splendour and rural charms of her country seat at Wilton prompted writers to envisage it during the 1590s as the main focus for her literary activities. Behind this fulsome image, however, lay the reality of a large aristocratic household, frequented by relatives, friends, distinguished guests, employees and other personages. In assessing the scope and significance of her literary reputation it is first necessary to determine the level of intimacy involved in the Countess's relationships with individuals from each of these categories.

From the scraps of evidence concerning the Countess's personal life which have survived, it becomes clear that she placed great importance upon the well-being of her family and friends. Her earliest known letter, written in about 1578, conveyed her apologies to the Earl of Leicester for not keeping him informed of her new husband's state of health. Almost twenty years later, on 29 September 1597, she penned an impassioned missive to Robert Cecil, in which she defended the Earl from a charge of slandering another person.[36] She was no less energetic in looking after the interests of her brother, Robert, who was appointed Governor of Flushing in the summer of 1589. On 9 September 1590, the Countess wrote to her sister-in-law, Barbara, offering to send her own nurse over to Flushing to assist in the latter's imminent confinement. Several years later, she did her best to facilitate her brother's return to England. Robert's secretary, Rowland Whyte, remarked of one of her letters sent to the Lord Treasurer, William Cecil, early in 1598: 'I never read anything that could express an earnest desire, like unto this.' In other surviving examples of her presumably extensive correspondence, she wrote to Julius Caesar, the Master of Requests, supporting the suit of a 'poor complainant' of her acquaintance; to the Earl of Essex, offering friendly solicitations for a voyage upon which he was about to embark from Plymouth; to Robert Cecil, concerning marriage proposals for her eldest son, William; and to the Queen herself, profusely thanking her for treating William graciously on his introduction to court life.[37]

Some of her letters also provide hints of the ways in which her own compositions may have circulated among her closest friends. During the early 1590s, she wrote to Edward Wotton (1548-1626), the scholar and diplomat mentioned in the Defence of Poetry as Philip Sidney's companion at the court of the Emperor Maximilian II in Vienna in 1574/5. She requested him to send her his copy of 'a certain idle passion which long since I left in your hands', since she had lost her own version of it. In a later letter, addressed apparently to Tobie Matthew (d.1628), Archbishop of York, she promised that 'my translation shall be very shortly with you', and also sent to him another work remarking: 'as this copy is the first, so also is it to be the last.'[38]

During the late 1590s the Earl of Pembroke's failing health began to cause serious concern. His condition oscillated between decline and recovery through 1600; and just before his death in January of the following year, Robert Sidney wrote from Baynard's Castle to Cecil: 'I fear his friends shall not have him long, and when he is gone I shall lose him, to whom of all men (my father and mine elder brother excepted) I have been most bound.' In view of this intimacy, it is interesting to note that the paper in Robert's autograph notebook of poems has been dated c. 1593-1601, the period when he was in closest touch with his sister. Although the inscription, 'For the Countess of Pembroke', on its first page may have been a postal direction rather than a dedication, it is clear that, like his elder brother, Robert appreciated Mary Herbert reading his poems in manuscript.[39]

The Countess and Robert are also known to have shared their literary interests with Sir John Harington of Kelston, the translator of Orlando Furioso. Harington was one of their distant relatives and the first Earl of Pembroke had stood as a godparent at his christening in August 1561. This kinship presumably assisted the development of his informal friendship with the Sidney family. The keen interest which Robert and his sister took in Harington's literary pursuits is demonstrated by a long letter which Robert penned to him in about 1600. In this letter, which was delivered personally by the Countess - 'my sister beareth this in privacy, and therefore so safe' - Robert implied that Harington's recent return to England after military service in Ireland would provide him with more time for poetry, and remarked: 'let me have proofs of your employ, and send me verses when you can.' In the same letter, Robert revealed that he had been actively involved in presenting Elizabeth with literary gifts from Harington's own pen: 'Your present to the Queen was well accepted of; she did much commend your verse, nor did she less praise your prose.' He also added: 'I do read Ariosto, and commended the translator to all friends, which you mark as the best good will I can show you.'[40] It may have been in response to such generous assistance that Harington penned a dedicatory epistle probably to the Countess and Robert for a now unidentified work which concluded: 'The work as yet I wish not seen of other,/ But of your self and of your noble brother'.[41]

Sometimes, members of Mary Herbert's household offered her samples of their literary endeavours. Gervase Babington, one of the chaplains at Wilton, dedicated three theological works to her and her husband in the 1590s.[42] Similarly, Thomas Howell, a humble ladies' man-servant in her employ, regarded himself virtually as the Herbert's honorary family versifier, dedicating a printed collection of his rather unimpressive verses to the Countess in 1581. In this miscellany, entitled Howell's Devises, he even fashioned the Herbert motto, 'Ung je servirey' into a simple assertion of the social and moral worth of family patronage, in a poem beginning 'To serve but one, a constant courage shows,/ Who serveth more, he rightly serveth none.'[43]

Another writer equally committed to the concept of

family patronage was Abraham Fraunce who had entered Shrewsbury School in January 1571/2 under the personal sponsorship of Philip Sidney. This support enabled him to continue his studies at St John's College, Cambridge, after which he entered Gray's Inn, where he remained until 1588. At about this time, he took up a position in the Court of the Council of the Marches of Wales. Between August 1590 and April 1591, the Earl of Pembroke sought unsuccessfully to ease Fraunce, whom he described as a 'pleader at the bar', into the position of Queen's solicitor in Wales; but Fraunce died unexpectedly soon afterwards.[44] In return for this lifelong support, he honoured the Sidneys and the Herberts as the sole patrons of his literary works, addressing no less than six printed volumes to the Earl and Countess of Pembroke between 1587 and 1592. It has to be admitted, however, that none of these works was of any great literary merit. Fraunce devoted much of his poetic energies to fostering the ultimately futile cause that sought to subject modern tongues to the discipline of Latin metres, as Latin had been to Greek. Both Philip Sidney and his sister experimented with quantitative metres but Ben Jonson justifiably expressed little respect for such projects in his peremptory aside: 'Abram Francis in his English hexameters was a fool.'[45]

The literary achievement of Samuel Daniel was of a totally higher order. Daniel proudly placed the beginnings of his poetic career firmly within the environs of Wilton House, his 'best school', whereof he would ever 'hold a feeling and grateful memory'. At Wilton he claimed to have obtained 'the first notion for the formal ordering' of his poetry and his early dedications repeatedly suggest that the Countess was in no small measure responsible for his commitment to literary endeavour. Daniel's arrival at Wilton as a tutor to her children probably took place soon after the publication of Newman's pirated edition of Astrophil and Stella (1591). Like Sidney, Daniel had suffered the indignity of having his 'secrets bewrayed to the world, uncorrected'. In the following year, the stationer, Simon Waterson, counteracted Newman's edition with an authorised text of Delia, containing fifty corrected sonnets and Daniel's own prose dedication to the Countess of Pembroke. This address was markedly tentative in tone, implying that, since the Countess would obviously be taking steps to protect her brother's poems, she might well be persuaded to look favourably upon Daniel as Sidney's fellow-sufferer from the injustice of piracy.

If this was Daniel's method of ingratiating himself with Mary Herbert, it appears to have been extremely successful. Daniel replaced the tentative 1592 prose dedication to the Countess with a much more fulsome dedicatory sonnet in the 1594 edition of Delia. He now appeared to be enjoying Mary Herbert's personal interest and loyally offered all of his poems to her in retrospection with the lines:

> Great patroness of these my humble rhymes,
> Which thou from out thy greatness doost inspire:
> Sith only thou hast deign'd to raise them higher,
> Vouchsafe now to accept them as thine own.[46]

In contrast to Daniel, who viewed literature as a means of attracting the attention of influential patrons, Thomas Moffet came to Wilton in 1592 as the Earl's physician with his social position already assured through a distinguished career in medicine which had included treating Philip Sidney himself. He adopted Wiltshire as his home county and represented Wilton in the Parliament of 1597. The Earl paid Moffet an annual pension and he was senior enough to act as one of the seven witnesses to Pembroke's will, drawn up in January 1596. After the Earl's death, according to Aubrey, he 'lived in his later time at Bulbridge (at the west end of Wilton - it belongs to the earl of Pembroke) at the manor-house there.'[47]

Viewing himself as a professional employee and a country gentleman, Moffet was already in receipt of adequate financial remuneration for his skills and it is probable that he sought from the Countess neither material rewards nor further appointments. Instead, he would have been flattered by her literary interest in his compositions and appreciative of the prestige of her friendship. In his Nobilis or a View of the Life and Death of a Sidney (c.1594), Moffet gratefully recorded Philip's interest in his career and recalled knowing some of Sidney's most intimate friends, including Dyer, Brounker and Greville. This elegiac treatise, addressed to the young William Lord Herbert and urging him to emulate his uncle's example, was as much an expression of allegiance to Philip's surviving relatives and friends as a tribute to the man himself.[48] A few years later, Moffet dedicated to the Countess his charming narrative poem, The Silkworms and their Flies (1599), presenting it as a gentleman's literary exercise, designed to amuse his high-ranking female friends. In these verses, Mary Herbert and her ladies were presented within a pastoral framework in the dramatised story of Pyramus and Thisbe, whose souls were transformed into silkworm moths. In March 1599, John Chamberlain remarked that 'The Silkworm' was 'no bad piece of poetry', and it is difficult to imagine the Countess being anything but pleased with this unusual literary gift.

It was a sign of particular privilege for a writer to be able to indicate a familiarity with his patron's own literary interests and, in the case of the Countess of Pembroke, several were keen to hint at their first-hand knowledge of her compositions. In 1594 Henry Parry, one of the chaplains at Wilton House, praised her metaphrase of the Psalms; as did Samuel Daniel who in dedicating to the Countess his play Cleopatra, noted: 'Those Hymns that thou dost consecrate to heaven, /Which Israel's singer to his God did frame' (57-8).[49] It was, however, Thomas Moffet who revealed by far the most detailed knowledge of the Sidney family's private literary activities during the 1590s. In his 'Nobilis', he made reference to Philip's now lost 'letters of most excellent style, in metrical and prose form which he addressed to the Queen, to friends, but particularly to your honoured mother [the Countess].' He also seems to have been familiar with the majority of Sidney's other works. Furthermore, he was aware not only of Philip's and the Countess's literary endeavours but also those of her brother, Robert, and her niece, Elizabeth, Countess of Rutland, Philip's only child.

A few other writers associated with Wilton House may also have had access to Philip Sidney's manuscripts. As early as 1581, Thomas Howell was pleading in his Devises for a wider circulation of the Arcadia; and in his Arcadian Rhetoric (1588) Abraham Fraunce lifted quotations from manuscript versions of the Arcadia and Astrophil and Stella. Inevitably, a sprinkling of writers without any known Sidney/Herbert connections, notably Robert Greene, Thomas Lodge and George Puttenham, also appeared to be aware of the Arcadia before its first appearance in print in 1590. They may even have been able to get their hands on manuscripts from outside the family circle. After all, at least one had already gone astray by November 1586 when Ponsonby contacted Greville. However, during the decade following Sidney's death, the Countess's households at Wilton and Baynard's Castle, along with those of Robert Sidney, Fulke Greville and the Countess of Rutland, remained the most likely locations where writers might gain access to

Sidney's literary works before they became generally available in print.

THE MYTH OF PATRONAGE

Those writers who were fortunate enough to form a personal association with the Countess could derive considerable advantages from her interest in their work. However, only a handful of individuals are known to have ever achieved such a relationship. Generally, aristocratic patronage involved a patron's personal assistance only for a minority of writers, and they were usually those who either lived within the patron's household or were privileged to mingle with members of the nobility on terms of friendly intimacy. For the rest, panegyric dedications brought no guarantee of either acceptance or reward, nor did patrons necessarily consider themselves responsible for the contents or quality of works which were prefaced by their names. Numerous literary tributes were addressed to members of the aristocracy on a purely speculative basis - many of them achieving nothing.

A misunderstanding of this aspect of patronage-hunting has sometimes led to an unwarranted scepticism in assessing the Countess of Pembroke's significance to late-Elizabethan literature. Her illustrious reputation appears, at first sight, incompatible with the small number of writers who are known to have gained admittance to Wilton House. Furthermore, several of the works addressed to her were of little literary value. The ex-soldier, Thomas Churchyard, and the clergyman, Nathaniel Baxter (who apparently also had an inclination towards petty larceny) led the way in dedicating to the Countess verses which were almost entirely devoid of poetic merit.[50] Turning to her own compositions, it has to be admitted that, by and large, they are more expressive of Mary Herbert's devotion to her brother's memory than of an independent creative talent. Surveying the whole of her career, Mary Ellen Lamb recently put forward the argument that, 'the Countess of Pembroke's patronage has been especially exaggerated'.[51]

In some respects, this view is an entirely correct one. Since the late nineteenth century, for example, there has been a critical tendency to interpret the Countess's translation of Garnier's Antonius as an indication of her desire to instigate a dramatic 'school' of neo-Senecanism which aspired to rival the popular drama of Marlowe and

Shakespeare. This view has determined Mary Herbert to be responsible for motivating the composition of Daniel's Cleopatra (1594) and Philotas (1605), Thomas Kyd's Cornelia (1594), Samuel Brandon's The Virtuous Octavia (1598) and Greville's two Turkish moralities, Alaham (c. 1601) and Mustapha (c. 1596-1610), along with his lost 'Antony and Cleopatra'. T. S. Eliot expressed the widely held belief that 'the Countess of Pembroke tried to assemble a body of wits to compose drama in the proper Senecan style, to make head against the popular melodrama of that time ... the shy recluses of Lady Pembroke's circle were bound to fail.'[52]

Daniel did indeed draw inspiration from the Countess's example when writing his Cleopatra, as he acknowledged in its 1594 dedication:

> Lo here the work the which she did impose,
> Who only doth predominate my Muse:
> The star of wonder, which my labours chose
> To guide their way in all the course I use.
> She, whose clear brightness doth alone infuse
> Strength to my thoughts, and makes me what I am;
> Call'd up my spirits from out their low repose,
> To sing of state, and tragic notes to frame.

Continuing her plot-line; 'thy well grac'd Anthony / ... Requir'd his Cleopatra's company', Daniel created a heroine who faced tragedy with dignity and courage, an interpretation which was presumably designed to please the Countess. Samuel Brandon, however, is a much more shadowy character about whom little is known. To his Octavia, dramatising the thoughts of Antony's deserted wife, was appended a verse 'Letter from Octavia to Antonius', along with its reply, which paralleled Daniel's similar letter in his Poetical Essays (1599).[53] It may also be of significance that Brandon's play appeared under William Ponsonby's imprint, in the same year as his edition of Sidney's 'collected works'.

Nevertheless, apart from Daniel and perhaps Brandon, there is every reason to believe that neither the Countess, nor Kyd, Greville and two other dramatists, Sir William Alexander and Lady Elizabeth Carey, whose plays have been compared to Mary Herbert's Antonius, ever had the slightest intention of forming a dramatic school. It is unlikely that the Countess even knew Kyd, and his Cornelia (1594), a hasty and unimpressive piece of work, was dedicated to Bridget Radcliffe, Countess of Sussex, who was not, as has sometimes been suggested, Mary Herbert's aunt. Similarly, Brandon's interest in the Antony and Cleopatra story did not prompt him to dedicate it to the Countess of Pembroke. Instead, he offered his Octavia (1598) to ady Lucia Audelay, probably the wife of the Earl of Castlehaven, and his two verse epistles to Mary Thinne, mistress of Longleat.[54] As regards the rest, even a cursory study of the dramas written by Greville, Alexander and Lady Carey reveals that they owed little, if anything, to Mary Herbert's translation in terms of style or content.

In all likelihood, Daniel was most responsible for initially creating this confusion. Immediately following his arrival at Wilton, he invested a considerable amount of poetic energy in asserting the Countess's role as a literary patroness and, by implication, his own importance to her. In the dedication prefacing Cleopatra (1594), he gave thanks for her support and promised to seek the means of repaying her: 'I must so work posterity may find, / How much I did contend to honour thee.' One of the ways in which he hoped to do this, we may suspect, was through endowing the Countess's interest in Garnier with a significance which she herself probably never intended. In Daniel's eyes, her Antonius set an example for those writers who wished, 'to chase away this tyrant of the North, / Gross Barbarism', a 'hideous beast', which had been first challenged by Philip Sidney. Through Philip's and Mary's combined leadership of English poets, Daniel thought, the rest of Europe 'might know how far Thames doth outgo / The music of declined Italy'. Added to his hope was the suggestion that the Countess's patronage of Daniel would ensure her everlasting fame even 'when Wilton lies low levell'd with the ground'. In other words, Daniel's composition of his Cleopatra and his insistence that the Countess and her brother had been fired by a missionary zeal to reform English poetry, may have been no more than a pleasing, but none the less calculated, act of patronage-seeking.

A recognition of the mistaken assumptions which have clouded modern criticism of the Countess's Antonius serves to emphasise the futility of looking for circles of writers surrounding her. Such an assemblage, in all probability, simply did not exist. Like many other literary patrons from the ranks of the aristocracy, the Countess possessed a number of close friends and employees who were interested, to varying degrees, in amateur composition. At the other end of the spectrum, her rank, kinship and involvement in the publication of her brother's works, as well as some of her own, endowed her with an enviable public reputation as a major literary figure. In response, some writers who could claim no form of personal contact with her felt fully justified in addressing their works to her on a purely speculative basis. William Smith, for example, presented her with an attractive manuscript of flower poetry, 'A new year's gift, made upon certain flowers', while admitting in his dedication: 'My Muse presumes to offer you, / although unknown, yet dutious love, and true.'[55] William Gager, Barnabe Barnes, Thomas Churchyard, Henry Lok, Francis Meres, Charles Fitzgeoffrey and Francis Davison all celebrated the Countess's literary reputation without providing any indication that they had ever met her.[56] Others, such as the musician, Thomas Morley, who dedicated his Canzonets (1593) to Mary Herbert, and Gabriel Harvey, who claimed a familiarity with a mysterious 'excellent gentlewoman, my patroness', in Pierces Supererogation (1593), hinted at some sort of personal acquaintance with the Countess, even though no evidence can now be discovered to support their claims. It appears that, occasionally, some writers openly squabbled in their rivalry for Mary Herbert's interest and favour. Thomas Nashe had sought to ingratiate himself with the Sidneys through his preface to Newman's 1591 edition of Astrophil and Stella; and he was ready to snap and snarl at any potential rival for their favour. In this preface, he ridiculed Nicholas Breton, whose lament for Sidney, 'Amoris Lachrimae', had just been published. Elsewhere he poked fun at Gabriel Harvey for having recommended to the printer, John Wolfe, such a worthless volume as Barnes's Parthenophil and Parthenophe, in which a dedicatory sonnet to the Countess had been included. Nor was Nashe alone in promoting such undignified tussles. Abraham Fraunce also weighed in with his amusing dismissal of the Harvey brothers in the comic tale of the three 'Academic Gardeners', Damoetas (John), Pasnip (Richard) and the Thistle (Gabriel).[57]

Clearly, we must agree with Mary Ellen Lamb that it is palpably untrue to suggest, in the words of Pearl Hogrefe, that Mary Herbert 'gave practical help and encouragement to many writers when she became the Countess of Pembroke and lived at Wilton House.'[58] After all, it is difficult to imagine how a considerable number of hopeful courtier-writers in London could have considered it worth their while to trek into the depths of rural Wiltshire on the strength of a single speculative dedication. Such writers, of course, always lived in the hope that their dedications might elicit a favourable response but many were obliged to resign themselves simply to admiring her from afar. Nevertheless, beyond the walls of the Wilton estate, the Countess remained a figure of considerable significance to the reading-public at large, most of whom presumably knew nothing about her personally. Mary Herbert's idealised identity as the surviving sister of an honorary Protestant saint also blended readily with the Tudor tradition of female pietism, endowing her with a remarkable spiritual potency, comparable to the aura of semi-divinity which surrounded Queen Elizabeth. The depiction of the Queen and the Countess in literary panegyrics demonstrates the commitment of the sixteenth-century mind to the concept of a complete and perfect individual, possessing all the virtues and graces. Writers strove in their dedications to Mary Herbert to create a magnificent and lasting image of nobility, piety and beneficence. She was compared to the Duchess of Urbina [sic] by Breton, and to Augustus' sister by Meres. Some turned to the classical precedents of Minerva (Howell, Nashe, Drayton and Fitzgeoffrey) and Urania (Spenser), while others conjured with anagrams of her name like Greville's Myra (Mary) and Drayton's Meridianus (Mari Sidnei). In view of her close association with Philip Sidney, her strongest appeal was undoubtedly to pastoral poets who invested her with the traditional perfection and purity of such country maidens as Amaryllis (Dyer), Cinthia (Baxter), Clorinda (Spenser) and Pandora (Drayton). Abraham Fraunce coined the name Pembrokiana for her, and as late as the 1640s, William Basse was still resolutely singing the praises of Poemenarcha (Mary Herbert) and her beloved Philisides (Philip Sidney).[59] Although the Countess of Pembroke's image was as much a creation of myth and symbol as of reality, her reputation as a patron of letters was a literary fact of life for several generations of English writers.

THE LITERARY HEIRS OF PHILISIDES

Although it was both pleasing and convenient for late-Elizabethan writers to regard the Countess of Pembroke as her brother's 'goodly image living evermore', the naming of a worthy male successor to Philip's literary role was not so obvious. In 1591 Nashe expressed his doubts over whether any prominent courtier could ever be found to match Sidney's idealised reputation as a literary patron: 'But thou art dead in thy grave, and hast left too few successors of thy glory, too few to cherish the sons of the muses, or water those budding hopes with their plenty, which thy bounty erst planted.'[1] Expressing the conventional despair of elegiac lament, these words also underline a genuine problem faced in the 1590s by writers who had envisaged Sidney as the new Maecenas of vernacular literature. Where was his successor to be found?

Apart from his sister, Philip's closest literary associates had been Edward Dyer and Fulke Greville, 'a happy blessed Trinity', as he once described their friendship. Neither, however, possessed the social status or creative productivity to emulate Sidney's burgeoning literary reputation. Nor were writers able to turn to any other members of Philip's immediate family circle. Sir Henry Sidney had once advised his younger son, Robert, to 'follow the direction of your most loving brother ... imitate his virtues, exercises, studies, and actions.'[2] But it does not appear that any significant literary collaboration ever took place between them. Besides, Robert was appointed as Governor of Flushing in July 1589, a post which kept him out of England for long periods during the next decade. Similarly, Philip's brother-in-law, Henry, second Earl of Pembroke, a cultured and erudite man, succeeded Sir Henry Sidney in 1586 as President of the Welsh Council, and was thereby also isolated from the mainstream of English court life. More significantly, the Protestant alliance led by the Earl of Leicester in the early 1580s all but disintegrated soon after Philip Sidney's demise. Leicester himself died in 1588 and his brother, Ambrose, Earl of Warwick, in 1590. Sidney's father-in-law, Sir Francis Walsingham, also died in that year. Warwick was childless and Leicester's heir, Lord Denbigh, had died in 1585, reviving briefly Sidney's own hopes of succeeding to his uncle's fortune and position. Another staunch supporter of the alliance, Francis Russell, second Earl of Bedford, also died in 1585; as did his son and heir, leaving his grandson, Edward, an unpromising minor, to become the third Earl. By 1590 there was an urgent need to find both a political and literary successor to Philisides.

In a codicil to his will, Sidney bequeathed 'to my beloved and much honoured lord the Earl of Essex, my best sword'. Robert Devereux, second Earl of Essex (1566-1601), was the new, young favourite of Queen Elizabeth. His father had fought in Ireland during Sir Henry Sidney's governorship and, although the latter privately regarded the Earl with considerable suspicion, believing that he wished to displace him as overall military commander, Essex had proposed just before his death in 1576 a marriage between his daughter, Penelope, and Philip Sidney. It is unlikely that the Sidneys would have viewed this match seriously, although two years later, the Earl of Leicester secretly married Robert Devereux's widowed mother. Robert had fought bravely in the Low Countries campaign and was already firmly associated in the public mind with Sidney's heroic death in 1586. In the following year, the Queen appointed him as Master of the Horse, the position with which she had signified her favour for Leicester soon after her accession. In view of such associations, Sidney's gift of his 'best sword' became, as F.J. Levy notes, 'strongly symbolic, for Essex inherited not only the weapon but the policy it was intended to defend'.[3]

In foreign affairs during the early 1590s, Essex enthusiastically espoused the cause of armed aggression towards Spain, a policy which, at least initially, was much more attractive to post-Armada England than it had been to the Queen in the previous decade. Furthermore, unlike Sidney, Essex was both a nobleman in his own right and a successful courtier who felt confident of Elizabeth's continuing favour.

In 1590 he married Sidney's widow, Frances Walsingham, a union which greatly pleased those who envisaged him as Philip's successor. In his Polyhymnia, an account of the accession-day tilts held on 17 November 1590, George Peele depicted Robert Devereux, "Yclad in mighty arms of mourner's hue', as still lamenting the loss of Sidney:

> And all his company in funeral black,
> As if he mourn'd to think of him he mist,
> Sweet Sidney, fairest shepherd of our green,
> Well lett'red warrior, whose successor he
> In love and arms had ever vowed to be.[4]

Several of Sidney's family and closest associates also began to consider Essex as the major inheritor of Philip's political ambitions and patronage. Fulke Greville acted as one of his advisers during the 1590s and lived for a time at the Earl's London residence. Edward Dyer was also briefly associated with Essex. The Countess of Pembroke wrote an informal letter to him on behalf of her husband, sending their good wishes for his safety during one of his expeditions. In 1593 her brother, Robert Sidney, borrowed £1,000 from Essex, and regarded the Earl as an influential ally when attempting to obtain leave from his uncongenial posting at Flushing. His belief appeared to be well founded, since in 1597 Essex (unsuccessfully) put Sidney's name forward for the important position of Warden of the Cinque Ports. Robert's wife, Lady Barbara, was also a close friend of the Countess of Essex; and Roger Manners, Earl of Rutland, the husband of Philip Sidney's daughter, Elizabeth, was another of the Earl's intimates.

Robert Devereux's academic and courtly training had endowed him with many of the qualities expected of an English Maecenas. Educated largely under the direction of his guardian, Lord Burghley, as a ten years old child he could already write fluently in Latin and French. He matriculated in 1579 from Trinity College, Cambridge, eventually becoming Chancellor of that University in 1598 as Burghley's successor. A considerable proportion of his closest associates were distinguished scholars. One of his secretaries was Henry Cuffe, the Oxford Tacitean; another academic, Henry Savile, dedicated his acclaimed 1591 translation of Tacitus to the Earl. Other friends included Anthony and Francis Bacon, the latter acting as his political adviser; the diplomat Henry Wotton, and the founder of Oxford

University's Library, Thomas Bodley. A group of actors performed under the protection of his name in the early 1580s, and Henry Wotton warmly commended his skill in designing 'impressas and inventions of entertainment'. Wotton also recalled that Essex would frequently 'evaporate his thoughts in a sonnet'; and some of his lyrics were probably performed before the Queen at court.[5]

There was, however, one crucial disparity between the Earl of Essex and Sir Philip Sidney - the public esteem in which their respective literary talents were held. Robert Devereux's poetry was, according to his most recent editor, 'functional, autobiographical, and directed primarily to the Queen'. Only about ten poems or fragments of poems have survived which can be definitely attributed to Essex; and they do not seem to have enjoyed a wide circulation during his lifetime.[6] Although both men regarded writing as an activity distinctly secondary to the pursuit of their court careers, Sidney's monumental labours at Wilton and during other slack times marked him out as inimitable.

The vast majority of Tudor and Stuart dedications were addressed to individuals who had probably never experienced the slightest desire to put pen to paper themselves. Such patrons were envisaged by their clients as the purveyors of influence and material rewards rather than as a source of encouragement or literary criticism. But to be Philip Sidney's literary successor was a totally different matter. By the mid-1590's some informed courtiers were publicly expressing the view that Sidney's unique literary gifts rendered him irreplaceable from among the ranks of the English aristocracy. One of his close friends, Lodowick Bryskett, wrote in the Astrophel collection of elegies:

> Phillisides is dead. O luckless age
> ...
> Alas who is left that like him sings?
> When shall you hear again like harmony?
> So sweet a sound, who to you now imparts?
>
> (111, 122-4)[7]

It was, however, not just literary considerations which limited Essex's efficacy as the heir to Sidney's reputation as a patron and national hero. At the heart of the problem lay the Earl's monopolistic attitude towards the dispensing of patronage, combined with an unshakeable faith in his own opinions. While still only in his early twenties, Robert

Devereux's favour with the Queen and his extensive estates endowed him with great powers of patronage which, according to Conrad Russell, he 'exercised indiscriminately', and 'was largely responsible for a considerable revival of bastard feudalism'.[8] At court he persistently sought posts for candidates who stood no feasible chance of being appointed, such as Robert Sidney for the Wardenship of the Cinque Ports, and the Attorney Generalship for Francis Bacon; tactics which brought little credit to him and even less to his hopeful protégés. While frequently loyal to his friends, Essex remained mindlessly indifferent to the essentially pragmatic nature, even for aristocrats, of preferment seeking. Those who hoped that he would take over the Earl of Leicester's patronage of Puritans were also disappointed because Essex was primarily interested not in causes but rather in his own prestige. He lent his name to the adherents of a whole range of religious camps, including some Puritans like George Gifford; but also staunch Anglicans, such as the Queen's chaplain, Matthew Sutcliffe; along with Archbishop Whitgift; and even several discontented Catholic recusants who later ensnared themselves in the Gunpowder Plot.[9] Inevitably, Essex's desire to control all the major political offices by filling them with a network of trusted henchmen, led him into numerous acrimonious disputes with other influential patrons, most notably, Robert Cecil and, as we shall see, the Earl of Pembroke in Wales.

'HOW TO OBTAIN A BENEFICIAL'

In a study of this scope, it is inevitable that certain important aspects of aristocratic patronage can only be examined briefly. The heavy dependence of churchmen and theologians upon the nobility for their livelihoods is just such an area of interest. The vast majority of religious works produced between 1558 and 1603 contained an address or dedicatory material; and perhaps more than in any other kind of literature, the writer expected the recipient to take a personal interest in the contents of the book. Those privileged to preach at court or in the great houses of the aristocracy presented printed copies of their sermons to distinguished members of the congregation. Minor works of biblical exegesis or translations of theological tracts from the continent were gratefully dedicated to patrons who had provided their authors with livings or preferment. The maintenance of Protestantism also prompted the production of huge quantities of polemical writings. Examining the Earl of Leicester's sponsorship of Puritan and anti-Catholic writers, Eleanor Rosenberg concluded that, 'the dissemination of propaganda was the most powerful single purpose behind the production of patronized religious writing in this period.' Regarded as yet another possible heir to the patronage of Leicester and Sidney, Thomas Egerton was envisaged in dedicatory tributes, Louis Knafla explains, as 'a future leader of evangelical Protestantism in England and Continental Europe'. His patronage was sought by Oxbridge theologians, anti-Catholic propagandists, Puritan preachers, and rural curates and ministers from his own native area, the northern Welsh borderlands.[10]

As President of the Council in Wales from 1586, the second Earl of Pembroke, called 'the eye of all Wales' by Thomas Wiliems of Trefriw, was nominally responsible for the enforcing of uniformity within the Welsh Church. His council held jurisdiction over religious offences in Wales and the Marches, and his presidency began with an energetic drive against recusants.[11] Pembroke's name was also associated with the most notable Welsh Puritan of the period, John Penry, who in 1588 dedicated to the Earl his tract, An Exhortation unto the Governors and People of Wales, violently denouncing the alleged corruptions and incompetence of the clergy. According to Penry, best known for his role in the Mar-Prelate tracts, the Welsh Church was in a 'reprobate and accursed estate of woeful damnation', due to the ignorance of its ministers and the indifference of its episcopacy. He held Pembroke personally responsible for this state of affairs, suggesting that, if he could not find a solution to the problem, he should resign. A short but intense controversy ensued, resulting in Penry publishing a revised edition of his tract, answering some of the criticisms of his opponents. Pembroke is not known to have published any official response to Penry's accusations, even though the latter continued to lament the corruptions of the Welsh clergy until he was imprisoned in May 1593 and executed soon afterwards.[12]

In his Exhortation, Penry denounced how in Wales, 'our livings are impropriated, possessed by swine, as non-residents and hirelings'. This complaint was already familiar to Pembroke, due, in no small measure, to the efforts of Gervase Babington, one of his household chaplains. Babington was a copious writer, although his frequently reprinted works of biblical exegesis are of interest today not so much for their theology as for their powerful analysis of the failings of the late-Elizabethan patronage system; in particular, the stranglehold which the aristocratic laity had come to exert over ecclesiastical preferment. His controlled arguments and lucid prose share a common motivation with Spenser's satiric description in his Mother Hubberd's Tale (1591) of the most effective way to obtain a lucrative church living:

> For that the ground work is, and end of all,
> How to obtain a Beneficial.
> First therefore, when ye have in handsome wise
> Your self attired, as you can devise,
> Then to some Noble man yourself apply,
> Or other great one in the world's eye. (485-90)

Born in about 1550, Babington was educated at Trinity College, Cambridge, before moving to Oxford where he was appointed as a university preacher in 1580. A few years later he was informed that he had been selected to be one of the Earl of Pembroke's family chaplains which entailed a move to Wilton House and provided him with the opportunity of preaching in Wales. Babington's absorption into a powerful aristocratic patronage network made him acutely aware of the controversy over ecclesiastical preferment which later so incensed John Penry. After the dissolution of the monasteries, a considerable number of Church livings became the gift of the Crown and the laity. Aspiring clerics were frequently totally dependent upon the favour of a well-placed patron who could intercede with the sovereign or a great nobleman to gain lucrative preferment for them. In the May eclogue of The Shepherd's Calendar, Spenser describes how this process gradually turned influential churchmen into manipulative courtiers:

> That not content with loyal obeysance,
> Some gan to gape for greedy governance,
> And match them self with mighty potentates,
> Lovers of Lordship and troublers of states. (120-3)

At a lower level, abuses were just as widespread, most commonly involving either patrons embezzling ministers' wages or clergymen trading their integrity for a more subservient form of self-advancement.

Babington's tract, <u>A Very Fruitful Exposition of the Commandments</u>, dedicated to Pembroke in 1583, opens with a firm denunciation of the most glaring injustices suffered by many clergymen. In a hard-hitting address to the 'Gentlemen in Glamorganshire', he laments, 'the neglect that aboundeth every where to furnish the rooms allotted thereunto with sufficient men both for gifts and goodwill to discharge the duties of true ministers.' He goes on to complain of unscrupulous patrons retaining parts of the stipends due to ministers and of them having little concern for the well-being of the Church, concluding unequivocally: 'it is love in the minister to his God to feed his sheep. So it is assuredly in the patron to cause them to be fed'. <u>Mother Hubberd's Tale</u> also seeks to open its readers' eyes to such abuses and presents a similar picture of humble clergymen being forced, 'T'accept a Benefice in pieces riven' (540):

> For some good Gentlemen that hath the right
> Unto his Church for to present a wight,
> Will cope with thee in reasonable wise;
> That if the living yearly do arise
> To forty pound, that then his youngest son
> Shall twenty have, and twenty thou hast won.
>
> (525-30)

Babington, however, does not satisfy himself merely with personal observations but also confronts those who mismanage the system with the conclusive authority of legal judgements. Regarding the endowing of preferments, he refers to common law which states that a patron: 'hath but <u>Ius Donationis</u>, and the ordinary <u>Ius Admissionis</u>: and therefore compelleth the patron to bestow it in a time or else to loose it by lapse, apparently therein denying him any leave to retain it either in whole or part for ever to himself.' Furthermore, under ecclesiastical law, patrons are '<u>advocatos ecclesiarum</u>, <u>vicedominos</u>, <u>custodes</u>, <u>gardianos</u>', which as Babington points out, are not titles of ownership but merely, 'names of fidelity, government and careful preservation of the Church'.

The most remarkable quality of Babington's discussion of these problems is his candour; even when his generalised criticisms could have reflected on those patrons whose influence was all important to him. Despite living at Wilton House and probably at Cardiff Castle, he deplores, 'that cloak and cover and cause of so much oppression, the cloth and liveries of superiors'.[13] This is a surprisingly pointed comment from one who owed his living to patrons who still clad their acting companies, musicians and other personal servants in cloth bearing the family crest. Nevertheless, Babington gained rich rewards from the system which he found so flawed. In 1581 he was the warden of St Giles's Hospital at Wilton and after 1585 held the living of several parishes in Wiltshire. Through Pembroke's influence he was elected as Bishop of Llandaff in August 1591. At the same time he was widening considerably his sphere of court contacts since in 1590 he preached a semon before the court at Greenwich which was published in the following year with a dedication to the members of the Privy Council.[14] His next progression occurred in March 1595 when he was enthroned as the Bishop of Exeter. He seems to have gained the support of John Whitgift, Archbishop of Canterbury, for this preferment, since he wrote to Robert Cecil on Babington's behalf. In 1597 Babington made his final move to become Bishop of Worcester, a position which he held until his death in 1610.

Babington's criticisms of the late-Elizabethan patronage system boldly attacked the structure which supported his own career. But as he rose to power and began to exert influence on behalf of others, even he was not above reproach for the very faults which he had once so forcefully condemned. It appears that his appointment to Exeter involved the tacit surrender to the Crown of certain valuable lands belonging to the Bishopric. He also earned the wrath of the citizens of Exeter by alienating the manor of Crediton at Colebrooke, formerly the seat of a branch of the Herbert family, in favour of Sir William Killegrew, whose family were long-time beneficiaries of the Cecils. A contemporary lampoon, lamenting these times, 'when bishops sell lands from their posterity', describes Babington as a deceiver who 'can preach well', but yet 'loveth the world more'. Even Babington's stern condemnation of the retention of preferments by patrons did not prevent Robert Cecil in 1608 from criticising him, then Bishop of Worcester, for exactly the same fault.[15] Despite these reservations, the most important consideration here is not to judge Babington's own merits and failings but rather to record his uncompromising assessment, alongside those of Penry and Spenser, of the aristocracy's involvement in the ecclesiastical patronage system during the last quarter of the sixteenth century.

THE ARISTOCRACY AND DRAMATIC COMPANIES

Although Babington was unequivocal in his condemnation of 'the cloth and liveries of superiors', such insignia were of the utmost importance to one specific group of aristocratic servants. Noblemen had traditionally held dramatic entertainments in their households to mark family celebrations or seasonal festivities, but their official patronage of acting companies during the last quarter of the sixteenth century was a direct result of a desire for a more centralised state control. In 1572 the 'Act for the Punishment of Vagabonds' decreed that 'common players' were obliged to be able to demonstrate themselves as 'belonging to any Baron of this Realm' or 'other honourable Personage of greater Degree', or run the risk of being declared 'rogues, vagabonds and sturdy beggars'. In response to these restrictions, James Burbage (d.1597) wrote to the Earl of Leicester on behalf of a group of actors who were already performing under his protection. Hoping to be nominally retained as 'household servants and daily waiters', Burbage emphasised that he and his colleagues desired no 'further stipend or benefit at your Lordship's hands', but only their liveries and 'your honour's licence to certify that we are your household servants'.[16]

Burbage's plea was successful. On 10 May 1574 his company received a royal patent, the first of its kind to be issued for adult performers. Now officially recognised as Leicester's servants, they were authorised to play 'comedies, tragedies, interludes, and stage plays, together with their music', in both London and the provinces. Other companies were then able to seek a nominal association with aristocratic households, performing under the protection of the Lord Chamberlain (Lord Hunsdon), the Lord Admiral (the Earl of Nottingham), and the Earls of Sussex, Warwick, Essex and Oxford. The next stage in the process of turning strolling entertainers into professional actors and courtly servants was the formation in 1583 of the Queen's Men, an élite group of players drawn from among the best talent in the aristocratic companies. Clad in scarlet coats to signify their royal patronage, the Queen's Men were renowned in London and granted privileged treatment by the city authorities in the provinces.[17]

By the end of the 1580's, the names of some of the most distinguished members of the aristocracy were publicly associated with popular drama. But in most cases, it is unclear as to how personally involved the English nobility were willing to become with common players. 'It is probably not an over-statement', writes Andrew Gurr, 'to say that to the aristocracy they were at best befriended parasites.'[18] Nevertheless, performances at court during the Christmas seasons of 1574 and 1575 by the Earl of Leicester's Men imply that their patron had been influential in obtaining these 'bookings'. They may have also contributed to Leicester's famous entertainment of the Queen at Kenilworth in mid-summer 1575. Similarly, Thomas Radcliffe, Earl of Sussex, became Lord Chamberlain in July 1572; and by the following winter his company were performing at court. In some rare instances, noble patrons even enjoyed taking a first-hand involvement in dramatic productions. Edward de Vere, Earl of Oxford, was recorded as an actor in a Shrovetide device at court in 1579; and Francis Meres described him in Palladis Tamia (1598) as a playwright and one of 'the best for comedy amongst us', although none of his dramatic compositions is known to have survived. William Stanley, Earl of Derby (1561-1642), was also a devotee of the stage and was recorded in June 1599 as then 'busy penning comedies for the common players'.[19]

Plays were mostly performed at Elizabeth's court in the old Banqueting House in Whitehall but the nobility also had opportunities to see popular drama elsewhere. The Theatre, Rose and Globe are known to have had separate 'lords' rooms' in their galleries which were partitioned off and close to the stage. Few specific details are known about the attendance of the aristocracy at such venues. Information is more abundant concerning the growing importance of the Blackfriars precinct as a centre of theatrical life from the time Richard Farrant rented a hall there in 1576 for performances by his Chapel Children. The Earl of Pembroke's London residence, Baynard's Castle was only a short walk from this area; the Lord Chamberlain and Lord Hunsdon had lodgings within its precinct. The Queen and her entourage visited the Blackfriars on 16/17 June 1600 for the wedding of Lord Herbert (a cousin of the Pembrokes) and Anne Russell, at which a masque, The Lost Muse, was performed. She returned on 29 December 1601 to see a play at Lord Hunsdon's residence. A few years earlier, James Burbage had proposed to establish a new playhouse in the Blackfriars, and although eventually successful, the scheme was initially opposed because of the annoyance it would cause, 'to all the noblemen and gentlemen thereabout inhabiting'. Elsewhere, members of the aristocracy sometimes welcomed players into their own homes to perform before their friends and guests. In November 1578, and again in May 1580, Leicester's Men played on Lord North's estates in Kirtling. Similarly, in 1589 the Queen's Men were at the Earl of Derby's at Latham and also at another of his houses at Knowsley.[20]

Late-Elizabethan public theatre offered rich returns to playhouse owners, such as James Burbage, his sons Cuthbert and Richard, and Francis Langley; and to its 'sharers', those dramatists and actors, most notably William Shakespeare and Edward Alleyn, who held a direct financial interest in their companies. But for the vast majority of 'hireling' actors the rewards remained small and the future uncertain. Life outside the major companies, headed by the Queen's, the Lord Admiral's and the Lord Chamberlain's Men, sometimes held little to recommend it, even when the protection of a nobleman's name was available. The sketchy history of the Earl of Pembroke's Men, encompassing the highs and lows of theatrical life, provides ample justification for this view. Probably drawn together from fragments of other companies, James Burbage, acting on behalf of a miscellaneous group of players, may have applied directly to Henry Herbert for their right to use his name as Pembroke's Men. If this was so, an association between the two families developed which lasted until the death of James's younger son, Richard, in 1619.[21]

Pembroke's Men were recorded at court during the 1592 Christmas season and performed versions of some Shakespeare plays, as well as Marlowe's Edward II. They toured extensively in the provinces during the early 1590s but apparently without much success. On 28 September 1593 Henslowe noted that the players had been reduced to pawning their costumes. Four years later, a reconstituted company under Pembroke's patronage entered into an agreement with Francis Langley to play at the Swan for a year. These players were responsible for the staging of the scandalous Isle of Dogs which resulted in the imprisonment of Ben Jonson who had written parts of it, along with some of the actors. Often fragmented, sometimes controversial and probably a financial failure, Pembroke's Men disappears from dramatic records after 1600.[22]

Inevitably, modern interest in this minor company has grown out of all proportion to its contemporary significance on account of the possibility that Shakespeare himself had once been among their number. According to the title-pages of some early quarto editions, Pembroke's Men are known to have performed versions of Titus Andronicus, 2.3. Henry VI and The Taming of the Shrew. Although perhaps the majority of scholars have preferred to envisage Shakespeare gaining his early dramatic experience in either the Queen's or Lord Strange's company, before establishing himself in the Lord Chamberlain's Men, a suspicion has often been expressed that for a time he wrote and perhaps also played for Pembroke's Men. Clearly influenced by J.Q. Adams's A Life of William Shakespeare (1923), E.K. Chambers tentatively concurred with this view. During the last twenty five years, however, the case for this association has been more confidently argued. A.S. Cairncross strongly advocated Shakespeare's membership of what he took to be the precursor of Pembroke's Men, the Strange/Admiral combine, a theory which received further elaboration from R.E. Burkhart.[23] A. Gurr also pointed to textual evidence which may indicate that Shakespeare was a member of 'the 1592 Pembroke's Company'. On the other hand, S. Schoenbaum judiciously regarded his membership of Pembroke's Men as no more than 'romantically appealing'; while B. Morris bluntly described all such theories as 'a glittering tower of conjecture'.[24]

The simple fact of the matter is that the name of Pembroke's Men on some early Shakespeare quartos can in no way be taken to indicate his membership of this company. Some of these plays were also performed by other groups of actors before their publication; and there is a strong possibility that Pembroke's Men relied heavily upon 'memorial reconstructions' of Shakespeare's work, presumably because they possessed neither authorial nor authorised manuscripts themselves. It is impossible, therefore, to demonstrate from these sources that Shakespeare benefited directly from the Earl of Pembroke's nominal patronage during the early 1590s.

There is no doubt that the aristocracy were of considerable use to actors and dramatists during the 1590s, providing both essential protection and various forms of employment. However, it is also clear that, unlike the close bonds of sympathy which many poets envisaged between themselves and Philip Sidney, there was little sense of a shared endeavour among members of the nobility and acting companies. Certainly, the Earls of Derby and Oxford appear to have enjoyed being involved with theatricals. But for the most part, aristocratic patronage of late-Elizabethan drama was carried out on an official rather than a personal level. Members of the nobility, as far as we can tell, had little impact upon the quality of plays performed commercially before 1603. Nevertheless it should not be forgotten that the performance on the public stage of plays by Kyd, Marlowe, Shakespeare and other Elizabethan dramatists was possible, under the prevailing legislation, only through the sponsorship of the aristocracy.

THE END OF A REGIME

In 1599 plans were being made for a royal visit to Wilton House which ultimately never took place, perhaps because of the uncertain health of both the Queen and the Earl of Pembroke. It is possible that the Countess penned for this occasion the 'Astraea Dialogue' and her dedicatory address to Elizabeth prefacing the Sidney Psalms, in addition to commissioning a presentation volume of the Psalms from the writing-master, John Davies of Hereford. Her dedicatory address is set within an overtly political context. The figure of David is compared to that of Elizabeth as the protector of national security, deciding 'what Europe acts in these most active times' (8):

> Kings on a Queen enforst their states to lay:
> Main-lands for Empire waiting on an Isle;
> Men drawn by worth a woman to obey;
> One moving all, herself unmov'd the while. (81-4)[25]

In reality, national and international affairs were a source of considerable disquiet both to the country in general and to the Countess's immediate family circle. There has been a tendency in the past for historians to paint an overly depressing picture of England in the 1590s, enervated by fin de siècle depression and disillusion. But it is clear that a series of bad harvests, escalating inflation and enclosure problems engendered considerable discontent in the country; while at court distinct cracks were beginning to appear in the patronage system on account of the huge official fees and monopolies held by a privileged minority of public servants. From 1593 onward, rebellion in Ulster placed a serious strain on the royal exchequer, and in the spring of 1597 it was realised that Philip of Spain was assembling another armada at Corunna. To compound these problems, speculation was steadily mounting as to whether

James VI of Scotland, Lady Arabella Stuart, the Spanish Infanta, or some other less likely candidate would follow a Queen who continued to inhibit Parliament by resolutely refusing to name or confirm her successor. Another important succession struggle surrounded Lord Burghley, the key-stone of the late-Elizabethan patronage system, whose failing health obliged him to devolve more and more of his administrative duties onto his son, Robert.

These were also far from happy times for the Herberts and Sidneys. From the beginning of his Presidency of Wales, the Earl of Pembroke had struggled, but with little success, to eradicate various abuses from the Council, particularly the increases in fees demanded by officials for drafting or approving documents. He was also suspicious of the powerful lawyer party on the Council which, in turn, increasingly sought to contest his influence. Renowned as a blunt and impulsive man, Pembroke's imperious manner and marked lack of diplomatic skills were partly to blame for such problems. He once sent a heated missive to Elizabeth which his secretary, Arthur Massinger, the father of the dramatist, Philip, flatly refused to hand over, considering it unwise to have 'so passionate a letter delivered unto the Queen'. The Earl's frequent promotion of his relatives and loyal protégés was another source of disquiet. In 1600, for example, he appointed as deputy lieutenants Sir William Herbert of Swansea for Glamorgan, William Herbert of Welshpool and Richard Herbert of Park for Montgomery, and Matthew Herbert for Monmouthshire. Fulke Greville was notoriously overladen with appointments, acting by 1593 as a Councillor, Secretary, Clerk of the Council and sole keeper of the Signet. Resentment was aggravated in 1598 when, contrary to the regulation that the Secretary should reside in Wales, Greville became Treasurer for the Wars and the Navy in England. The greatest threat to Pembroke's power, however, came from the ambitions of the Devereux family in Wales, led by Robert, second Earl of Essex. Their interest lay primarily in exerting influence over appointments and, as has been noted, Essex often revealed a total disregard for established procedures in seeking favour for his own people. Pembroke once complained that Devereux greeted one of his recommendations for an office with 'scoffing laughter', and after 1595 they were locked in a bitter struggle for power in Wales.[26]

Although by 1598 Pembroke was expected soon to retire, he remained as President of Wales for another two years, probably wishing to ease his brother-in-law, Robert Sidney, into the post when an opportunity arose. After almost a decade as Governor of Flushing, Robert considered that an appointment which had once been regarded as a useful apprenticeship in royal service had turned into a virtual exile from the real centre of power. Some of Robert's most melancholy poems, riddled with images of failure, disease and despair, may have been written at this period, and there are some striking parallels between the language of these poems and some of Robert's letters, explaining the problems of his Governorship. In the summer of 1598, the Earl of Pembroke requested the Queen's permission to convalesce at Wilton and to be released from his duties in Wales. But Elizabeth did not agree, preferring instead to send him one of her own doctors. By the following spring, Herbert's condition was worsening and Robert Sidney, temporarily in London, begged Cecil to grant him extended leave from his post in Flushing, in order to assist his sister during her husband's illness.[27]

In a world where the public prestige of a nobleman played a large part in determining his attractiveness to writers, it is unsurprising that Pembroke received few literary addresses during the 1590s. In 1592, however, William Gager, the editor of the Oxford _Exequiae_ (1587) volume of Sidney elegies, made determined efforts to ingratiate himself with the Herberts. Gager was a nephew of Sir William Cordell, the Master of the Rolls, and while studying at Oxford had attracted the attention of the Earl of Leicester. His play _Meleager_, based upon the legend of the hunting of the Calydonian boar, was first performed at Oxford in 1582 and restaged in 1585. A printed text of the play appeared in 1592 with a Latin prologue and epilogue, addressed to the Earls of Leicester and Pembroke, who had been present at the later performance, along with Philip Sidney. In the same year, his tragi-comic melodrama based upon the _Odyssey_, entitled _Ulysses Redux_, was published with a dedication to Thomas Sackville, Lord Buckhurst.[28]

Henry Herbert's other literary associations during the last decade of his life stemmed almost entirely from his duties in Wales. In 1593 the Welsh grammarian, Henry Salesbury, dedicated to him one of the earliest grammars, in Latin, of the Welsh language.[29] In the following year, George Owen, a historian of Pembrokeshire, compiled a manuscript catalogue of all the Earls of Pembroke. This project was of direct personal interest to Owen because he claimed to be himself a descendant of the fifteenth-century Earl of Pembroke.[30] Finally, in 1597 Herbert approved the appointment of John Salusbury as deputy Lieutenant of Denbigh, an individual chiefly remembered as the dedicatee of Robert Chester's poetic miscellany, Love's Martyr (1601), in which Shakespeare's 'The Phoenix and the Turtle' first saw print.[31]

Men of letters were also beginning to take an interest in the Earl's eldest son and heir, William Lord Herbert. After being tutored at Wilton by Hugh Sanford, and perhaps Samuel Daniel, he was sent to university. His introduction to collegiate life came at the age of twelve when in September 1592 his father took him to Oxford for the Queen's visit, and he attended a banquet given for the royal retinue by the President and fellows of Magdalen College.[32] It was, however, from New College that William and his younger brother, Philip, matriculated on 9 March 1593. Their arrival was celebrated by William Thorne, later renowned as an Hebraist and orientalist, who dedicated a theological tract, Ducente Deo (1592), to William. Thorne, a Wiltshire man, had recently been elected a fellow of New College and proudly recalled how his college had produced the Peplus volume of Sidney elegies which had been dedicated to the Earl of Pembroke.[33] Two years later, another Wiltshire man, Henry Parry, dedicated to William his Victoria Christiana, an account of a Church assembly held at Oxford in 1591. Eventually becoming Bishop of Worcester, Parry's earlier career had included a period as chaplain at Wilton House in the late 1580s, and he clearly knew the family well. In his dedication he praised William's tutor, Hugh Sanford, and commended the Countess's completion of the Sidney Psalms, as well as lamenting the trials of the Earl's Presidency in Wales. In terms strikingly similar to Thomas Moffet's advice to William Herbert in his Nobilis (c. 1594), Parry also encouraged the young Lord to imitate the example of his illustrious uncle, Sir Philip Sidney.

William left Oxford in 1595 without taking a degree, although his scholarly and literary pursuits were perhaps not totally neglected afterwards. Late in 1599, for example, Robert Sidney's agent, Rowland Whyte, wrote to him at Wilton, requesting a copy of the Spanish romance, Amadis de Gaule, from his mother's library.[34] Nevertheless, from the summer of 1597, when William was introduced to court life, his sights were firmly fixed upon seeking royal favour and powerful friends. He took up residence in London in the spring of 1598, and in the following year intended to 'follow the camp' at the annual musters with a large personal retinue. Picking up on these military concerns, Robert Barret, a veteran of the Low Countries campaigns, prefaced his <u>Theory and Practice of Modern Wars</u> (1598) with dedicatory addresses to William and his father, reminding the former of the bravery of his grandfather, the first Earl of Pembroke, and his uncle, Sir Philip Sidney.[35]

Rowland Whyte kept a close eye on the young Lord's behaviour, no doubt realising that with the steady decline in Henry Herbert's health, William could soon prove to be a powerful friend to the Sidneys. Some reservations, however, were expressed over his commitment to the all important task of seeking favour at court. 'My Lord Herbert is a continual courtier', Whyte wrote, 'but doth not follow his business with that care as is fit; he is too cold in a matter of such greatness.' He confirmed this opinion a few days later, remarking: 'there is a want of spirit and courage laid to his charge, and that he is a melancholy young man.' But in November 1600 William was granted the favour of a private audience with the Queen, a gesture for which Elizabeth was lavishly thanked by his mother; and even Whyte began to believe that he would 'prove a great man in court'.[36]

It was also necessary for William Herbert's family to find a suitable wife for him. The negotiations opened in the autumn of 1593 when Sir George Carey, son and heir of Lord Hunsdon, the Lord Chamberlain, proposed a match between William and his daughter, Elizabeth. The former, however, appears not to have been impressed by his prospective bride; and Sir George later complained that the Earl of Pembroke's financial demands to sanction the match had been unreasonable. In view of the Earl's precarious state of health, his family grew suspicious of Carey's motives. Rowland Whyte informed Robert Sidney: 'Truly I heard, that if my Lord of Pembroke should die, who is very "pursife" and "maladise", the tribe of Hunsdon do lay in wait for the wardship of the brave young lord.' These negotiations ended acrimoniously but in 1597 fresh talks were opened with Lord Burghley for a marriage between his granddaughter, Bridget Vere, and William. Once again, financial terms proved an insurmountable barrier, although there is also the possibility that neither Burghley nor William Herbert held much enthusiasm for the match. Two years later, Robert Sidney and Whyte were strongly advocating another marriage scheme for William, this time with a niece of Charles

Howard, Earl of Nottingham and the Lord Admiral, who would have been a powerful ally for Robert at court. These proposals met with just as little success as the others, prompting Whyte to remark wearily: 'I don't find any disposition at all in this gallant young Lord to marry.'[37] It should also be noted that there is still no conclusive evidence to support the theory that Shakespeare was summoned by the family at about this time to cajole young William out of his marital shyness with such stern warnings as, 'Die single, and thine image dies with thee'.[38]

For the last five years of his life, William's father, the second Earl, was a sick and melancholy man. On Christmas Eve 1595 he sent a poignant note to his friend, Sir Francis Hastings, in which his seasonal greetings were tempered with the sad lament: 'I dream of nothing but death, I hear of little but death, and (were it not for others' further good) I desire nothing but death.'[39] His condition steadily worsened until he was by late 1599 little more than a semi-invalid. Both his son, William, and Robert Sidney began to grow anxious over the distinct possibility of the Earl's offices being awarded after his death to aspiring individuals from outside the family circle. During the winter of 1600/1 it became apparent that Henry Herbert did not have long to live. Robert Sidney, with his eye on the Presidency of Wales, sought permission from the younger Cecil to stay at Wilton with the Earl, 'to whom of all men, my father and elder brother alone excepted, I have been most bound.'[40] A few days before his father's death in the early hours of 18 January 1601, William made a similar request in a letter to Robert Cecil, with the intention of ensuring that he received his inheritance undiminished. This missive was reinforced a few days later by another, begging Cecil to intercede on his behalf with the Queen, 'whom if it please not to deal very graciously with me, I shall prove a poorer Earl than I was before a Lord.'[41]

In the following months, William Herbert was to become even more acutely aware of the importance of gaining royal favour. From the autumn of 1598 he had actively sought out the friendship of Robert Devereux. During the winter of 1599 two of Essex's closest associates, the Earl of Southampton and Sir Charles Danvers, were entertained at Ramsbury, one of the Herberts' houses near Wilton. William Herbert continued to consort with members of Essex's circle during 1600. But with the collapse of the Earl's rebellion on 8 February 1601, it became essential for him to clarify his allegiance. Robert Sidney was instructed to agree terms of surrender with the rebels and William Herbert was probably never in any real danger. Nevertheless, he wisely wrote to Robert Cecil, condemning 'this wicked action', and totally disassociated himself from the rebels, 'men I cannot call them'.[42] Along with Essex were executed Danvers and one of the second Earl of Pembroke's most persistent opponents in Wales, Sir Gelly Meyrick.

It was perhaps fortunate that by the time Essex's rebellion took place, the young Earl of Pembroke was already out of circulation at court, due to another unwise association. In June 1600 he had attended the wedding festivities at the Blackfriars of his kinsman, Lord Herbert, son of the Earl of Worcester. A masque was performed after dinner, in which the leading female dancer was Mary Fitton, one of the Queen's ladies. Early in February 1601 news seeped out that she was pregnant, and although William Herbert admitted paternity, according to Cecil, he 'utterly renounceth all marriage'. The child died soon after its delivery in March but Herbert was placed briefly in the Fleet and then banished from court. Two months later it was thought wise for him to withdraw to Wilton House, a move which he regarded as little less than a journey into exile. On his arrival there he immediately requested permission from Cecil to travel abroad, remarking: 'I have not yet been a day in the country, and I am weary of it as if I had been a prisoner there seven year.' The Queen, however, did not forgive such transgressions easily. All William Herbert could do was to kick his heels in the country, awaiting the new reign.[43]

'THIS SAD-JOYFUL CHANGE'

By mid-summer 1601 King James VI of Scotland and Robert Cecil had begun a secret correspondence which facilitated James's peaceful accession to the English throne two years later. The smoothness of this transition was reflected in the literary celebrations marking the coronation on 25 July 1603 and James's subsequent entry into London, delayed by the plague until March 1604. In entertainments by Ben Jonson and Thomas Dekker, and arches designed by Stephen Harrison, James was heralded as the long-awaited sovereign who would reunite all the British Isles. Although he was conventionally depicted as an English Caesar, special care was taken to represent the King as a purveyor of peace rather than war. Samuel Daniel's A Panegyric Congratulatory proclaimed:

> ... and now in peace therefore
> Shake hands with Union, O thou mighty State,
> Now thou art all Great-Britain and no more,
> No Scot, no English now, nor no debate;
> No borders but the Ocean and the shore.

It was fitting that Daniel's royal panegyric reached print together with his treatise on poetic form, a Defence of Ryme (1603), addressed to the Earl of Pembroke, since James's devotion to learning and poetry was already renowned. Intelligent, well-read and disputatious, he had been tutored by the famous Scottish scholar, George Buchanan, and his talented associate, Peter Young. Sometimes misrepresented as a clumsy and self-opinionated pedant, in reality, James viewed learning and scholarship as essential attributes of good kingship. He wished to be regarded as the British Solomon, nurturing native talent and attracting foreign writers and artists. Daniel explained that [God] 'Taught thee to know the world, and this great Art /Of ord'ring man, <u>Knowledge of Knowledges.</u>'[1] James responded with enthusiasm to this challenge by publicly asserting his confidence in the wisdom and opinions of learned men. He employed Ben Jonson to entertain his court with masques; consulted the antiquary and scholar, Sir Robert Cotton, over peace with Spain and the Catholic plot of 1605; and dedicated his own defence of lay monarchy to one of the great European patron princes, the Holy Roman Emperor, Rudolph II.

While Daniel, Jonson and other writers sought to attract the King's interest through their literary tributes, members of the aristocracy were similarly obliged to scramble for positions and favour at the new court. Robert Cecil and Lord Henry Howard, his intermediary in the succession negotiations with James, were already building up the patronage networks which would dominate the first decade of Jacobean court life. Many others also expected rewards. The nobility under Elizabeth had been starved of honours and grants. The new King, particularly one from another country, had little choice but to dispense them liberally. Furthermore, there were now numerous Scotsmen at the English court, many holding positions in the newly created royal bedchamber, who expected to benefit from their journey south. The pursuit of favour in the Queen's household was no less competitive. Casting a cynical eye over this 'feminine commonwealth', the Earl of Worcester informed the Earl of Shrewsbury in February 1604:

> First, you must know we have ladies of divers degrees of favour; some for the private chamber, some for the drawing chamber, some for the bed-chamber ... My Lady Bedford holdeth fast to the bed-chamber; my Lady Harford would fain, but her husband hath called her home. My Lady Derby the younger, the Lady Suffolk, Ritche, Nottingham, Susan, Walsingham, and, of late, the Lady Sothwell, for the drawing-chamber; all the rest for the private-chamber, when they are not shut out, for many times the doors are locked; but the plotting and malice amongst them is such, that I think envy hath tied an invisible snake about most of their

necks to sting one another to death.[2]

The accession of James provided William Herbert with a chance to put behind him the Mary Fitton scandal. John Davies of Hereford, a friend of William's former tutor, Hugh Sanford, addressed a wide range of verses to members of the Herbert family between 1602 and 1617. In his Microcosmos (1603), he advised the young Earl:

> Pembroke, to Court (to which thou wert made strange)
> Go, do thine homage to thy Sovereign,
> Weep, and rejoice, for this sad-joyful change[3]

Pembroke signed the proclamation declaring James's succession to the throne of England; and in April 1603 he joined the swelling throng, escorting the King on his progress from Scotland to Whitehall. When the press of courtiers became too great for James, he limited access to the royal bedchamber to a favoured few, including William Herbert. He soon received another indication of the King's favour when, shortly before the coronation, James created him a knight of the Garter. At the coronation itself, the Venetian ambassador recorded how the 'Earls, Council, and the Barons' kissed the King's hand and touched the crown. He added, with some astonishment: 'The Earl of Pembroke, a handsome youth, who is always with the King and always joking with him, actually kissed His Majesty's face, whereupon the King laughed and gave him a little cuff.'[4]

London was hit by the plague in late summer 1603 and a western progress was hastily planned which included Pembroke's country residence, Wilton House. James was there on 29 and 30 August and for part of the autumn, spending a great deal of time in his favourite pursuit of hunting. Although the court moved from one country house to another, James remained especially fond of Wilton. On 2 December the King's Men were summoned there from Surrey to act before their patron. This group, formerly the Lord Chamberlain's Men, formed the company to which Shakespeare and Burbage belonged. In reward, John Heminge received on behalf of the company a payment of £30. Contrary to a popular legend, almost certainly a nineteenth-century fabrication, suggesting that Shakespeare himself was in attendance for a performance of As You Like It, it is not known which play or plays were performed.[5]

Philip Herbert was even more successful than his elder

brother in catching the royal eye. Before James's coronation, he was appointed as a Gentleman of Queen Anne's bedchamber and made a Knight of the Bath. Gossip about the King's favour for Philip grew when late in 1603 he received, along with Sir James Hay (d. 1636) and Sir John Peynton, a grant for the transport of cloth, rumoured to be worth not less than £10,000.[6] Hoping to cash in on this favouritism, Davies of Hereford dedicated another of his miscellanies, Wit's Pilgrimage (1605?), jointly to Herbert and Hay:

> Sith God and King, and your minds' sympathy
> Have made you two, an undivided one,
> (One, as of two, love makes an unity)
> I cannot give a gift to one alone.[7]

Philip's promising court career was also commended by one of his kinsmen, William Herbert of Glamorgan, who compiled a poetic commemoration of great figures in English history, entitled A Prophecy of Cadwallader (1604). After praising the memory of such illustrious personages as King Henry V and the fifteenth-century Earl of Pembroke, he reminded Philip Herbert of the need to retain royal favour: 'Pursue thy first designments (noble knight) / Affect thy Country, and admire thy king.' Such advice, however, appears to have been needless. Robert Cecil's letters of 1605 are filled with references to Philip's intimacy with James; and on 4 May he was created Earl of Montgomery.[8]

The marriages of William and Philip further strengthened their positions at court. After prolonged negotiations, conducted largely by the ubiquitous Hugh Sanford, a match was agreed between Pembroke and Mary Talbot, the daughter of the powerful and very rich seventh Earl of Shrewsbury. Edward Hyde, Earl of Clarendon, later remarked that Herbert, 'paid much too dear for his wife's fortune by taking her person into the bargain', but the marriage provided him with some useful connections. In particular, his bride's father had been a close friend of Burghley and his son was a trusted associate of Robert Cecil. The ceremony took place on 4 November 1604, followed just under two months later by Philip Herbert's marriage to Susan Vere, the daughter of the Earl of Oxford. Their courtship had been conducted secretly but, in contrast to Queen Elizabeth's usual reaction to such behaviour, James expressed nothing but pleasure over this union.[9]

The first two years of James's reign were prosperous times for the Herbert brothers. Furthermore, their education and family connections endowed them with a ready-made reputation for a love of learning and the arts. Davies of Hereford described William as, 'Nephew to Sidney (rare worth's richest pearl)'; while William Herbert of Glamorgan reminded Philip of 'That man of men whose fatal name you bear'. In the last year of Elizabeth's reign, Francis Davison, the son of her Secretary of State, dedicated A Poetical Rhapsody to the new Earl of Pembroke, making prominent play of his lineage: 'Thou worthy son, unto a peerless mother, / Thou nephew to great Sidney of renown.' In 1603 the stationer James Shawe, formerly apprenticed to William Ponsonby and therefore familiar with the Sidney circle, dedicated to Pembroke an English translation of Jean Hotman's tract on diplomacy and politics, The Ambassador. Hotman (1552-1636), a diplomat, lawyer and Huguenot controversialist, had become a close friend of Philip Sidney after meeting him in 1582. Presumably with Sidney's diplomatic ambitions in mind, Shawe represented his nephew, Pembroke, as 'fit for the managing of these, and the like high service'.[10] The trust and affection with which James publicly treated William and Philip Herbert during the early years of his reign prompted some admirers of Sidney to think that, at last, two worthy heirs to Philisides had been found.

'THE KING'S AND QUEEN'S ENTERTAINMENTS'

Following James's accession, three of the leading acting companies were transferred from aristocratic to royal service. The Chamberlain's became the King's Men, while the Admiral's and Worcester's came under the protection of James's eldest son, Prince Henry, and Queen Anne. The Children of the Chapel were also renamed as the Children of the Queen's Revels. During the first decade of the reign, the yearly number of performances of plays at court was far greater than in Elizabeth's time, rising from over ten in 1603/4, James's first Christmas season, to a maximum of twenty-three in 1609/10. Between 1 November 1604 and 31 October 1605, for example, Shakespeare's company, the King's Men, gave royal performances of six of his plays, including The Merchant of Venice which James saw twice. Although Jonson asserted that Shakespeare's plays did 'take' the King, Dudley Carleton, a well informed commentator, was of the opinion that James usually evinced 'no extraordinary pleasure' in drama. The real royal enthusiast was Queen Anne whose devotion to the spectacular arts led her to become the prime instigator of that much studied form of theatricals, the Jacobean court masque.[11]

Queen Anne's first masque was organised to welcome Prince Henry when he joined the royal progress southwards at Winchester in the autumn of 1603. No details of this entertainment have survived but a French onlooker noted that the Queen was already planning more theatricals for the forthcoming winter season. The twelve days of Christmas, from the Nativity to the Epiphany, were traditionally a period of high revels, shared by royalty, nobility, visiting foreign dignitaries and other well-placed courtiers - an ideal time for ambitious members of the aristocracy to rub shoulders with their King and Queen on terms of cordial festivity. Although the physically ungainly King wisely eschewed dramatic performance, Anne frequently danced in her own 'Queen's masques'. Among the most prominent of the male performers were James Lord Hay; Ludovic Stuart, Duke of Lennox; various members of the Howard family; and, predictably, the Herbert brothers, William and Philip. James's first Christmas season at the English court was marked on New Year's night by an anonymous 'Masque Brought in by a Magician of China', and Daniel's The Vision of the Twelve Goddesses, performed on 8 January 1604. Although the text of this first masque is lost, descriptions of its staging indicate that the author had been commissioned to represent James's joyful acceptance by his new subjects. Pembroke was almost certainly the first masquer who gave the King an 'impresa' in a shield with a 'sonnet in a paper to express his device'. He then presented James with a jewel, rumoured to be worth £40,000, as a gift to proclaim the love and loyalty of the English nation. At the same event, Philip Herbert was exploiting to the full the effects which his physical charms were having upon the King. When he was asked for an interpretation of his device, 'a fair horse colt in a fair green field', Philip explained that it signified, 'a colt of Bucephalus's race and had this virtue of his sire that none could mount him but one as great at least as Alexander.' Delighted by such innuendoes, James 'made himself merry with threatening to send this colt to the stable.'[12]

As James's eye settled upon his younger brother, William Herbert drew closer to the Queen. According to

Camden, while Anne 'had her favourites in one place, the King had his in another. She lov'd the elder brother, the Earl of Pembroke; he the younger, whom he made Earl of Montgomery.' This friendship soon led William into collaborations with the Queen over the design and staging of court entertainments. He probably played a part, along with the Countess of Bedford, in recommending Daniel for the commission which resulted in The Vision of the Twelve Goddesses. He also lent to Anne the services of his former tutor, Hugh Sanford. Sir Thomas Edmondes observed:

> Both the King's and Queen's Majesty have a humour to have some masques this Christmas time, and therefore, for that purpose, both the young lords and chief gentlemen of one part, and the Queen and her ladies of the other part, do severally undertake the accomplishment and furnishing thereof; and, because there is use of invention therein, special choice is made of Mr Sanford to direct the order and course for the ladies.[13]

Although such specific references to the involvement of members of the nobility in the planning of court entertainments are rare, there is little reason to doubt that the Herbert brothers threw themselves wholeheartedly into the staging of early-Jacobean masques. Philip's nuptial celebrations on 27 December 1604 included a masque at night, 'Juno and Hymenaeus', lasting for three hours. Although the text is lost, the Revels Accounts state that it was 'presented by the Earl of Pembroke, the Lord Willowby and 6 Knights more of the court'.[14] Philip himself was a keen performer, appearing in Jonson's Hymenaei (5 January 1606), after the marriage of Robert, Earl of Essex, the son of the Elizabethan conspirator, to Lady Frances Howard, the daughter of the Earl of Suffolk; and in The Haddington Masque (9 February 1608), marking the wedding of John Viscount Haddington and Lady Elizabeth Radcliffe.

Among the female performers, Susan Vere, who became the Countess of Montgomery in December 1604, was also winning admiration for her masquing skills. She was Flora, representing 'the beauties of the earth', in Daniel's The Vision, and played alongside her sister-in-law, Lady Anne Herbert, and Robert Sidney's daughter, Lady Mary Wroth, in Jonson's The Masque of Blackness (Twelfth Night 1605). She appeared at least once more in a work by Daniel, as the

Nymph of the Severn in his <u>Tethys Festival</u> (5 January 1610), but she was most prominent in masques by Jonson. She danced in <u>Hymenaei</u> and <u>The Masque of Beauty</u> (10 January 1608), and appeared as the Scythian Thomyris in <u>The Masque of Queens</u> (Candlemas 1609). Jonson gratefully celebrated her long association with his entertainments in an epigram, describing her as 'A new <u>Susanna</u>, equal to that old'; a tribute which was warmly commended by George Chapman:

> Your fame (great lady) is so loud resounded,
> By your free trumpet, my right worthy friend;
> That, with it, all my forces stand confounded,
> Arm'd and disarm'd at once, to one just end.[15]

In 1605 Jonson urgently needed to reap some practical benefits from these distinguished court connections. Already under suspicion for representing in <u>Sejanus</u> the vices of a Roman court presided over by a homosexual, he was imprisoned for his part in writing <u>Eastward Ho!</u> which satirised James and his Scottish favourites. From his cell, he addressed pleas for assistance to as many powerful courtiers as possible, including Pembroke and Montgomery, writing to the former in terms which claimed a degree of personal intimacy:

> Neither am I or my cause so much unknown to your Lordship, as it should drive me to seek a second means, or despair of this to your favour. You have ever been free and noble to me, and I doubt not the same proportion of your bounties, if I can but answer it with preservation of my virtue and innocence; when I fail of those, let me not only be abandon'd of you, but of men.[16]

Although it is not known if Pembroke was able or willing to take any steps to assist Jonson, the authors of <u>Eastward Ho!</u> were released soon afterwards. By November 1605, despite his Catholicism, Jonson was being used by the Privy Council in their investigations into the Gunpowder Plot.

Another form of courtly festival in which the Herbert brothers excelled was the exercise of arms through tilts and barriers. According to Aubrey, tilting had been 'much used at Wilton in the times of Henry Earl of Pembroke and Sir Philip Sidney'. William Herbert tilted on every King's Day (24 March), and at his wedding to Mary Talbot in 1604, there

was 'an extraordinary show; at which time a great many of
the nobility and gentry exercised, and they had shields of
pasteboard painted with their devices and emblems.'[17]
Pembroke and Montgomery were prominent in the pageantry
which greeted the arrival in England of the Queen's brother,
Christian IV of Denmark, in the summer of 1606. John
Davies of Hereford penned a welcoming panegyric, Bien
Venu, which he dedicated jointly to the two chief royal
favourites, Philip Herbert and James Hay. William Herbert,
meanwhile, was a member of the party which went by barge
from Greenwich to Gravesend with James to meet the
Danish King. A lavish series of tilts were held in Greenwich
Park on 5 August to honour Christian, himself an
outstanding performer, in which the Herbert brothers joined
with the Earls of Arundel and Lennox as the 'Four Knights
Errant dominated by the Fortunate Island, Servants of the
Destinies'. The dramatist, John Ford, compiled an account
of these events, published under the title, Honour
Triumphant (1606), and dedicated to the Countesses of
Pembroke and Montgomery.[18]

Although William Herbert knew both Daniel and Jonson
and was an admirer of Inigo Jones, there is no evidence that
either he or his brother ever personally involved themselves
in the composition of the poetry and music or the design of
the sets and elaborate machinery used in court entertainments.[19] A close involvement in court revels, however,
provided the ambitious courtier with an enjoyable means of
making a favourable impression on the King and Queen.
Also, the presence upon the stage or in the audience of
Earls, Countesses and other nobles was just one ingredient,
along with the rich costumes, fantastic mechancial devices
and trompe l'oeil perspectives, in the creation of an illusory
display, geared to the greater glory of the monarchy. At the
moment on New Year's Night 1603/4 when William Herbert
knelt before the King in the 'Masque Brought in by a
Magician of China' and presented him with a choice jewel,
he was to be seen as an aristocratic observer of courtly
etiquette and, at the same time, an actor in a dramatised
panegyric, representing his nation's acceptance of its new
ruler. For an individual so clearly set on seeking royal
favour as the young Earl of Pembroke, such an advantageous
opportunity to place himself, both literally and symbolically,
at the very centre of court life was not to be ignored.

'THE REMNANT OF ANOTHER TIME'

Daniel's and Jonson's accession panegyrics and early court entertainments purveyed confident images of peace, prosperity and national unity, presided over by a wise sovereign. But, in reality, their experiences at the Jacobean court were in sharp contrast. At first, the publication of A Panegyric Congratulatory, followed by the commission for The Vision of the Twelve Goddesses, and his £10 a year appointment as licenser to the Children of the Queen's Revels, augured well for Daniel's literary career. Within two years, however, the optimism of A Panegyric Congratulatory had been dissipated by the sad despair of his address to Prince Henry, prefacing his play, Philotas (1605), in which Daniel now envisaged himself as 'the remnant of another time'. This tragedy dealt with the summary trial and execution of the noble soldier, Philotas, whom Alexander the Great had suspected of conspiring against him. Staged in 1604, shades of the Essex rebellion were soon detected in the play. Although Daniel protested to a Privy Council investigation that he had written the first three acts well before the events of February 1601, his sharp condemnation in the last two acts of misdirected monarchic power were much less easy to defend. Deprived of his office as licenser to the Queen's Children, Daniel revoked his earlier celebration of Jacobean patronage, preferring to take refuge in the memory of the last years of Eliza:

> For since that time, our songs could never thrive,
> But lain as if forlorn; though in the prime
> Of this new raising season, we did strive
> To bring the best we could unto the time.[20]

Daniel had left Wilton in about 1594/5, perhaps through some sort of disagreement but probably simply because William and Philip Herbert had departed for Oxford. He found other patrons - Fulke Greville, Lord Mountjoy, the Countess of Cumberland and the Earl of Hertford - but Wilton House always occupied a special place in his memory. In 1611 he revised the dedication of his play, Cleopatra, itself much altered in its 1607 edition, to Mary, Dowager Countess of Pembroke, for inclusion in his Certain Small Works. His praise was generous but unmistakably tinged with a nostalgia for a lost ideal. He recalled, 'the, then delicious Wilton' as that 'arbour of the Muses', where he had learned 'to apprehend how th'images / Of action and of greatness figured were.' The Dowager Countess was also the dedicatee of his unfinished poetic history, The Civil Wars in which Daniel, tired and disappointed with his lack of progress as a courtier, described himself as 'having nothing else to do with my life, but to work whil'st I have it.'[21]

Daniel's only other major commission for a court entertainment, Tethys' Festival (1610), was a fluent and well constructed piece of work. It seems, however, that Daniel was never really suited temperamentally to the role of royal panegyrist. A Panegyric Congratulatory had counselled James to emulate the moderation of King Henry VII, and Tethys' Festival also invoked his memory. But by 1610 the court masque had become a celebration of conspicuous expenditure. Daniel had been concerned since Elizabeth's reign with the need for a 'reformation' of court masques and he remained uneasy over what he saw as a tendency towards undiscriminating royal panegyrics at James's court. Jonson was no mere time-serving flatterer of royalty but, unlike Daniel, he had no doubts over his own ability to celebrate the new regime through spectacular drama. Even if Jonson held any private reservations over the character of the King or his policies, he was still capable of publicly committing himself to the concept of pacific kingship.[22] After 1605 his position at court, built upon the commissions for The Masque of Blackness (1605), Hymenaei (1606), The Masque of Beauty (1608), The Haddington Masque (1608), The Masque of Queens (1609), and his various celebrations of Prince Henry, almost entirely eclipsed that of Daniel. Clearly, royal favouritism provided the determining factor in the court careers of Daniel, who never fully attained it, and Jonson, who regarded it as official confirmation of his self-elected position as England's premier poet. But favouritism almost always brings with it suspicion of the patron's motives, hostility towards those who enjoy it, and a general resentment of the system which permits it. Hence, as Daniel's fortunes sank, he maintained his reservations over the representation of James's sovereignty, entered into literary quarrels with Jonson, and took refuge in the memory of an earlier and supposedly better patronage system.

Jonson was only one among many to attract the enmity of rivals by attaining royal favour. The entourage of Scottish courtiers, who had followed James down from the north, also aroused considerable envy and distrust.

Eastward Ho!, staged in 1605 by the Children of the Queen's Revels, has already been mentioned; and in February 1606 another of their plays, John Day's The Isle of Gulls was deemed to be again mocking them. Two years later, the French Ambassador complained that Chapman's dramatisation of the intrigues of Charles Gontaut at the court of Henri IV, The Conspiracy and Tragedy of Charles Duke of Byron, attacked the French court and satirised the English King, 'his Scottish mien, and all his favourites astonishingly'.[23] It is interesting to note that all of these plays were performed at the Blackfriars, close to the Earl of Pembroke's London residence, Baynard's Castle.[24]

After the extravagance of the first Christmas season, the Privy Council put forward a proposal to curtail drastically court entertainments. But this suggestion fell on deaf ears. Queen Anne greatly enjoyed the preparations and spectacle of such occasions, and the King valued the ideals of monarchy which they promulgated. There seemed to be no end to the extra expenses incurred in the functioning of the early-Jacobean court. The already steep rises in the personal expenditure of the royal family over that of an abstemious, spinster Queen were greatly accentuated by the establishment in 1606 of a separate household for Anne, and the considerable expansion of Prince Henry's after 1610. In addition, several related factors - a swelling political élite, a loosening of the King's control over office-holding, a marked tendency towards life and hereditary tenure for middle-range officers, and the increasing potency of rival aristocratic patronage networks - served to place an almost intolerable strain on the court patronage system.[25]

Built upon royal favouritism and bolstered by the factious in-fighting of ambitious nobles, the early-Jacobean court patronage system was bound to engender discontent. No matter how miserly Queen Elizabeth had once been considered, she was now remembered as a sovereign whose authority had not been continually compromised by partiality and prodigality. In a letter cataloguing the drunkenness, brawling, fornication and vomiting occasioned by the entertainments at Theobalds in honour of King Christian IV in 1606, Sir John Harington pointedly remarked: 'I have much marvelled at these strange pageantries, and they do bring to my remembrance what passed of this sort in our Queen's days ... I never did see such lack of good order, discretion, and sobriety, as I have now done.'[26] After 1604 the memory of Elizabeth's reign increasingly pervaded the minds of discontented writers, prompting a flurry of satiric attacks on James's court, in such works as Michael Drayton's The Owle (1604), Thomas Heywood's If You Know Not Me (1605), and Richard Niccols's popular poems, The Beggar's Ape (written 1607, printed 1627) and The Cuckow (1607).

THE SIDNEIANS AND SPENSERIANS

During the last few years of Elizabeth's reign, Daniel and Drayton, the literary heirs of Sidney and Spenser, had been regarded as the prospective leaders of English poetry in the new century. The clergyman and poet, Charles Fitzgeoffrey, confidently wrote in 1596:

> Spenser, whose heart inharbours Homer's soul
> If Samian Axioms be authentical.
> Daniel, who well maist Maro's text control
> With proud plus ultra true note marginal:
> And golden mouth'd Drayton musical,
>> Into whose soul sweet Sidney did infuse
>> The essence of his Phoenix-feathered Muse.

Five years later, in his collection of Latin epigrams and epitaphs, Affaniae (1601), Fitzgeoffrey again linked these four poets, addressing consecutive elegies to Sidney and Spenser, and then, on the next leaf, celebrating Daniel and Drayton as their literary successors.[27] By 1605, however, Daniel was already in the shadow of Jonson. Drayton had also seriously blundered by celebrating James's accession in his poem, 'To the Majesty of King James', without first offering the expected elegy on Elizabeth. Furthermore, his biting attack on the 'regnum Cecilianum' in The Owle, followed by a fierce denunciation in the eighth eclogue of his Pastorals (c. 1606) of the Countess of Bedford for favouring a rival poet (perhaps Jonson), served only to alienate him from two of the most influential figures in the King's and Queen's circles.[28] The first major revival of 'Spenserian' poetry did not take place until after 1612. But it is clear that the origins of some of its most important characteristics - the sense of a lost golden world, a disillusionment with court life and a scepticism towards monarchic authority - lay in the views formulated by its father-figures, Daniel and Drayton, during the first three years of James's reign.

At the same period, the laments for the loss of Philip

115

Sidney, which continued unabated, were beginning to be endowed with a more specific tone of political disquiet. In 1604 William Herbert of Glamorgan had satisfied himself in A Prophecy of Cadwallader with placing Sidney in England's literary pantheon, alongside Chaucer, Gower, Lydgate and Spenser. Only two years later his perspective on Sidney was radically altered in England's Sorrow, or a Farewell to Essex. This volume of poetry, comprising a series of historical laments, was an overt work of Elizabethan nostalgia, celebrating the old 1580s line of Protestant militancy. It also paid tribute to Robert Devereux (1591-1646), the son and heir of the second Earl of Essex, who had been restored to the title by James on 18 April 1604. Two years later, Essex married Lady Frances Howard, the daughter of the powerful Earl of Suffolk. Robert Cecil had been considered by some of the second Earl of Essex's supporters as chiefly responsible for the Queen's decision to execute the Earl. This marriage into the family of Cecil's allies, the Howards, was designed to heal some of these political wounds. Six months later, Cecil's own son took as his bride another of Suffolk's daughters. But the Venetian ambassador was probably not far from the truth when he noted in his account of the wedding: 'Essex has an infinite number of friends all devoted to the memory of his father, all of whom are ready to attempt anything to avenge the death of so noble a gentleman.'29

It is clear that the Sidney/Essex association was firmly in Herbert of Glamorgan's mind as he compiled England's Sorrow. The collection begins with a series of poems in praise of the second Earl of Essex; his brother, Sir Walter Devereux (d. 1591); Queen Elizabeth; Robert Dudley, Earl of Leicester; and Sir Philip Sidney. He also makes prominent play of the second Earl of Pembroke's name, and, perhaps with the weddings of 1606 in mind, honours both William and Robert Cecil. Other important personages from English history, such as Henry V and Sir Thomas Wyatt, are praised but by far the largest section of the collection is given over to Sidney. Celebrating his three distinct roles as perfect courtier, Protestant warrior and patron of the arts, Herbert offers some consolation for his loss:

> But thou [Sidney] art dead, I would it were not sin,
> And I would wish thou wert but newly born,
> Thou wert, as if indeed thou hadst not been,
> Too soon we saw the night of such a morn;

Oh hadst thou never died, or ne're been born,
But being dead, fair heaven's grant I see
One to excel, who now is like to thee.[30]

This heir is none other than William, third Earl of
Pembroke, whom Herbert compares in the poem to his
grandfather, the first Earl: 'Whose name and virtue like his
grandsire may / Be ever great, his name shall never die.'

England's Sorrow exemplifies the marked attention
being paid to the memory of Sidney and Essex during the
first decade of James's reign. John Davies of Hereford also
linked the names of the two men in his lament for the
'renowned late English military knights' (no 184) in his
Scourge of Folly (1611). Of course, some writers were
prompted to recall Sidney for purely personal considerations. Nathaniel Baxter, who claimed to have been Philip's
Greek tutor, compiled a curious poetic volume, Sir Philip
Sidney's Ourania (1606), considering a miscellany of topics,
including astronomy, botany, alchemy and medical science.
Baxter's execrable poetry was designed to milk patronage
from Sidney's relatives. In one passage, as indecorous as it
was badly written, he invoked the ghost of Sidney to
pressurise the Dowager Countess of Pembroke into showing
him favour. On a more dignified level, Gervase Markham's
The English Arcadia (1607), drawing upon the plot of
Sidney's fiction, may be regarded, along with Sir William
Alexander's famous Supplement, printed in the 1613 folio of
the Arcadia, as the work of genuine admirers of Sidney's
prose style.

Other writers, however, were intent upon endowing
their veneration for Sidney with a political significance.
When John Day was summoned in 1606 by the Star Chamber
to explain the unflattering references to Scottish favourites
in his play, The Isle of Gulls, he argued that he had simply
been drawing his ideas from Sidney's Arcadia. And, to some
extent, this was true; since the play contained a Duke
called Basileus and his favourite, Dametas. But Day's Duke,
like James, devoted far too much time to hunting; while the
inordinate power granted to Dametas (in the Arcadia,
Basilius' chief herdsman) alienated both scholars and
soldiers from the court.[31]

In 1607 the poet and antiquary, Richard Carew,
dedicated to the Earls of Pembroke and Montgomery his
English adaptation and continuation of Henri Estienne's (or
Stephens's) Apologie pour Herodote. Carew had known

Sidney personally when they had been together as students at Christ Church, Oxford. During his European travels, Philip had developed a firm friendship with Estienne (1531-98), renowned as a Greek scholar and printer. Carew explained in his preface how Estienne had sought to imitate the example of the Greek historian, Herodotus, a recorder of the bizarre and intriguing, by publishing in 1566 an anthology of 'our strangest modern histories'. Examining 'the rusticity of former times, and the fashions of foreign countries', the Apologie under its English title, A World of Wonders, promised its readers a banquet of lively characters and unusual observations. Carew, however, produced a volume which was a startling dichotomy. On one level, it was mere sensationalism at its most lurid, titillating its readers with stories of murder, cruelty, cannibalism, sodomy, bestiality and cuckoldry. But it also had a more serious intent. At the time of its compilation, James was earnestly pursuing a policy of appeasement with Spain. In 1604 the Infanta Anne, daughter of Philip III, had been proposed as a bride for Prince Henry. In response, Carew used his dedication to the Herbert brothers to remind them that in this volume they would find Estienne's proof of 'the gluttony, lechery, cruelty, felony, blasphemy, stupidity, and the like cardinal virtues of our good Catholics of the Romish hierarchy', adding on his own account, that 'their Catholic religion is nothing but catholic corruption, and Catholic Papists, catholic heretics.'[32]

Carew's and Day's works demonstrate how pointedly the memory of Sidney could be used to cloak their own responses to Jacobean court politics and religious policy. As open discontent with the court patronage system grew during the early seventeenth century, Sidney's legendary perfection as a courtier was increasingly emphasised. Represented by Davies of Hereford as 'Our little world's great paragon of fame', and by Herbert of Glamorgan as 'a man yborn to govern men', Sidney was posthumously confirmed by Jacobean poets as a leader of Protestant nationalism.

'THE GREAT EXAMPLE OF HONOUR'

In 1607 the stationer, Edward Blount, dedicated a translation of Lorenzo Ducci's The Courtier's Art jointly to 'the right honourable and most noble brothers', William and Philip Herbert. During the next two decades, Richard

Carew, William Shute, Thomas Charde, Leonard Digges, Walter Sweeper and others followed suit, creating an impression that the Earls of Pembroke and Montgomery consciously collaborated in their patronage of literature.[33] In reality, this was far from being the case. Aubrey described William as 'a good scholar' who 'delighted in poetry'. In contrast, he insisted that Philip 'did not delight in books, or poetry', preferring outdoor pursuits to the company of scholars and poets. Clarendon confirmed this view, representing William as endowed with 'a good proportion of learning', while Philip 'pretended to no other qualifications than to understand horses and dogs very well',[34]

Equestrian skills were of great advantage to those wishing to ingratiate themselves with a King who much preferred the thrills of the chase to reading state papers. Gervase Markham dedicated the first two books of his treatise on horsemanship, Cavelarice (1607), to Prince Henry and later instalments to the Earl of Montgomery and his kinsman, Edward Somerset, Earl of Worcester, both renowned for their expertise in tilting and hunting. Pembroke was also an enthusiastic participant in such activities, as John Ford's Honour Triumphant (1606) makes clear. But it was Philip Herbert who reaped most reward from his skills on horseback. As Clarendon remarked, Philip 'had the good fortune, by the comeliness of his person, his skill, and indefatigable industry in hunting, to be the first who drew the King's eyes towards him with affection.'

Philip's intimacy with James occasionally brought him into personal contact with scholars; when, for example, he accompanied the King to Oxford in 1605. During this visit, Philip and William were both granted honorary MAs. Matthew Gwinne's Latin comedy, Vertumnus, played before James at St John's, was dedicated to Montgomery on its publication in 1607. This address, however, made little attempt to depict Philip as a serious patron of learning. It was probably intended merely as an acknowledgement of Gwinne's former associations with the family, through his work for the 1590 edition of the Arcadia. Besides, during its performance, the King had been so weary from hunting earlier in the day that he fell asleep; and it appears that the rest of the royal party was in a similarly fatigued condition.[35]

Several other dedications made to Philip Herbert before 1610 convey the impression that their authors were not seeking to tax the intellect of a saddle-weary royal favourite. In about 1605, the young John Reynolds of Exeter, later to earn notoriety for his anti-Spanish satires, dedicated to the Earl and Countess of Montgomery a still unpublished romance, 'Love's Laurel Garland'.[36] From the publication of the Arcadia, up to and beyond The Countess of Montgomery's Urania (1621) by Lady Mary Wroth, the Herberts were closely identified with the romance tradition. Reynolds's romance, however, was a much less substantial work, recounting the various amorous adventures of a Princess Diaphania and Prince Philisander. Despite the reverential nod to Sidney perhaps implied in his hero's name, Reynolds made no great claims for his work, offering it as merely 'the first essays' of an amateur. Of a similarly modest quality was a printed romance dedicated to Philip Herbert, John Hind's Eliosto Libidinoso (1606), a melodramatic 'pot-boiler' tracing the tragic love of a Cyprian prince, Eliosto, for his father's second wife, Cleodora, resulting in their shared imprisonment and execution. Three years later, the prolific satirist and hack-writer, Samuel Rowlands, dedicated to Montgomery his versification of the folk-tale, Guy Earl of Warwick. Hastily compiled and of negligible literary quality, it was an immediate and lasting best-seller. Slightly more 'up-market', the pamphleteer and poet, Anthony Nixon, addressed to Philip a volume of popularised history, The Wars of Swethland (1609), tracing the struggle between Sigismond, King of Poland, and his uncle, Charles, King of Swethland (Sweden).

The works dedicated during the same period to the Herbert brothers jointly, or especially to Pembroke alone, were of an entirely different order. The Kentish merchant turned poet, Josuah Sylvester, addressed a sonnet to William in his translation of the Divine Weeks (1608) of the Huguenot poet, Du Bartas, whose first Week of contemplative poetry Philip Sidney had once begun to translate. Sylvester was an ardent admirer of Sidney, Essex and Prince Henry; and he went to considerable lengths to depict Pembroke, 'so graceful, useful, both in court and state', as a worthy member of this Protestant line of descent. A similar perspective was adopted by George Chapman when his translation of the first twelve books of Homer's Iliad was published in about 1610. Opening with a poetic epistle to Prince Henry, the volume also contained sixteen dedicatory sonnets, including ones to Robert Sidney and the Earls of Pembroke and Montgomery. After praising William's 'godlike learning', Chapman reminded Philip of the example of his illustrious namesake:

> There runs a blood, fair Earl, through your clear veins
> That well entitles you to all things noble;
> Which still the living Sydnian soul maintains,
> And your name's ancient noblesse doth redouble. [37]

The Anglicised Italian, Robert Gentili, addressed to Pembroke in 1607 a legal tract, In Titulos Codicis ... Disputationes Decem by his father, Alberico, regarded by many as the founder of international law. The elder Gentili had come to England from Italy in the mid 1580s as a Protestant refugee. Through the personal patronage of the Earl of Leicester, who was then Chancellor of Oxford University, he began to lecture there, instigating a revival of the study of civil and Roman law in England. Keen to express his gratitude, Alberico had awarded fulsome praise in his De Legationibus Tres (1585) to both Leicester and his political heir, Philip Sidney, whom he described as the 'perfect ambassador'. Robert's 1607 dedication, intended as a tribute to the generosity which his father had received from Pembroke's relatives, provided yet another reminder of the heady days of militant Protestantism in the 1580s.[38]

By far the most common concern of the dedications addressed to Pembroke during the first decade of James's reign was the question of religious allegiance and its implications for national security. Some works, such as Richard Carew's translation of Estienne's A World of Wonders (1607), were riddled with passages of full-blown anti-papist satire, reminiscent in language and tone of Edwardian Protestant propaganda. Operating on a more subtle level, John Healey's translation of Joseph Hall's Mundus Alter et Idem, a prose satire recounting an imaginary journey to the Antipodes, maintained an unwavering hostility towards Catholicism beneath a broader moral concern for the human condition.[39] A third form of anti-Catholic polemic was offered jointly to Pembroke and Robert Sidney in 1612 by William Crashaw, the father of the poet Richard, when he addressed to them a revised edition of his translation of Niccolo Balbani's biography of his friend, Galeazzo Caracciolo, Marquis of Vico, who, like Sidney, had died in 1586. Crashaw had been educated at St John's College, Cambridge, a hot-bed of English Puritanism, and had earned for himself the reputation of a powerful preacher. Balbani had been an adherent to Genevan

Calvinism and his life of Caracciolo, a nephew to Pope Paul IV, traced the marquis's 'conversion from popery' to 'his true religion'. Working from Beza's Latin version, Crashaw produced under the English title, <u>News from Italy of a Second Moses</u>, a lucid rendering of Balbani's compelling contribution to Protestant hagiography.[40]

Crashaw was also closely involved in the publication of John Healey's English translation of that favourite of Calvinist reformers, St Augustine's <u>The City of God</u> (1610). A second edition appeared in 1620, this time addressed jointly to the Earls of Pembroke, Arundel (his brother-in-law) and Montgomery, and revised throughout by Crashaw. In his dedicatory address, Crashaw claimed that Healey had first undertaken the project at his suggestion, hence giving him the right to correct his occasionally loose interpretation of the text. Healey's 'looseness', we may suspect, lay as much in his failure to exploit the polemical potential of Augustine's writings as in his relative lack of scholarship. In his 1620 dedication, for example, Crashaw made great play of denouncing the concept of Purgatory as a ludicrous Popish invention, as well as reminding his readers of the important contributions made by Augustinian theologians, led by Calvin, to the Protestant Reformation. It is clear from his two dedications that Crashaw hoped to persuade Pembroke to patronise an ambitious campaign of Protestant propaganda, designed to counter the threat posed by James's pro-Spanish policies. In the preliminaries to his translation of Balbani, Crashaw explained that this volume was being published as a sample of a larger scheme, 'to collect and put forth (as one antidote against this poison) the true stories and lives of the true, but especially the later Saints and holy men of God.' Nothing, however, appears to have come of this interesting plan to produce a Jacobean 'Book of Martyrs'.

The importance attached to Pembroke's name as a literary patron between 1604 and 1611 reflected his growing stature as a courtier and royal servant. At the beginning of the reign, James had awarded him the lucrative keepership of various lands and the offices of Steward of the Duchy of Cornwall and Lord Warden of the Stanneries of Devon and Cornwall. He was also appointed Lord Lieutenant of Cornwall, giving him administrative and military power over a large part of the South-West of England. To these offices was later added the Governorship of Portsmouth.[41] Although these appointments were indicative of the King's continuing favour, the Herbert brothers found their position threatened after 1607 by the rise of a minor Scottish courtier, Robert Carr, whose handsome looks caught James's eye when he broke his leg while tilting before the King. James saw much of Carr during his convalescence and soon afterwards made him a Gentleman of the Bedchamber. He was knighted in 1607 and created Viscount Rochester in 1611. Possibly in response to such favouritism, Pembroke engaged in an acrimonious public quarrel with the Earl of Argyll over a matter of court precedence, threatening to 'run him through with his rapier'. His brother, Montgomery, came to blows with another Scotsman, William Ramsay, at Croydon races. Both of these confrontations took place in 1610, the year in which proposals were put before the Commons to exclude all Scots from court.[42]

By 1611 the ambitions of the various factions at court were becoming more polarised. Salisbury was still James's chief minister but the failure of his Great Contract, designed to reform the whole financial system, seriously weakened his position. Scotsmen, such as Argyll, Ramsay and Hay, continued to challenge their English rivals for James's favour. Although inimical English laws against the Scots were repealed, the King remained bitter and disappointed over the hostility towards his proposals for an Anglo-Scottish union. His involvement in European politics was another source of disharmony at court. James wished to effect a diplomatic reconciliation to the Catholic-Protestant conflict in Europe; in part, by marrying his daughter, Princess Elizabeth, to the Catholic Prince of Piedmont. When this scheme fell through, he turned to the possibility of a union of England and Spain through the marriage of Prince Henry to the Spanish Infanta. These plans were supported by the Earl of Worcester, Lord Knollys and various members of the Catholic Howard clan, led by the Earls of Northampton, Suffolk and Nottingham. But they were strongly opposed by Prince Henry himself and Salisbury; Thomas Egerton, Lord Ellesmere; the Earl of Southampton; the new Archbishop of Canterbury, George Abbot; and the Earl of Pembroke, who was elected to the Privy Council in 1611.[43] Robert Cecil's health, however, was rapidly declining, and Pembroke was coming to be regarded as his closest friend and political confidant. According to the envious Earl of Northampton, Salisbury now 'wished never to be separated from the Welsh Earl [Pembroke]'; and John Chamberlain reported that, 'all business 'twixt the King and [Salisbury] in his absence passes by the Earl of Pembroke, who is <u>communis</u> <u>terminus</u> between them.'[44]

In 1611 Jonson's Roman play, <u>Catiline</u>, representing the moral and political corruption of courtiers and the failure of senatorial government, was played by the King's Men at either the Globe or the Blackfriars theatre, with Burbage, Heminge and Condell among its cast. Tracing the struggle between the conspirator, Catiline, and his noble opponent, Marcus Tullius Cicero, later Consul of Rome, the play was deemed too long and sombre by its first audiences. In response to this lukewarm reception, Jonson prefaced the 1611 quarto edition of the play with a dedication to 'the great example of Honour and Virtue', William, Earl of Pembroke: 'In so thick and dark an ignorance as now almost covers the age, I crave leave to stand near your light and by that to be read.' Jonson laid his case before the authority of Pembroke's literary judgement, as Daniel had done eight years previously in his <u>Defence of Ryme</u>. But Jonson's words were more than just an angry dramatist's riposte to the 'noise of opinion'. His dedication was a forthright attempt by the leading writer at the Jacobean court to establish Pembroke publicly as a noble arbiter of morality and taste, standing resolutely against the corruptions and ignorance of the times, like Cicero against Catiline. During the next decade, the identification or absence of 'virtue' and 'nobility' became key concepts in Jonson's representations of court society; a concern which was firmly established in both the text of <u>Catiline</u>: ' 'Twas virtue only, at first, made all men noble' (II.127), and in its dedicatory celebration of Pembroke's 'Honour and Virtue'.

ENGLAND'S LOST RENAISSANCE

In 1603 Daniel's <u>A Panegyric Congratulatory</u> had envisaged an ideal court society in which 'grace and favour shall not be dispos'd, / But by proportion, even and upright'. 'Temp'rate soberness' would prevail over 'loathsome surfeits', encouraging men to strive 'for the Republic' rather than pursuing only 'private hopes'. The standards set by King James and Queen Anne, fostering a court prone to favouritism and extravagance, were far removed from Daniel's prophecies of a new golden age. Nevertheless, his growing disenchantment with the Stuart court after 1603 was not totally without hope. The address, 'To the Prince', prefacing <u>Philotas</u> (1605), opened with Daniel's cautious optimism that Henry Frederick, then eleven years old, would ultimately live up to his vision of discerning and temperate kingship:

> To you most hopeful Prince, not as you are,
> But as you may be, do I give these lines:
> That when your judgement shall arrive so far,
> As t'over-look th'intricate designs
> Of uncontented man: you may behold
> With what encounters greatest fortunes close,
> What dangers, what attempts, what manifold
> Incumbrances ambition undergoes.   [45]

It is understandable that James's eldest son and heir elicited high hopes from royal panegyrists. But it is altogether much more surprising that, as he passed through adolescence, Henry began to live up to these expectations. By the time he was eighteen, he was being hailed as a statesman of international significance and as Britain's outstanding royal patron of the arts. After being created Prince of Wales in 1610, his household, centred at St James's Palace, was recognised as providing a marked contrast to those of his parents. It presented itself as a model of order and sobriety. Swearing was fined and banquets were intended to 'pass with decency and decorum, and without rudeness, noise or disorder'.[46] 'His Highness's household', Sir Thomas Chaloner observed, 'was intended by the King for a <u>Courtly College</u>, or a <u>Collegiate Court</u>.' According to John Cleland, 'the <u>Academy</u> of our noble Prince', was soon esteemed as 'the true <u>Panthaeon</u> of Great Britain.'[47] Despite his youth, Henry was drawn by an elevated concept of royal magnificence to recruit artists, architects and engineers from abroad whose skills could provide him with the trappings of a spectacular Renaissance court, matching those of Italy, Spain or the Holy Roman Empire.

The range of the Prince's literary and artistic interests can only be briefly indicated here. During the Christmas season of 1603/4, his nominal patronage was lent to a group of players, formerly known as the Admiral's Men. Among their playwrights were George Chapman, who entered the Prince's household as a 'sewer-in-ordinary', a minor domestic post; and Michael Drayton, whose immense verse history of England, <u>Polyolbion</u> (1612), was addressed to the Prince. Henry was taught languages by John Florio, an essential skill in view of the international flavour of his correspondence; and he studied music under the direction of Antonio Ferrabosco. Jonson observed in 1609: 'these gentler studies, that go under the title of Humanity, is not the least honour of your wreath'. Daniel's praise of Henry in Philotas (1605), may have later played some part in winning for him, in preference to Jonson, the commission for Tethys' Festival (1610). It was, however, Sylvester who became Henry's first 'poet pensioner' in about 1606. Almost certainly contrary to his father's wishes, the Prince entered into correspondence with Sir Walter Raleigh, who had been sent to the Tower in 1603 for supposedly having conspired against James in the Bye Plot. Raleigh wrote for Henry, The Prince, or Maxims of State, a perceptive and world-weary tract of statecraft; and it is probable that the Prince read drafts of his monumental History of the World, even though the two men apparently never met. Edward Wright tutored Henry in mathematics; Thomas Lydiat was appointed as his cosmographer and chronographer; and Francis Bacon was impressed by his interests in science. In the visual arts, the Prince employed Inigo Jones as his Surveyor of Works, and managed to lure from Florence the renowned Italian architect, Constantino di Servi. The Frenchman, Solomon de Caus, an engineer and garden designer, was appointed in 1610 as Henry's 'Architect' at £100 a year, twice Jones's stipend. The Prince also gave employment to several portrait painters, most notably Robert Peake and Isaac Oliver, whose work celebrated his imperial image in various classical and military poses.[48]

As the portraits of the Prince and many of the dedications offered to him suggest, his future role in European affairs was becoming a prominent concern by 1610. From the age of thirteen, Henry had been kept informed of international events by Robert Cecil who sent him selected ambassadorial dispatches to read. After his investiture as Prince of Wales, he was determined to support a more militant, or at least active, role for Britain in European affairs than that proposed by his father's foreign policies. Prince Henry's Barriers made prominent play of Henry's chosen name for tilting, 'Moeliades' (an anagram of 'miles a deo'), and associated him with St George as a Protestant soldier. The imagery depicting the Prince was also frequently tinged with a strong Elizabethan flavour. In Daniel's Tethys' Festival, Henry was presented with Astraea's sword, linking him with the 'peace through war' policies of Elizabethan militant Protestancy.[49]

By 1610 Jonson was expressing his doubts to Henry over the wisdom of an aggressive foreign policy. But there were now others who spoke stridently of the hopes which the Protestant nation were investing in their soldier-prince. Henry strictly excluded all Catholics from his household; and from this essentially domestic gesture grew an expectation that the Prince would eventually seek to counter the growing power of European Catholicism. The translator, Samson Lennard, who had seen action with Sidney at Zutphen, prayed that he might 'live to march over the Alps, and to trail a pike before the walls of Rome, under your Highness' standard.'[50] Lennard envisaged Henry as the inheritor of an ideological political descent from Elizabethan times, through the Earl of Leicester, Sir Philip Sidney and the Earl of Essex. It is debatable whether the Prince himself would have wished to lead a 'Holy War' in Europe against Catholicism. But his keenness to promote close ties between England and her Protestant allies was unmistakable. He greeted with great enthusiasm the proposals for a match between his sister, Princess Elizabeth, and Frederick, the Protestant Elector Palatine. When Frederick arrived in England in October 1612 to collect his bride, Henry was reported to have expressed his resolve to travel back with his party to Europe to find for himself the future Queen of England.

Henry involved himself prominently in the festivities which greeted the Elector but was forced to take to his bed on 15 October through the gathering effects of a fever which he had tried to ignore. His condition rapidly worsened and late in the evening of 6 November the Prince died, probably from typhoid fever. His demise left his family and household distraught. Two months later, James was still prone to cry out, 'Henry is dead, Henry is dead', as the memories flooded back. The Prince's funeral surpassed even that of Sir Philip Sidney in its sombre splendour and pomp. Amidst an 'Ocean of Tears', Henry was laid to rest in Henry VII's chapel at Westminster Abbey; a choice emphasising the bonds which King Henry IX would have forged between the Tudor and Stuart dynasties. English writers gave vent to an unprecedented outburst of lamentation. Four university anthologies, two volumes of funeral sermons and over fifty elegies were printed between 1612 and 1614.[51] Thomas Campion's haunting lyric, 'How like a golden dream you met and parted', recalling the friendship between Henry and the

Elector Palatine, stood as an epitaph to the hopes for a European Protestant Union. Another of Campion's elegies, printed in his <u>Songs of Mourning</u> (1613) and set to music by Giovanni Coprario, inevitably draws its reader's mind back over a quarter of a century to recall the comparable sense of despair and unfulfilled promise evoked by the death of Sidney - Prince Henry's most notable predecessor as a leader of militant English Protestantism and aristocratic patronage of the arts:

> When court and music call'd him, off fell arms,
> And, as he had been shap't for love's alarms,
> In harmony he spake, and trod the ground
> In more proportion than the measur'd sound.
> How fit for peace was he, and rosy beds!
> How fit to stand in troops of iron heads,
> When time had with his circles made complete
> His charmed rounds! All things in time grow great.[52]

'THE PRIMUM MOBILE OF OUR COURT'

With the rise of Robert Carr, Philip Herbert had the good sense to concede his position as a royal favourite without an unseemly struggle; a move which ensured that he continued to benefit from James's bounty. In April 1612, Carr, now Viscount Rochester, joined the Privy Council. After Salisbury's death in May, the King decided to act as his own secretary, using Carr as his assistant. The entry of an untried and inexperienced favourite into the centre of political affairs was a startling new development. Courtiers rushed to ingratiate themselves with Carr; and one observer noted that he had become the 'primum mobile of our court, by whose motion all the other spheres must move, or else stand still.'[1]

Due to the period of mourning for Henry, the wedding of Princess Elizabeth to Frederick could not be held until St Valentine's day 1613. The Inns of Court staged two masques in celebration: one by Chapman for the Middle Temple and Lincoln's Inn; the other by Francis Beaumont, with Francis Bacon as its 'chief contriver', for the Inner Temple and Gray's Inn. At court, Campion's The Lord's Masque, sponsored by the Earls of Salisbury and Montgomery and Lord Hay, celebrated this union which drew Britain into the centre of European affairs. Numerous nuptial odes and tracts were published, and, although many were still tinged with sadness for the loss of Henry, hopes were high that within a few years Frederick would become the King of Bohemia, endowing him with the rank and power which Prince Henry had once expected to be his own.

The other major court wedding of 1613 was that of Robert Carr to Frances Howard, the daughter of the Earl of Suffolk. Inconveniently, Frances was already married to the son of the Elizabethan Earl of Essex. She succeeded, however, in gaining a divorce, after a series of sordid investigations, on the grounds of her husband's impotence. Many, including George Abbot, Archbishop of Canterbury, who had conducted the marriage ceremony of Elizabeth and Frederick, were unconvinced by the legality of this separation. But the King was adamant that Carr should have his way. One major impediment remained, in the form of Carr's closest political adviser, the Protestant courtier, Sir Thomas Overbury, who feared that such a union would negate his own influence and place Carr under the sway of the Catholic Howards. This problem was solved by having Overbury consigned to the Tower, supposedly for refusing James's command to take up diplomatic duties in France or Russia, but really to take him out of circulation for a while. Pembroke, incidentally, played a small but significant part in this incarceration. James had first sent Archbishop Abbot to offer the diplomatic posting to Overbury, but when he refused, Pembroke and Ellesmere, the Lord Chancellor, then visited him together in an attempt to pressurise him into agreement.[2]

On 4 November, to match Carr's status to that of his spouse, James created him Earl of Somerset. Pembroke and Carr had shown little liking for each other during the previous year but on 17 November Sir Robert Naunton reported that Pembroke had wisely decided for the moment to avoid antagonising such a powerful favourite.[3] On 26 December Carr and Frances Howard were married in the Banqueting House at Whitehall. In the evening, Pembroke and Montgomery danced in Campion's The Squire's Masque. The Dean of Westminster delivered a flattering sermon on the virtues of the female members of the Howard clan, and even Archbishop Abbot made an appearance. Jonson provided a humorous entertainment, The Irish Masque, and verses for a challenge at tilt, despite having already celebrated the inviolable bonds of matrimony in Hymenaei for Frances's first marriage to the Earl of Essex. Jonson had been abroad for Princess Elizabeth's wedding and was keen to re-establish his reputation as the court's leading masque writer. Besides, Frances's father, the Earl of Suffolk, in his capacity as Lord Chamberlain, offered Jonson the unusually large sum of £200 for his services. Francis Bacon, with his unerring eye for the main chance, offered to the couple his Masque of Flowers on Twelfth Night 1614. John Donne penned an 'Epithalamion' and expressed a willingness to write a prose defence of Frances's divorce. George Chapman hopefully considered Somerset as a patron who could help him to recoup some of his losses following the death of Prince Henry.[4]

Prominent courtiers were also obliged to angle for Somerset's favour; and the Howards were proving by far the most successful in this venture. Led by Thomas, Earl of Suffolk; Henry, Earl of Northampton; and Charles, Earl of Nottingham, they were generally regarded as pro-Catholic and anti-Parliament, even though they did not constitute a solid political faction in the modern sense. Northampton played a leading part in securing Frances Howard's divorce, mocking Essex as 'My Lord the gelding', and manoeuvring Overbury into the Tower. Although he was not averse to double-dealing even his own relatives, Northampton saw Robert Carr's favour with the King as a means of building up the Howards' patronage network throughout the court and beyond. Opposing them were the Archbishop of Canterbury; the Earls of Southampton and Pembroke; Thomas Egerton, Lord Ellesmere; and various discontented Protestant noblemen who regarded a reliance on Parliament as preferable to an increased intimacy with Spain. By 1614 rumours were spreading that Catholic aggression towards the Protestant states in Germany was planned, much to the consternation of English courtiers such as Pembroke who retained a keen interest in the welfare of Elizabeth and Frederick. To make matters worse, James was thought to be adopting a strictly non-interventionist policy in Europe, in response to pressure from the Howards and Somerset.[5]

PEMBROKE THE POLITICIAN

It was during this particular crisis that Pembroke first began to attract attention as a major political figure at court, an aspect of his reputation which has been much misunderstood. Although some recent studies, notably by Robert Ruigh and Conrad Russell, have confirmed his extensive influence in parliamentary affairs during the latter half of James's reign, his determination and strength of character have remained open to doubt.[6] Clarendon began the process, claiming that Herbert's 'natural vivacity and vigour of mind' were sapped by an excessive indulgence in 'pleasures of all kinds'. Francis Bacon also observed that, 'for his person he was not effectual'. The nineteenth-century historian, S.R. Gardiner, completed the picture of a languid, young aristocrat, 'a wealthy man with nothing to seek for himself', by noting that he had 'no force of character ... with an intelligence greater than his power of will, he was the Hamlet of Charles's court.' Falling in with this view, Sidney Lee concluded that 'as a statesman, Pembroke lacked force of character', an impression which has remained prevalent. In 1941, for example, Phyllis Bartlett dismissed him as 'a self-centered, pleasant, and futile sort of individual'. Tresham Lever, the historian of the Herbert family, saw him as one who above all, 'liked an easy life; anything, or almost anything, for peace was his motto.' As recently as 1986, Derek Hirst concluded that Pembroke was 'not the stuff of which determined opposition was made'.[7]

I believe, however, that the third Earl of Pembroke's political skills and character have been seriously misrepresented. Even as a young man at James's court, his determined pursuit of royal favour is not suggestive of an ineffectual character. Nor did he lack the ambition to thrust himself into public affairs. He regarded the demise of Salisbury as an opportune time to assume a more public role in court politics. Pembroke was widely considered to be Robert Cecil's close friend - he even wrote an epitaph for him - and, along with his brother, Philip, carefully watched over his sick-bed.[8] However, at least to his enemy Northampton, the motives for this solicitude were perfectly clear. Soon after Salisbury's death, he warned Robert Carr: 'The little lord [Salisbury] when at Bath, wished never to be separated from the Welsh Earl [Pembroke], who is likely to prove an alchemist [take over his offices].' Pembroke also vied with Carr for the Mastership of the Horse, a position previously held under Elizabeth by both Leicester and Essex. By the end of 1612 he was recognised as a leading opponent of the proposed Spanish match for Charles with the Infanta; and he became a firm advocate for the calling of a Parliament which he believed would be able to influence James in this respect.[9]

Several of the literary dedications made to Pembroke between 1612 and 1614 acknowledge his developing status at court, and suggest that he was now envisaged by some writers as a worthy successor to the Leicester-Sidney-Essex-Prince Henry chain of Protestant political descent. This is the impression conveyed by the ex-soldier and translator, William Shute, in two works addressed jointly to Pembroke and Montgomery. The first, a translation of Thomas de Fougasses's The General History of Venice (1612), had been dedicated in the original to Prince Henry's great hero, Henri IV, whom he once described as 'my second father'. In August 1611 the Prince had also expressed an interest in Venice itself, discussing its fortifications with the Venetian ambassador. In addition to its military importance in the Adriatic, Venice played a significant role in the imperial ambitions of radical English Protestants. Diplomatic relations, broken off during Elizabeth's reign, were resumed after James's accession. Henry Wotton, previously the Earl of Essex's secretary, was sent out as Ambassador. He favoured an alliance between the Protestant powers and the more 'liberal' Catholic states of Venice and Savoy, as a means of securing powerful support in Italy for their opposition to Spain and the Habsburgs. A rift which developed between Venice and the Papacy accentuated English interest in these proposals. It is therefore, possible that Prince Henry had been intended as the original dedicatee of Shute's translation.

Shute's second work, a translation of Maurice, Prince of Orange's The Triumphs of Nassau (1613) had a more immediate claim to the Herbert brothers' attention through its references to Philip and Robert Sidney's exploits in the Low Countries. Shute explained that these triumphs belonged 'in some sort to your Lordships, many of these actions being performed by your noble uncles ... you have a most exact commentary of your own upon this work ... Viscount Lisle.' But, once again, Prince Henry would have been the most suitable patron for the book. Along with Henri IV, Maurice had formed his ideal military hero. Their portraits were the only two displayed in Henry's gallery at St James's Palace. The Prince had greatly admired Maurice's leadership of the forces of the United Provinces against Spain which led in 1609 to a twelve-year truce and a virtual recognition of Dutch independence. Henry had also been an active student of Maurice's military expertise, employing his engineer, Abraham van Nyevelt, and studying the history of his campaigns.[10]

The Cambridge graduate and artist, Henry Peacham, was another admirer of the Prince who turned his attention to the Earl of Pembroke in 1612. Peacham's emblem book, Minerva Britanna, was dedicated to Henry and made prominent play of the imperial ambitions of his household. It contained an interesting range of emblems addressed to prominent Jacobean courtiers, including one to Pembroke.[11] A similar approach was taken by Josuah Sylvester, a keen promulgator of the Leicester-Sidney-Essex-Prince Henry inheritance, whose hopes of preferment had been left in ruins by Henry's death. After 1612 Sylvester undertook a somewhat desperate programme of multiple dedications, addressing hopeful poems to Pembroke and several of his current political allies, including Robert Sidney, Viscount Lisle; George Abbot, Archbishop of Canterbury; Thomas Egerton, Lord Ellesmere; Henry Wriothesley, Earl of Southampton; and Frances Howard's former husband, the Earl of Essex. Little came of these efforts and by 1617 he was working for the Merchant Venturers at Middelburg in Zeeland where he died a year later.[12] George Chapman and John Donne, both staunch admirers of Prince Henry, also considered it worth their while to solicit favour from the Herberts.[13]

The Earl of Pembroke's increased prominence as a political figure at court coincided with the first major revival of Spenserian poetry between 1612 and 1614. In the wake of the deaths of Salisbury and the Prince, and the resulting scramble for power and patronage, pastoral poets such as Michael Drayton, William Browne and Christopher Brooke expressed their unease over contemporary court society by adopting the familiar 'persona' of the simple and honest shepherd, and endowing it with the role of a Protestant moral commentator and visionary. The first part of Drayton's Poly-Olbion (1612), dedicated to Prince Henry, celebrated the attractions of the English countryside as opposed to the vicissitudes of court politics. Browne's Britannia's Pastorals (1613) spoke more directly through its depiction of the sufferings of various Protestant heroes, particularly the Elizabethan Earl of Essex, languishing in a Spenserian Vale of Woe.[14]

The connections between the Jacobean Spenserians and the Herberts were strong since Drayton had long expressed in his poetry an ardent admiration for Philip Sidney and the Countess of Pembroke. Browne, according to Anthony Wood, was actually employed after 1624 by the Herberts.[15] These two poets were also closely associated with the prolific satirist, George Wither, another admirer of Prince Henry, whose Obsequies (1612) on his death had been dedicated to Robert Sidney. Wither's Abuses Stript and Whipt appeared in the following year.[16] It comprised a series of poems on the corruptions of courtiers, avidly read for its exposure of the financial and moral abuses reputedly prevalent among James's highest office-holders. There seems little doubt that the Earl of Northampton was one of its main victims, and it was probably at his instigation that Wither was imprisoned

in 1614. Pembroke may have pulled some strings to counteract this order since over twenty years later, in A Collection
of Emblems (1635), Wither reminded Philip Herbert of his
gratitude to, 'Your much renowned brother, as a chief / In
bringing to my waned hopes, relief.' He went on to explain
how Pembroke had not only facilitated his release but also
sought to 'rehabilitate' him into court favour, describing how
King James:

> ... took offence
> At my free lines; He [Pembroke] found such means
>   and place
> To bring, and reconcile me to his Grace;
> That, therewithall, his Majesty bestow'd
> A gift upon me, which his bounty show'd.[17]

Wither's dilemma was presumably greatly eased by the
death of Northampton in 1614, as was Pembroke's own
political position at court. Even on his death-bed,
Northampton's mind had been firmly fixed on court intrigue.
A few hours before he died, he wrote to Somerset, insisting
that 'the Earl of Pembroke and the Lord Lisle should not
have any of his offices', as they were his enemies.[18] After
his death, the King decided to end the Treasury Commission
established in 1612, and appointed Northampton's nephew,
the Earl of Suffolk, as Lord Treasurer. Robert Carr
succeeded to Suffolk's previous post as Lord Chamberlain, a
position which Pembroke, with Queen Anne's support, had
also sought.

Something had to be done by Pembroke and his
associates to counter Somerset's escalating influence.
Anthony Weldon states that the Earls of Pembroke and
Hertford, along with Herbert's close friend, the Countess of
Bedford, plotted to divert James's attention to a new
favourite, a handsome but penniless youth called George
Villiers. Pembroke even had to give Villiers some of his
cast-off fineries so that he could make an appearance at
court.[19] By November 1614 the King was hooked and only
after determined efforts was Somerset able to block Villiers's
appointment to the royal Bedchamber. John Chamberlain
observed on 1 December 1614 that preparations were in
hand for Jonson's masque, The Golden Age Restored: 'the
principal motive whereof is thought to be the gracing of
young Villiers and to bring him on the stage.'[20] Pembroke
also promoted his appointment as a cupbearer which

increased his contact with the King. In April 1615 a supper-party was held at Baynard's Castle to formulate further plans. The Queen herself persuaded James to appoint Villiers as a Gentleman of the Bedchamber which was duly done on 23 April. During the summer, James went on a long progress which included a visit to Wilton House, a sign of Pembroke's continuing favour at court. Villiers accompanied the royal party and by the end of August he had developed a firm hold over the King's affections.[21]

Somerset was already deeply worried by the threat posed by Villiers when rumours began to circulate which ensured his downfall. At the beginning of 1615, Secretary Winwood received reports that there were suspicious circumstances surrounding the death in 1613 of Sir Thomas Overbury while in prison. The Chief Justice, Sir Edward Coke, immediately began investigations, and by the end of the month he had assembled enough evidence to implicate Somerset and his Countess in a murder case. The Earl of Montgomery was one of the lords who questioned Frances Howard with the object of obtaining a confession that she had procured Overbury's death through slow poisoning. At the trials held in May of the following year, the Earl and Countess of Somerset were found guilty of murder, although James decided to commute their sentences. Their assistants, Weston and Mrs Turner, were not so fortunate and went to the scaffold. Sir Jervis Elwes, Lieutenant of the Tower, was also hanged and his estates turned over to Pembroke who apparently returned them intact to his widow and children. After a shared confinement in the Tower until January 1622, Robert Carr and Francis Howard were released and withdrew from court to the isolation of the country.[22]

The scandals over the Essex divorce proceedings, the murder of Overbury and James's astonishing leniency towards the Somersets, occasioned a flurry of satiric literature. Anagrams were coined, such as 'Frances Howard - Car finds a whore' and 'Thomas Overbury - O! O! a busie murther.' Scurrilous poems were passed from hand to hand:

A page, a knight, a baronet and an Earl
Were match'd in England to a saucy girl
Was ever such a match seen four to four
A wight, a witch, a murderess and a whore.

John Davies of Hereford published a satiric tract, dedicated to Pembroke, detailing Overbury's agonising death. In the theatre, it seems likely that Middleton's The Witch (1616), presenting a lurid display of court corruptions, sexual intrigue and potions to prevent the consummation of a marriage, sought to exploit the contemporary fascination with the seamier details of Frances Howard's first marriage.[23]

The fall of such an important favourite placed some writers in an exceptionally difficult position. A few remained openly loyal, such as the Scottish courtier, Sir Robert Aytoun, who composed in Latin elegiac couplets an imagined epistle from Frances to Carr which represented the couple as star-crossed lovers. Others, including Chapman and Daniel, also continued to regard Somerset as worthy of their praise, motivated probably by personal interest. Jonson included his nuptial masques for both of Frances Howard's weddings in the 1616 Folio of his works, although direct references to the Somersets were suppressed.[24] More generally, however, the marital intrigues and fall of Carr engendered among many writers an intense disillusion with court life, which, increasingly, they dared to express in manuscript and print.

'YOU LOVE NOT ALONE THE ARTS BUT THE MEN'

On 23 December 1615, Pembroke took over the Lord Chamberlain's staff, an appointment strongly influenced by Queen Anne whose own Chamberlain was the Earl's uncle, Robert Sidney. Broadly speaking, James's household consisted of three distinct departments: the Chamber, presided over by the Lord Chamberlain; the Household, under the control of the Lord Steward who supervised the basic material needs of the King and his court; and the Stable, headed by the Master of the Horse. The Lord Chamberlain's duties were extensive, including the appointment and control of the King's personal servants, guards and pursuivants, as well as the officers of the Armoury, the Ordnance, the Wardrobe and the Mint. He was also responsible for the allocation of lodgings at court, the reception and hospitable treatment of foreign dignitaries, and the arrangement of royal progresses. Bearing a white staff, the symbol of his office, the Lord Chamberlain was expected to maintain order at banquets, dramatic entertainments and within the royal entourage. It has been calculated that Pembroke's total stipend, comprising his salary, diet allowance, livery, brokerage and other fees, came to over £4,800 a year, one of the highest declared incomes enjoyed by a court official.[25]

One immediate effect of taking up this appointment was that Pembroke began to attract the attention of those seeking ecclesiastical preferment, since the Lord Chamberlain held overall responsibility for the supervision of the royal chapel and the appointment of James's chaplains. Sermons were the most apposite kinds of writing for such individuals to offer, and after December 1615 their dedications came thick and fast. Taking only a few examples, Thomas Adams, described by Robert Southey as 'the prose Shakespeare of Puritan theologians', dedicated A Divine Herbal (1616) to William Herbert, apparently with some success since he later addressed another collection of sermons in 1625 and his folio Works in 1629 to the Earl.[26] Bartholomew Parsons, a relative of the Jesuit Robert Parsons, acted as chaplain to the Bishop of Salisbury and held several Wiltshire livings. He offered to Pembroke his sermon, The Barren Tree's Doom (1616), preached on 5 August to commemorate James's escape from the Gowry Conspiracy in 1600. Clearly, by 1616 Adams and Parsons envisaged the new Lord Chamberlain's patronage as a route to court preferment, a view shared by Richard Sheldon, John Hitchcock, William Dickenson, Robert Bruen, Edward Chaloner and other churchmen.[27] Even a humble page of the royal chamber, one Benjamin Agar, presented Pembroke with his manuscript notes, 'as they were taken memoriter', of a sermon preached before the King by James Montagu, Bishop of Bath and Wells, who had officiated at the wedding of the Earl of Somerset and the Countess of Essex two years previously.[28]

The Office of Works, responsible for royal building programmes, was also ultimately answerable to the Lord Chamberlain, and Pembroke took a keen personal interest in its projects. These involvements frequently placed the Earl in the company of Inigo Jones. In 1618 Herbert and Jones both had seats on a Royal Commission examining the designs for Lincoln's Inn Fields and a chapel which was to be built there. Pembroke and Robert Sidney, as respective Lord Chamberlains, may have also been concerned with Jones's work for Queen Anne's palace at Oatlands, Surrey in 1616/17; the Queen's House at Greenwich in 1616/18; Holyrood House, Edinburgh in 1617; and with the designs for a new Star Chamber.[29] In 1620 the King visited Wilton House again, and on being told about Stonehenge, requested that a history should be made of it. Jones himself recalled:

> I was sent for by the right Honourable William then
> Earl of Pembroke, and received there his majesty's
> commands to produce out of mine own practice in
> Architecture, and experience in Antiquities abroad,
> what possibly I could discover concerning this of
> Stoneheng.[30]

E.K. Chambers stated that the Lord Chamberlain was
'incomparably the most important figure at court in all
matters concerned with entertainments.' Although much of
the organisation was entrusted to deputies, Pembroke was
responsible for the 'emptions and provisions for masks given
at the royal expense', and was expected to regulate the size
and behaviour of their audiences.[31] The players and
musicians employed at court were also under his control. It
is difficult to determine how closely Pembroke chose to
involve himself after December 1615 in the staging and
production of court drama. However, it is known, for
example, that on 2 November 1624 he sponsored a performance of 'Rule a Wife and Have a Wife, for the ladies, by
the King's Company'.[32] As regards the public theatre, the
interests of the sovereign and the privy council were likewise represented by the Lord Chamberlain, who presided
over the licensing of plays and the control of their printing
by the Revels Office. Its Master charged a fee, usually
between £1 and £2, for issuing performing or printing
licences, and exercised authority over all matters of censorship and the staging of plays during Lent or when plague
conditions prevailed. One of Pembroke's cousins, Sir Henry
Herbert, the brother of George the poet, bought the office
through the Earl's influence from Sir John Astley in July
1623 for £150 a year. On 7 August Sir Henry was at Wilton
for a visit by James and noted proudly: 'It pleased the King,
at my Lord Chamberlain's motion, to send for me unto his
chamber ... and to knight me, with my Lord Marquis
Hamilton's sword ... and to receive me as Master of the
Revels.'[33]
William Herbert was also willing to involve himself
personally in the affairs of the leading company of players,
the King's Men. In 1617 some of their members went into
the provinces and, using copies of letters patent belonging
to their parent company, set up a group which tried to pass
itself off as the real royal company. Pembroke responded by

circulating a stern letter, ordering 'all Justices of Peace' to apprehend the offending actors, and to send them with their letters patent directly to him. Two years later, at the request of John Heminge, he insisted that the King's Men should continue to receive their accustomed allowances, even though Lionel Cranfield, the new Master of the Wardrobe, wished to cut them in his efforts to reduce court expenses.[34] Such interventions were probably prompted not only by Pembroke's performance of his official duties but also by his friendly intimacy with the players. On 13 March 1619, Richard Burbage, one of the most prominent members of the King's Company, died. Over two months later, Pembroke lamented in a letter to James Hay, Viscount Doncaster, that he had avoided attending a play at court, 'which I being tender-hearted, could not endure to see so soon after the loss of my old acquaintance Burbage'. The Earl probably also knew the sixty-years-old Edward Alleyn, whom he joined, along with Inigo Jones, in a party sent to greet the Spanish Infanta on her expected arrival in England in 1623. In the same year, Alleyn married the daughter of another of Pembroke's literary friends, John Donne.[35]

When in May 1619 a number of corrupt and unauthorised versions of plays belonging to the King's Men appeared, Pembroke wrote to the officials of the Stationers' Company, forbidding them to print any of their plays without the actors' consent.[36] This letter suggests that his unofficial influence, well before Sir Henry Herbert became Master of the Revels, was already recognised within the printing profession. It is clear from dedications by James Shawe and Edward Blount that he was regarded by Jacobean stationers as a patron of particular significance.[37] Sharing this view, Thomas Charde dedicated the posthumous collected Works (1615) of Bishop Gervase Babington (d. 1610) to the Herbert brothers. Another stationer, John Budge, offered to Pembroke a posthumous edition of Sir John Harington's Epigrams (1615).

There is an interesting line of descent among some of the stationers associated with the Herberts during James's reign. Both Blount and Shawe had been apprenticed to the publisher of most of Sidney's works, William Ponsonby. Blount continued Ponsonby's practice of publishing high-class literary texts, including volumes by Josuah Sylvester, John Florio and Samuel Daniel, who all sought the favour of William Herbert.[38] Blount's imprint also appeared on Matthew Gwinne's Latin play, Vertumnus (1607), containing verses to the Earl of Montgomery; and on Leonard Digges's translation of the Spanish romance, <u>Geraldo</u> (1622), addressed to both Pembroke and Montgomery. Digges, it will be remembered, carved himself a small niche in literary history by contributing commendatory verses to Blount's most ambitious professional involvement, the Shakespeare <u>First Folio</u> (1623), prefaced by Heminge's and Condell's renowned address to the 'Incomparable Pair of Brethen'.

Like Blount, his sometime business partner, Thomas Thorpe, was well aware of Pembroke's reputation as a patron of letters, and several volumes in which he had a professional interest were addressed to the Earl.[39] In 1609 John Healey dedicated to William Herbert his translation of <u>The Discovery of a New World</u> by the satirist and later bishop, Joseph Hall. Thorpe had originally entered this work in the <u>Stationers' Register</u> on 18 January, although it eventually appeared under Blount's imprint. Soon afterwards Healey joined a party of emigrants for the New World where, sadly, he died. Thorpe came into possession of some other unpublished manuscripts by Healey, and immediately set about getting into print his potentially lucrative translation of St Augustine of Hippo's <u>The City of God</u> (1610), dedicating it himself to Pembroke. Also in 1610, Thorpe addressed to John Florio, one of the editors of the 1590 <u>Arcadia</u>, Healey's translation of the <u>Handbook</u> or <u>Enchiridion</u> of the Roman Stoic philosopher, Epictetus. In this dedication Thorpe thanked Florio for the help he had given Healey in finding a suitable patron for an earlier work:

> For his apprentice's essay you procured (God thank you) an impregnable protection: He now prays the same patron (most worthy of all praise) for his journey-man's master-piece.

Florio knew the Herberts well and this 'essay' may have been none other than Healey's translation of Hall's <u>Discovery</u>. Significantly, six years later, a new edition of his translation of Epictetus was dedicated by Thorpe directly to Pembroke, 'as a legacy unto your Lordship'.

Between 1609 and 1616, it is clear that Thorpe was keen to publicise his admiration for Pembroke's interest in literature - perhaps the two men even knew each other. The possibility that Thorpe took it upon himself in 1609 to dedicate Shakespeare's <u>Sonnets</u> to 'Mr W[illiam] H[erbert]' cannot, therefore, be totally discounted. Nor, it should be emphasised, can this identification be conclusively proved from the available evidence. Thorpe's lapidary-style dedication: 'TO. THE. ONLIE. BEGETTER. OF. THESE. INSVING. SONNETS. Mr. W.H. ...', onced earned him the apt title of 'the Sphinx of literature', who 'thus far ... has not met his Oedipus'. This comment, made as long ago as 1865, still holds true.[40]

Writers sometimes revealed in their dedications an awareness that William Herbert was a patron who could offer practical assistance in negotiating the frequently perilous path from manuscript to print. In 1623 Joseph Hall implied that his volume had been commissioned by the Earl, requesting him, 'to receive from the Press what you vouchsafed to require from my pen.'[41] Similarly, in his dedication of the printed version of his study of David's Penitential Psalm (1617), Samuel Hieron recalled how he had recently presented a manuscript draft of the work to William Herbert, in acknowledgement of some form of employment: 'your Honour not only receiving this from me when I brought it to you, but after some fortnight's detainment with you for perusal, returning it back unto me with acceptance.'[42]

Occasionally, writers asked Pembroke to intervene directly in the affairs of the Stationers' Company and to arbitrate in literary quarrels over publication rights. In 1619 Ralph Brooke, York Herald and a jealous rival of William Camden, launched a strong attack in A Catalogue and Succession of the Kings on the printing of illicit editions of heraldic material. He wished to ensure that 'the undigested notes of dead heralds and painters' books (to the prejudice of the living) be not published by any'; and explained how the Lord Chamberlain's influence over the Stationers' Company could be of considerable assistance in this matter: 'It were therefore to be wished, that books of that kind should be examined by experienced officers, and therewith have your Lordship['s] allowance, before they pass the Press.'

On a more personal level, in 1619 Ludovico Petrucci, an Italian exile from the Inquisition who had found preferment at Oxford in 1609, sought assistance from Pembroke in his dispute with the stationer, William Jones. Petrucci had been forced to leave Oxford by some of its Puritan members who suspected him of Popish sympathies. In self-vindication, he wrote an Apologia which he planned to have published with some emblems of his own design. Jones had already begun work on this project when he fell out with Petrucci; possibly because the latter was unable to pay for the use of his press, or, as a noted Puritan, Jones grew hostile towards a suspected Papist. He retained some of the blocks which had been cut for Petrucci's emblems and published them, without permission, in another volume, The Mirror of Majesty (1618), dedicated to the Herbert brothers.[43] Petrucci retaliated by having his Apologia printed elsewhere and sending a copy, along with a manuscript letter in Italian explaining his predicament, to the Earl of Pembroke. However, no assistance seems to have been forthcoming and Petrucci may have died soon afterwards in the Fleet.[44]

Following the Overbury murder scandal, the moral standards of court life were savagely attacked by Robert Anton, William Browne and John Davies of Hereford.[45] Viewed as a palliative to Somerset's self-interested exploitation of royal favour, Pembroke found himself regarded as something of a focus for this discontent. Philip Massinger, the son of the second Earl's Secretary, Arthur Massinger, also addressed his complaints about court life to William Herbert in a short but powerful poetic epistle, 'The Copy of a Letter' (c. 1615). Massinger was trying to eke out a meagre existence as a dramatist, 'such as are poets born, are born to need'; and it seems that he had just begun to do some work for the King's Men, 'scarce yet allowed one of the Company'. Cleverly cast as a humble plea for favour from the Lord Chamberlain, Massinger's 'Letter' was a forthright condemnation of the indiscriminate scattering of panegyrical tributes at court:

> I would not for a pension or a place
> Part so with mine own candour; let me rather
> Live poorly on those toys I would not father,
> Not known beyond a Player or a Man.[46]

Clearly, Massinger had a point. Addressing Pembroke in 1616, Thomas Thorpe apologetically noted that they lived in 'this scribling age, wherein great persons are so pestered daily with dedications'. In his Advancement of Learning, Bacon sternly warned: 'Neither is the modern dedication of books and writings, as to patrons, to be commended: for that books (such as are worthy of the name of books) ought to have no patrons but truth and reason.'[47] Mid-Jacobean writers were seriously concerned that the sheer proliferation of panegyric tributes was not only diminishing the impact of their words but also demeaning their status as moral commentators on court life. Furthermore, the frequently undignified squabbles for favour among writers did little to commend their views. George Wither, for example, attracted the envious attention of the rhymester and so-called 'water-poet', John Taylor, who dedicated an epigram to Pembroke in his The Nipping or Snipping of Abuses (1614).[48] Incredibly, Taylor accused Wither, whom he called 'St George of Braggadochia', of seeking publicity by being imprisoned and claimed that Wither had advised him to do likewise. Taylor entered into a similarly indecorous tussle with another satirist, William Fennor, whose unmemorable poetic Descriptions (1616) were also dedicated to Pembroke.

In his Abuses Stript and Whipt (1613), Wither cast a cynical eye over the whole frenetic game of patronage-hunting by dedicating the volume: 'To himself, G.W. wisheth all happiness. Thou (even myself) whom next God, my Prince, and Country, I am most engaged to.' Yet, despite this brave proclamation of independence, Wither's judicious praise of William Herbert and other select patrons within the pages of this collection tacitly acknowledged that the lure of court patronage was still a literary fact of life for most ambitious writers. The continued rise of commercialism in the world of printing - in the form of controversial writings, broadside street ballads and their prose counterparts, chapbooks, 'moral' miscellanies, and cheap fiction - offered a periodic escape from the pursuit of influential courtiers, churchmen and city dignitaries. But no serious writer, committed to earning a living from his pen, could afford to neglect totally the unpredictable potential of hierarchical patronage. Even Bacon managed to balance his high-flown desire to have 'truth and reason' as his only patrons with a more expedient decision to dedicate his Essays to the Duke of Buckingham in 1625. What these writers were really objecting to was the proliferation of second-rate material in court circles which placed an impossible strain on the available patronage. As early as 1612 John Davies had complained: 'For, Time now swells (as with some poisonous weed) /With paper-quelkchose, never smelt in schools; /So, made for follies excess.'[49] In other words, there were simply too many clients pursuing too few rewards.

Jonson's depiction of Pembroke's personal excellence in his Catiline dedication presented an image in sharp contrast to the pervasive pessimism over court standards. Other writers began to follow this lead, depicting the Earl as an ideal courtier who reflected the golden age of Philip Sidney and the Countess of Pembroke, putting to shame the shoddy corruptions of their own times. In 1611 John Davies paid his respects to the 'honor'd name' of this 'learn'd and judicious lord'. Two years later, Joseph Fletcher insisted: 'your virtues do as much entitle your Nobleness: which two, in this age, do so seldom meet in one, as most usually to be great, and to be good, is required a double person.' George Wither, Josuah Sylvester and John Taylor echoed these sentiments, celebrating Pembroke's name as the epitome of greatness and goodness. By 1616 this idealised image was a pervasive one, adopted by Robert Anton, William Browne and William Fennor. Describing the Earl as, 'the most noble embracer, and encourager of goodness', Thomas Adams concluded: 'You are zealously honour'd of all those that know goodness; and have daily as many prayers, as the earth saints.'[50]

The 1616 folio edition of Jonson's Works, a format usually reserved for the Bible, collections of sermons, histories and important translations, opened with the dedication of his Epigrams, 'the ripest of my studies', to William Herbert, 'the Great Example of Honour and Virtue'. Reiterating the sentiments of his Catiline address, Jonson explained that he knew from experience to 'expect at your Lordship's hand the protection of truth and liberty while you are constant to your own goodness'. Pembroke's integrity and performance of his duties as Lord Chamberlain was also commended in Jonson's Christmas His Masque (1616) and For the Honour of Wales (1618). Similarly, in The Gypsies Metamorphos'd (1621), Jonson represented the Earl as the ideal literary patron:

> You know how to use your sword and your pen,
> And love not alone the Arts, but the men.
> The Graces and Muses every where follow
> You as you were their second Apollo.

It was, however, in his famous epigram, 'I do but name thee, Pembroke, and I find /It is an epigram on all mankind', that Jonson spelled out most powerfully William Herbert's growing importance to Jacobean poets. This collection has been usefully described as a 'book of moral heraldry', demonstrating Jonson's belief that hopes for the revitalising of moral standards at court lay in the hands of an élite minority of the aristocracy, respected for their 'worth, not merely blood'. The act of naming became a device for drawing attention to the means for realising this ideal society; and Pembroke stood out as, 'so great an exemplar of civic virtues that he must be the model for all who wish to keep England safe.'[51] Just as Spenser's dedication prefacing The Shepherd's Calendar had envisaged Philip Sidney as an outstanding leader of courtiers and poets alike, so nearly forty years later, Jonson sought to endow William Herbert with a similar moral and literary role.

'A DISPOSITION AFFABLE, GENEROUS AND MAGNIFICENT'

Explaining his decision to dedicate the Epigrams to William Herbert, Jonson remarked: 'I return you the honour of leading forth so many good and great names ... to their remembrance with posterity.' Denoting a real man, the name 'Pembroke' also became a focus for a moral code in which virtue was seen to elevate and distinguish an individual while vice reduced him to the anonymous masses of flawed humankind. Although based upon what was by all accounts a warm and lasting friendship, Jonson's representation of the Earl as 'an epigram on all mankind' was intended primarily as a didactic abstraction, an attempt to distil some of the hidden virtues out of a flawed court society and to encapsulate them in the person of one of its leading members.

But what of the real man, the private individual behind the public reputation? Inevitably, the dearth of the Earl's papers seriously impedes an assessment of his personal interests and tastes as a patron. It is known, however, that he sometimes turned his hand to poetry. A volume purporting to offer a selection of his work appeared in 1660 under the title, Poems Written by William Herbert, Earl of Pembroke. Its editor, the son of John Donne, was a dubious character, 'by profession a clergyman but by inclination a profiteer'.[52] The collection contained many poems which have been since ascribed to others, including Thomas Carew, Henry King and William Strode. The volume was addressed to Christiana, Countess of Devonshire (d. 1675), for whom Pembroke had written some of his poems. It appears that she had provided Donne with copies of those in her possession. Others had been acquired from the court musicians, Lawes and Lanier, who had previously set some of the Earl's lyrics to music.

Donne's motive in publishing, we may suspect, was to

make a quick profit rather than to bolster Pembroke's literary reputation. Nevertheless, the poems which can be ascribed to William Herbert with some degree of certainty do him no discredit and bear comparison with the spare-time effusions of other able aristocratic poets, such as the Earls of Oxford and Essex. Pembroke is at his best when writing about amorous intrigues and the vicissitudes of court life. In, for example, 'Why with unkindest swiftness doest thou turn /From me', he composes a dramatic monologue of an irritated and cynical courtier who finds on his return from a visit away from the court that his mistress, 'malicious as incontinent', has been unfaithful. His consolation, perhaps echoing Jonson's Epigram CII, is a wry rejection of court standards, 'Where vice in angel's shape does title wage /With ancient virtue', and of the fickle woman: 'Enjoy thou many, or rejoice in one, /I was before them, and before me none.'

Pembroke probably wrote largely for his own amusement and the entertainment of an intimate circle of friends. When his poems appeared in 1660 they were printed with others by Sir Benjamin Rudyerd, a trusted political associate. They seem to have enjoyed writing question and answer poems and may have set each other themes or even written side by side. This kind of informal literary relationship was also enjoyed by Ben Jonson who for a time was given £20 by the Earl at each New Year to buy books. Drummond of Hawthornden recalled one incident when 'Pembroke and his lady' were discoursing: 'the earl said that women were men's shadows, and she maintained them. Both appealing to Jonson, he affirmed it true, for which my lady gave a penance to prove it in verse.' The product of this episode was Jonson's song, 'That Woman Are But Men's Shadows', based upon a verse by Barthélemi Aneau.[53] Jonson also knew Rudyerd well enough to pay a light-hearted compliment to his poetic talents in Epigram CXXI: 'Rudyerd, as lesser dames, to great ones use, /My lighter comes, to kiss thy learned Muse'; and in the following epigram, he praised his capacity for 'holiest friendship'.

To this small group of literary friends can perhaps be added William Drummond himself since he may have also written answer poems in response to Pembroke's.[54] John Leech, one of the Earl's secretaries and a friend of Jonson, dedicated some of his Latin epigrams to William Herbert in 1620. Four years earlier, William Browne revealed his privileged knowledge of Pembroke's amateur versifying with the tribute, 'None can more rightly claim a poet's pen'. John

Donne is also known to have enjoyed the Earl's friendship. In 1619 he joined a diplomatic mission to Germany as its chaplain. In a letter to its leader, Viscount Doncaster, Pembroke added the postscript: 'I beseech your Lordship commend my best love to Mr Doctor Dunn.' Although the poem, 'To my Lord of Pembroke: Fye, Fye you sons of Pallas', is no longer thought to be by Donne, there seems every reason to suspect that they would have found each other's poetic pursuits congenial.[55]

'His vigorous and restless mind ranged over the whole life of his age', was John Buxton's assessment of Pembroke's intellectual capabilities.[56] Literary dedications, of course, should not be taken as exact indications of a patron's personal interests. But even if only some of the works addressed to Pembroke were read by him, their range - including poetry, drama, music, heraldry, emblems, translations from ancient and modern languages, theology, sermons, philosophy, statecraft, history, international law, mathematics, medicine, astronomy, geography, horsemanship and military tactics - implies that his tastes were thought to be eclectic and his judgement held in high esteem.

Once again, however, it must be noted that the loss of many of the Herbert family papers has deprived us of a clear picture of one of the most admired men at the Jacobean court. For example, only a few scraps of information have survived concerning his interests in the visual arts. In a literary sphere, Pembroke was honoured by the compilers of emblems, an art which had been introduced into England during Elizabeth's reign. Before becoming a tutor at Wilton, Samuel Daniel had translated Italian and French emblems, and may have shown his work to the young William Herbert. In 1608 Richard Rowlands, or Verstegen, an antiquary and Catholic recusant living in Antwerp, dedicated to Pembroke and Montgomery his translation of a book of emblems by Otto van Veen, the renowned teacher of Rubens. Four years later, Henry Peacham addressed an emblem to Pembroke in <u>Minerva Brittana</u> and praised his knowledge of painting and pen drawing in his <u>Graphice</u> (1612).[57] The Earl was a keen collector of paintings, using Inigo Jones to acquire works on his behalf between 1613 and 1615. In about 1620 he wrote expressly to his cousin, Sir Edward Herbert, then Ambassador in Paris, asking him to purchase a painting which he particularly desired. Surviving portraits of Pembroke by Abraham Blijenbergh (c. 1617

Powis Castle) and Daniel Mytens (c. 1625 Wilton House) demonstrate his employment of the skills of the fashionable court portraitists.[58]

As early as 1564, Pembroke's grandfather, the first Earl, had helped to finance the 'Jesus of Lubeck', captained by John Hawkins, on a speculative voyage to the coast of Guinea and the Spanish Indies. The third Earl's involvements in such projects were extensive, acting as a member of the King's Council for Virginia (1609); an incorporator of the North-West Passage (1612); Bermuda (1618) and Guiana (1627) Companies; and as a member of the Council for New England (1620). A list of holdings of members in the Virginia Company, compiled in about 1618, reveals that Pembroke's investment of £400 was second in size only to that of the immensely rich Company of Grocers.[59] A patron of William Herbert's status and influence could sometimes prove a distinct asset to the colonisers in England. In 1623 the Earl of Middlesex and the Crown nominees sought to have the Virginia Company's charter withdrawn. Pembroke almost certainly opposed this move, particularly since he was still a major investor; and he played a part in Middlesex's impeachment in the following year. He was also involved in obtaining a royal charter for the merchant Sir William Courteen who was seeking support for a scheme to colonise Barbados.[60]

Predictably, English writers readily responded to Pembroke's interest in New World ventures. The clergyman, Richard Thornton, presented the Earl with a manuscript account of a failed expedition to colonise a region of the Amazon, mounted by the Guiana Company in 1629. In 1624, at the prompting of Sir Robert Cotton, Captain John Smith addressed to Pembroke a History of Virginia and an account of his colonisation involvements.[61] William Herbert probably shared Prince Henry's view that colonisation and privateering could be used to counter Spanish power in an area which provided them with great wealth. He therefore supported Ellesmere's and Winwood's proposals in 1616 for Raleigh to be allowed to make one last voyage to the Orinoco in search of gold to fill the royal coffers. But it appears that the Earl's major objective in such matters, like most other adventurers, was financial profit.

Several of Pembroke's other interests also strictly fall outside the scope of this study since he regarded them primarily as financial speculations. He became a Governor of the Society of London for Mineral and Battery Works

(1604) and was also involved in the mines Royal Society. Metal smelting and mining in Wiltshire attracted his attention, along with the Waterworks at Trellick, Monmouthshire.[62] It was reasonable, therefore, for Rowland Vaughan to choose Pembroke as the patron of his schemes for social and agrarian reforms proposed in his fascinating volume, <u>Most Approved, and Long Experienced Water-Works</u> (1610). The author claimed the 'memory of three hundred years dependency' on Pembroke's family, insisting that the Vaughans had fought alongside the Herberts in such notable military engagements as Cressy, Poitiers, Agincourt and Banbury. His <u>Water-Works</u> proposed how this Welsh connection could be put to good effect by combining his ingenuity and entrepreneurial flair with the Earl's influence and financial support. Vaughan sought to 'raise a golden world (for common-wealth) in the Golden-Vale in Herefordshire', through extensive drainage and irrigation projects. Apparently with the approbation of two former Wilton House chaplains, Bishop Babington and Bishop Parry, he also wished to employ a godly minister whose preaching would counteract the harm already done in the area by the present incumbent, deemed by Vaughan to be a 'counterfeit Puritan'. It seems unlikely, however, that Pembroke would have been inclined to avail himself of Vaughan's concluding invitation for all interested parties to meet with him for further discussions over supper in the house of 'Master Wotton, a scrivener', in Fleet Street.[63]

The diversity of Pembroke's interests, combined with the appeal of his idealised image as a courtier, exerted a strong influence over later seventeenth-century assessments of his character by Hamon L'Estrange, Sir William Sanderson, David Lloyd, Anthony Wood, John Aubrey and the Earl of Clarendon. To Aubrey, he was 'a most noble person, and the glory of the court in the reigns of King James and King Charles'. Likewise, Clarendon celebrated how the quality of court life was enhanced by Pembroke's presence, insisting that through his tenure of office as Lord Chamberlain, 'the court appeared with the more lustre because he had the government of that province'. 'And sure', he continued, 'never man was planted in a court that was fitter for that soil, or brought better qualities with him to purify that air.' Pembroke's reputation as a patron received similar treatment. Aubrey deemed him to have been 'the greatest Maecenas to learned Men of any Peer of his time; or since. He was very generous and open handed.' Clarendon concurred, noting 'a disposition affable, generous, and magnificent, and commended his willingness to foster talent:

And as his conversation was most with men of the most pregnant parts and understanding, so towards any who needed support or encouragement, though unknown, if fairly recommended to him, he was very liberal.[64]

FRIENDS AND RELATIVES

The third Earl of Pembroke's reputation as a literary patron was enhanced by the distinction of his whole family circle in this respect. Philip Herbert, it has to be admitted, was rather less involved with writers, but even he received several joint dedications with his brother and wife, and a significant number of other dedications in his own right, including important translations of Boccaccio's Decameron (1620) and d'Urfé's Astrea (1620). He also shared his brother's interest in New World ventures, becoming a member of the Council for the Virginia (1612), East Indies (1614) and Guiana (1626) Companies, and an incorporator of the North West Passage Company (1612).

Pembroke's relationship with Sir Robert Sidney, created Earl of Leicester in 1618, had taken on an added significance after Salisbury's death in 1612. As already noted, William Shute declared in 1613 that they were the joint heirs of the Leicestrian tradition of Protestant militancy; a view also put forward by William Crashaw in 1612.[1] Although Robert Sidney's persistent financial difficulties and prolonged service overseas prevented him from ever becoming a major court patron of literature, his family associations elicited a wide range of tributes from Josuah Sylvester, Francis Quarles, John Davies of Hereford, Robert Dowland and George Wither. As a practising poet, he also shared his literary endeavours with his sister, Mary Herbert, his close friend, Sir John Harington, and perhaps even with William Herbert himself.

Thomas Howard (1585-1646), the 'Collector' Earl of Arundel, became Pembroke's brother-in-law through his marriage to Aletheia Talbot, the sister of Herbert's wife,

Mary. During the early years of James's reign, Arundel had entered prominently into court life, acting as a principal masquer in Jonson's Hymenaei (1606). In the following June, Arundel, Lennox, Pembroke and Montgomery performed together as the four knight-errants of the Fortunate Isles, in one of the entertainments held to honour the King of Denmark's visit to England.[2] But from 1607 onward, Arundel drew closer to Prince Henry's circle and withdrew from those of James and Anne. Clarendon greatly disliked Arundel and, with venom dripping from his pen, depicted him as 'a man supercilious and proud, who lived always within himself and to himself ... so that he seemed to live as it were in another nation'. He pointedly compared Arundel with Pembroke: 'a man of another mould and making, and of another fame and reputation with all men'.[3] Over certain political issues, notably the Spanish match in the early 1620s, Arundel and Pembroke were undoubtedly opposed. Clarendon's comments, however, are misleading. In reality, Arundel, the friend of Inigo Jones and Ben Jonson, appears to have shared with Pembroke a distaste for the excesses of court life. True, there is no evidence that any great cordiality ever existed between the two men, apart perhaps from their friendly rivalry over the acquisition of paintings. Nevertheless, the strength of their family links were well enough recognised; as William Crashaw demonstrated in 1620 by addressing his revised translation of St Augustine's The City of God to 'a triplicity of noble brethren', Pembroke, Montgomery and Arundel.[4]

Apart from Pembroke and Montgomery, prominence and much credit was brought to the Herbert family name by their cousins, the descendants of Sir Richard Herbert of Colebrooke. His great-grandson, also called Richard, married Magdalene Newport, the close friend of John Donne, to whom his 'Elegy 9. The Autumnal' is addressed. In 1609 Magdalene, then a widow, married a Wiltshire man twenty years her junior, Sir John Danvers; and it has been suggested that the couple may have first met through the Herberts of Wilton House. Magdalene's sons - the philosopher and poet, Edward, later Lord Herbert of Cherbury; George, the divine poet; Sir Henry, the Master of the Revels; Thomas, a seaman and author; and Charles, an amateur versifier - form one of the most remarkable family literary groupings of the period. In addition to Pembroke's official dealings with Henry as Master of the Revels, it is evident that they were also closely associated on a personal level. In 1626, at the christening of Henry's first child, both Pembroke and Montgomery stood as godfathers. Edward's dealings with his aristocratic cousins were rather more mixed. In February 1607 King James granted Montgomery Castle, rightfully the property of Edward, to his cousin, the Earl of Montgomery, who was then at the peak of his royal favour. It is probable that Edward was allowed to remain its tenant and in July 1613 he bought it back from Philip Herbert for £500. Despite this injustice, Edward Herbert appears to have remained on good terms with Philip's brother, Pembroke, and found him a useful ally at court before his appointment as Ambassador in Paris in May 1619.[5]

It was, without doubt, George Herbert who gained most from his family's intimacy with the Earls of Pembroke and Montgomery. As a young man, he enjoyed a brilliant academic career at Cambridge. In 1619 he attracted the King's admiration when, as University Orator, he offered thanks for the gift of a copy of James's Basilikon Doron to the university. According to Izaak Walton in his Life of Herbert, the King asked Pembroke the name of this impressive young speaker. The Earl replied that, 'he was his kinsman; but he loved him more for his learning and virtue than for that he was of his name and family.'[6] In July 1626, after abandoning the possibility of a court career and taking holy orders, George Herbert was installed by proxy as a canon of Lincoln Cathedral and prebendary of Leighton Ecclesia. These appointments were gained through the influence of Bishop John Williams, recently dismissed from his post as Lord Keeper, who was perhaps keen to curry favour with the Lord Chamberlain. The church at Leighton Ecclesia was badly dilapidated and Pembroke subscribed the large sum of £100 for its rebuilding. It is also likely that the third Earl was mainly responsible for George's presentation on 16 April 1630 to the living of Fugglestone-with-Bemerton, close to Wilton House, six days after Philip Herbert became the fourth Earl of Pembroke. George maintained a friendly contact with the Wilton household, visiting there Lady Anne Clifford, the fourth Earl's second wife, in 1632.[7]

George Herbert's election to the Montgomery seat in the 1624 Parliament was also due to the influence of his powerful relatives. And it is in the political patronage of the Earls of Pembroke and Montgomery that we find the clearest evidence of the efficacy of family ties in matters of preferment. From the mid-sixteenth century onward, the Earls of Pembroke had maintained, with the assistance of various branches of the Herberts, political power bases in Wales and Wiltshire. Family retainers and friends were absorbed into these networks, enabling the second Earl's physician, Thomas Moffet, to sit for Wilton in 1597; and his secretaries, Hugh Sanford and Arthur Massinger, to represent Wilton and Shaftesbury in the 1601 Parliament. The third Earl followed this electoral practice, as is evident from eight letters written between 1621 and 1628 to the Mayor and Aldermen of Wilton. Their purpose in each case was to indicate Pembroke's clear preferences for particular candidates. On 30 December 1623, for example, he wrote from Whitehall to the Corporation of Wilton:

> I have thought fit to recommend unto your choice my loving Cousin Sir Percy Herbert and my Steward Sir Thomas Morgan, whom if at my request you shall admit unto Burgesseships of that your Borough besides their care and sufficiency to steed you in anything, to the height of their abilities, you shall by this favour bind me in any thing wherein I, may, to show myself.

On 26 January 1624, Herbert and Morgan were duly elected.[8]

A few individuals were in the fortunate position of being able to regard the third Earl as both their main literary and political patron. A noted scholar and traveller in his youth, Sir John Stradling was elected as Sheriff of Glamorgan in 1607, an office which would have required Pembroke's approval. Perhaps by way of thanks, he dedicated an epigram jointly to William and Philip Herbert in the same year; and later addressed an unpublished political discourse to Pembroke.[9] In 1609 he was bequeathed by his great-uncle the castle and estate of St Donat's in Glamorganshire, near the Earl's Cardiff estates. A friendly association was presumably maintained, since in 1625 Stradling sat for Old Sarum, a Pembroke seat, along with the Earl's Secretary, Michael Oldisworth, who married one of Stradling's daughters. Bonds forged by literature, politics and marriage also played a significant part in the development of Sir Benjamin Rudyerd's political career. On 17 April 1618 he was appointed for life to the lucrative post of Surveyor of the Court of Wards. Sir James Whitelocke had no doubts that he had obtained the position by 'getting into the good opinion of the Earl of Pembroke and other noblemen'. Soon after this appointment, Rudyerd took the wise step of marrying Pembroke's distant cousin, Elizabeth, daughter of Sir Henry Harington. In 1620 he was first elected to represent Portsmouth through the influence of Pembroke, its Captain. He continued to sit for Portsmouth, 'my usual place' as he called it, until 1629. Subsequently, he was a member for Old Sarum and Downton (the latter with Edward Herbert): both were seats under Pembroke's control. In the House of Commons, Rudyerd frequently acted as a mouthpiece for his patron's views and his allegiance to Pembroke was widely recognised.[10]

This blending of political and literary interests sometimes extended into William Herbert's associations with women. His friendship with Lucy, Countess of Bedford, to whom he was distantly related, was strengthened by the practical consideration that he held the proxy of her (reputedly ineffectual) husband, the third Earl of Bedford, in the Parliaments of 1616 to 1626.[11] Pembroke and the Countess were also united by their strong affection for Princess Elizabeth, who became Queen of Bohemia in 1619. Their political views were usually in agreement, particularly over the Earl's strongly anti-Spanish policies in the early 1620s.[12] Clarendon sternly remarked that Pembroke 'was immoderately given up to women', but allowed that 'he was not so much transported with beauty and outward allurements, as with those advantages of the mind as manifested an extraordinary wit and spirit and knowledge, and administered great pleasure in the conversation.' The Countess of Bedford was just such a companion. Pembroke had dined with her and the Countess of Devonshire the night before he died. Their respective patronage of such writers as Jonson and Donne may have been more collaborative than we can now ascertain. Similarly, it would be interesting to know the extent of William Herbert's literary dealings with Philip Sidney's daughter, Elizabeth, Countess of Rutland (1584-1612), whom Jonson reckoned 'nothing inferior to her father' in poetry.[13]

Pembroke also enjoyed a close personal relationship with his cousin, Lady Mary Wroth, the eldest daughter of Robert Sidney. She and William Herbert were often together from the time of his first visit to London. When she married Sir Robert Wroth in 1604, Pembroke helped the Sidneys with her dowry. Following the death of her husband in 1614, she was beset with financial difficulties and lived for a time at Baynard's Castle, Pembroke's London residence. She bore him two illegitimate children, William and Catherine, a liaison which was openly acknowledged within the family. Edward, later Lord Herbert of Cherbury, addressed a poem to her, entitled 'A Merry Rime sent to the Lady Wroth Upon the Birth of my L. of Pembroke's Child, Born in the Spring.'[14] Lady Mary possessed an impressive record as a writer, being the first English woman to write a long work of prose fiction, The Countess of Montgomery's Urania, and a sonnet sequence, Pamphilia to Amphilanthus (published together in 1621); as well as a pastoral drama, Love's Victory. All three compositions reveal an intense preoccupation with the subject of love and infidelity which may have been accentuated by her affair with Pembroke.[15]

Lady Mary's choice of Susan Vere, Countess of Montgomery (1587-1629), as the patron of her Urania, draws attention to one of the most underestimated literary figures within the Herbert family circle. Lady Susan was the daughter of the Elizabethan poet-Earl of Oxford and was much admired for her performances in early-Jacobean masques. Other writers, such as Nathaniel Baxter, John Ford, Aemilia Lanyer and Josuah Sylvester, commended her contribution to the Herbert family's literary patronage network.[16] She was an admirer of John Donne's preaching skills, and in 1619 requested a copy of a sermon which he had delivered on 21 February at the Cockpit, a group of apartments where the Montgomerys had lodgings.[17] Anthony Munday indicated the extent to which she was willing to help literary men in their researches. He explained in the dedication to his translation of Amadis de Gaule (1618/19) how his difficulties in seeking out satisfactory editions from which to work were solved 'by the help of that worthy lady', who took the trouble to find for him, 'such books as were of the best editions'. In the light of such a comment, it is reasonable to surmise that the large number of romances dedicated to Lady Susan and Philip Herbert were motivated primarily by the Countess of Montgomery's enthusiasms.

The literary concerns of Pembroke's female friends demonstrate once again the important role played by women in aristocratic patronage of English letters. Nor should the Earl's mother, the Dowager Countess, be overlooked in this respect; even though after the death of her husband in 1601, she largely withdrew from court life. In 1613 she went abroad for almost three years. She was recorded at Flushing

and Antwerp in 1614, and visited Stuttgart before returning
to England in October 1616. For a time, she became the
target of idle court gossip. It was falsely rumoured that she
had married her travelling companion, Dr Matthew Lister.
Mary Herbert then retired to Houghton Conquest near
Ampthill in Bedfordshire which had been granted to her by
King James and redesigned from plans drawn up by Inigo
Jones. Aubrey claimed that it was 'built according to the
description of Basilius' house in the first book of the
Arcadia'. Between 1616 and her death in 1621 from the
small pox, she did little to attract public attention.[18]

Nevertheless, she remained, along with her brother,
Robert, a living link with Philip Sidney. Aemilia Lanyer
honoured her as 'great Penbrooke hight by name, /sister to
valiant Sidney'; Nathaniel Baxter named her 'Arcadian
Pastorella'; and in 1611 John Davies of Hereford was still
paying his respects to the 'ingenious sister of the never-too-
much renowned Sir Philip Sidney'.[19] The quality of the
literary works addressed to the Dowager Countess after
1601 was variable; ranging from Breton's unmemorable
meditations, The Ravished Soul and the Blessed Weeper
(1601) and Baxter's abysmal Sir Philip Sidney's Ourania
(1606), to Robert Newton's tedious The Countess of
Montgomery's Eusebia (1620). This mediocrity was, to some
extent, relieved by reprints of older works previously
addressed to her by Spenser, Thomas Morley and Babington,
along with Francis Davison's pleasing celebration of the
Sidneys in A Poetical Rhapsody (1602) - volumes which all
recalled the golden years of the 1580s and 1590s when her
reputation had been at its height.[20]

Ultimately, however, the Dowager Countess remained
of significance to Jacobean writers not on account of her
personal patronage or for the quality of the texts dedicated
to her, but because she provided a crucial link in a family
chain of literary inheritance. William Browne, for example,
wrote in his well known epitaph: 'Underneath this sable
hearse / Lies the subject of all verse: /Sidney's sister,
Pembroke's mother.'[21] By this time, it was virtually a
commonplace for the third Earl to be reminded, in the words
of the stationer, John Budge, of his 'Sidneian blood'. Thus, in
1619 Thomas Campion respectfully wrote in an epigram:
'Pembrochi viduam num tu Sidneida nosti'.[22] But Mary
Herbert's demise in 1621 greatly accentuated, among those
close to the family, a realisation that she had been the last
living representative of a lost, golden age. As a companion

piece to his epitaph, Browne penned an elegy which expressed his concern at the passing of a literary epoch and, at the same time, implied a sharp criticism of the standards of modern society:

> For should the world but know that thou wert gone,
> Our age, too prone to irreligion,
> Knowing so much divinity in thee,
> Might thence conclude no immortality.

Wilton House itself became a focus for much of the literary nostalgia triggered by the Dowager Countess's death. At the beginning of his career, Walter Sweeper, had been provided with a church living by the second Earl of Pembroke at Bewdley, Mary Herbert's birthplace. Two of his compositions, originally intended for dedication to the Dowager Countess, were published in 1622: an anti-Arminian tract, Israel's Redemption by Christ, now dedicated to Robert Sidney; and a devotional work, The True Noble-Man, addressed to the Earls of Pembroke and Montgomery. Like Browne, Sweeper regarded a sense of family continuity in patronage as all important. He described Mary Herbert in Israel's Redemption as 'the mother of two great Lords and Peers of this Realm, the Earls of Pembroke and Montgomery', and 'sister to that valorous learned knight Sir Philip Sidney'. In The True Noble-Man he commended the pious sobriety imposed upon Wilton by its former chaplain, Gervase Babington. This picture was confirmed by the posthumous 1622 reprint of his Works, with a preface recalling Babington's happy 'government' of the Earl of Pembroke's household. According to Sweeper, swearing was banished and 'the house-keepers and inferior servants well knew and practised the grounds of religion' - a picture strongly reminiscent of Prince Henry's establishment at St James's Palace after 1610. Like the Prince's household, the Wilton of the 1580s, 'for state and government somewhat resembled Solomon's Court', Sweeper remarked, and 'like a little university' it became an 'excellent nursery for learning and piety'. Mary Herbert's death confirmed this idealised reputation of Wilton House which was to prevail throughout the seventeenth century. Aubrey observed of its enduring fame:

> Wilton will appear to have been an Academy, as well as Palace, and was (as it were) the Apiarie, to

which Men, that were excellent in Arms, and Arts, did resort, and were carress't.[23]

'OUR HONOURABLE CHANCELLOR'

On 29 January 1617 the Earl of Pembroke was invited, by free election, to become Chancellor of Oxford University. He accepted this honour and was invested on 22 February at Baynard's Castle in a lavish ceremony attended by the Vice-Chancellor, several Bishops and graduates.[24] Following Queen Elizabeth's accession, the appointment of a series of lay Chancellors of Oxford and Cambridge had drawn the universities closer into the court patronage system. The Earl of Leicester (1564), Sir Christopher Hatton (1588), and Lord Buckhurst (1591) at Oxford, along with Sir William Cecil (1559), the Earl of Essex (1598), and Sir Robert Cecil (1601) at Cambridge, presided over ambitious royal plans for the full utilisation of the country's best intellects. King James maintained this policy, regarding the universities as 'the nurseries and fountains of our church and commonwealth'. By the time of Pembroke's election at Oxford, as successor to Thomas Egerton, Lord Ellesmere (d. 1610), the Chancellor was envisaged as the University's most important link with court and royal influence. He was also in a position to exert considerable control over patronage and preferment within the university. The Earl of Leicester was particularly active in this respect, seeking lectureships, degrees and incorporation for his own protégés, particularly Protestant refugees from the continent. He also gradually assumed responsibility for the appointment of the Vice-Chancellor and other university officers, as well as involving himself in the election of heads of houses and college fellows. One of his last acts as Chancellor was the establishment of a University Press, which, in return, became a major centre for the dissemination of printed literature favourable to the Earl's own political objectives.[25]

Like Leicester, Pembroke took seriously his responsibilities as Chancellor and made extensive use of his powers of patronage. In 1619 John Bainbridge was appointed as the first Savilian Professor of Astronomy at Oxford. In the following year he dedicated to Pembroke his Latin edition of Procli Sphaera Ptolemaei in which he warmly commended the Earl's desire to foster academic excellence at the university. He made special mention of the current revival of mathematics under the guidance of Sir Henry

Savile, Master of Merton College, and the founder of Bainbridge's Professorship. Pembroke appears to have given his full support to these schemes. When a volume of elegies was published by the university in 1622 to mark Savile's death, it was dedicated to the Earl in gratitude for his patronage of mathematics.[26]

Other dedications, penned by Nathaniel Carpenter, Thomas Godwin, Diggory Whear, Thomas James and John Prideaux, suggest that Oxford academics commonly viewed Pembroke's interest as a useful means of furthering their own careers.[27] In 1623 Edward Chaloner, a fellow of All Souls College, observed in the dedication of a collection of his sermons that the Earl was the first and most obvious choice for Oxford scholars seeking a patron: 'to whom should they fly for patronage, but to our honourable Chancellor'. Chaloner probably intended his dedication as a means of soliciting favour for his own academic advancement. In 1625 he again addressed a volume to Pembroke, 'in humble acknowledgement of your noble favours conferred on me'; this time from his new post as 'Principal of Alban Hall in Oxford'.[28] Similarly, in 1620 William Herbert instigated the appointment of one of his own kinsmen, Francis Mansell, as Master of Jesus College, despite strong objections from some of the fellows.[29]

Promising young students were also able to benefit directly from the patronage of the Chancellor. John Daniel Getsius, a Protestant refugee from the Palatinate, arrived at Oxford from Cambridge, bearing:

> commendatory letters ... much in his favour ... which being back'd with others from the most noble William Earl of Pembroke, Chancellor of that University, proved so beneficial to him and to four more of his countrymen, viz. Paul Wonecer, Marc Zeigler, Joh. Hoffman, and Joh. Voghtius, mention'd also in the said letters, that each of them had a pension of £18 per an.

The Earl also offered assistance to the son of the Brownist controversialist, Henry Jacob. Wood noted the reference which the Chancellor wrote to support 'Hen. Jacob a young scholar' who, according to Pembroke's testimony, had been tutored in the Low Countries by the famous Orientalist, Erpenius, 'in the study of good literature', especially in 'the oriental languages'. In 1619 Ben Jonson visited Oxford to receive an honorary M.A. degree, awarded on the recommendation of his friend, the Chancellor, and perhaps also as a tardy response to the dedication of his play, Volpone or the Fox (1607), to 'the two famous universities'.[30]

One Oxford institution, Broadgates Hall, went so far as to change its name in 1624 to Pembroke College as a compliment to the Chancellor. The new statutes of the college referred to his 'love of letters and lettered men, the patronage of whom the university in general, and his college in especial, commends to his protecting care'. The doctor and writer, Thomas Browne, then an undergraduate of the college, praised Pembroke as 'a most noble Maecenas' for giving his name to the new institution. The Earl became the college's Visitor and a member of its governing body. Although it was hoped that he would prove a great benefactor, his sole gift was 'a great piece of plate' which has since been lost.[31]

The Bodleian Library was more successful in gaining tangible benefits from the Chancellor's patronage. As early as 1609 Pembroke had given money to the library to purchase copies of 54 Spanish sermons. In 1633 Archbishop Laud donated at least 23 Latin and other miscellaneous manuscripts, containing a monogram which could stand for 'W.H[er]B[er]T.' It is possible that the Earl had been collecting Latin and West-European manuscripts which his family then passed on or sold to Laud. Pembroke's interest in acquiring such items appears to have been stimulated in 1628 when an extensive collection of Greek manuscripts, formerly owned by a Venetian, Giacomo Barocci, came onto the market. They were brought to England 'by Mr Featherstone the stationer', and deposited with Laud at London House. At the latter's instigation, they were purchased by the Earl for £700 and presented to the university in May 1629. It is known that Pembroke added to this collection a Javanese manuscript of his own; and it is probable that other manuscripts now in Bodley once belonged to him or were purchased at his expense.[32] Visitors to the Bodleian quadrangle may still see the most lasting tribute to Pembroke's Chancellorship of Oxford University: a life-size bronze of the Earl by Le Sueur which Thomas, the eighth Earl, presented to the library in honour of his distinguished ancestor.

Regarding himself as the chief protector of the university, Pembroke proved a determined and effective advocate of its rights and privileges. In early summer 1618, when he was briefly laid low by illness, the citizens of Oxford sought a new Charter of Corporation from the Crown, a move which was partly intended to loosen the University's control over their affairs. The Earl, however, heard of these plans and registered his strong objections to the granting of any privileges which 'did cross with the University Charters or Customs'. He succeeded in persuading the King to let him have the proposals examined in more detail by advisers, 'expert in their Charters and Customs'. They made several recommendations which prevented the citizens from infringing on the university's rights.[33] Ten years later, Pembroke once again intervened to protect its interests, which were this time being threatened by the Court of Common Pleas. He appealed directly to King Charles and advised him to 'appoint my Lord Keeper, my Lord Privy Seal and one of his principal secretaries to speak with the judges of that court ... for maintaining the privilege of the university'. Pembroke's confidence in his own influence was justifiably high by this stage. He seemed to have been optimistic that these privileges would remain inviolate, expecting 'no question but the present difference will have a fair end'.[34]

In matters of political preferment at Oxford, Pembroke predictably sought to exercise the power and influence invested in the Chancellorship directly to his own benefit. He could usually count on his choice of candidate being accepted for one of the two university seats; and a similar system operated at nearby Woodstock, for which one of his secretaries, Mr Taverner, sat in 1625/6 and 1627/8. However, his persistent desire to control both university seats, coupled with his occasionally high-handed electoral methods, became a source of considerable friction between the Chancellor and the members of Convocation during the 1620s. These problems came to a head in 1625 when his preferred candidate, Sir Thomas Edmondes, was chosen only after the Vice-Chancellor, serving Pembroke's interests, had blatantly ignored the dissenting voices at Convocation. But the complaints persisted and, at the order of the House of Commons, a by-election was held in which a rival candidate, Sir Francis Stewart, finally obtained the seat. Two years later, the Earl again wrote in favour of a candidate, Sir Henry Marten, although he was careful this time to emphasise that his letter was intended as a recommendation rather than an order. Marten was a popular choice with the university and, assuming that his seat was already safe, Pembroke tried to ease his secretary, Michael Oldisworth, into the second seat. The university, however, thought differently and selected Sir John Danvers. Apparently, not even the Chancellor could force the hand of Convocation when they considered him to have over-stepped the mark.[35]

Another difficulty facing Pembroke as Chancellor was the question of religious conformity at the university. After the Hampton Court Conference in January 1604, at which Puritans from both Oxford and Cambridge played a prominent part, James realised the importance of maintaining a strict policy of conformity within the institutions where so many of his churchmen and court office holders formed their earliest friendships and religious convictions.[36] At the time of Pembroke's election as Chancellor, steps were being taken to temper the spread of Calvinist doctrines within the university. Degree holders at Oxford were obliged to subscribe to the Three Articles, and attempts were made to ensure the attendance of all students at carefully regulated sermons in the university church of St Mary's. Wood reports that divinity students were schooled in 'such books as be most agreeable in Doctrine and Discipline to the Church of England', and it was planned to submit an annual report to the King on religious conformity at Oxford.[37] Pembroke responded energetically to this responsibility, even before his installation, by writing to the Vice-Chancellor, the Bishop of Bath and Wells, counselling 'a careful performance of those things which his Maiesty not long since did give you his royal directions.'[38] During his tenure of office, the Earl sought to keep himself well informed and perused accounts of Church Synods compiled by university men. Dr Ward, the Master of Sidney Sussex College, Cambridge, sent just such a document to Pembroke and, for his pains, received the gratifying response: 'if in any of your occasions my love may stand you in stead you shall find that you have not bestowed this courtesy on an unthankful person.'[39]

During the thirteen years of his Chancellorship, Pembroke's name was frequently invoked to preface works of religious interest. But since it was customary in dedicatory addresses to list all of the recipient's major titles and offices, it is usually difficult to ascertain whether his university role played any significant part in eliciting a dedication.[40] In some cases, however, authors made comments which implied that this was so. In The Grand

Sacrilege of the Church of Rome (1630), Daniel Featley (or Fairclough), formerly Archbishop Abbot's domestic chaplain, described his volume as 'those fruits of my studies, which grew under the shade of your Honour's protection in the famous nursery of religion and learning, the university of Oxford'. Some writers owed the publication of their work directly to the Chancellor's influence. James Wadsworth, who as a child had been educated in Spain by the Jesuits, described himself as 'unknown unto your Lordship', until he gained Pembroke's interest, 'by a relation made unto your Honour of my travels and observations beyond the seas', recounting how in 1622 he had been captured by Moorish pirates and sold into slavery. This manuscript 'relation' is now lost but Wadsworth, having being converted into an anti-Catholic propagandist and Jesuit-hunter, explained in the dedication of his autobiographical The English Spanish Pilgrim (1629), how the Chancellor had sent a letter to the Oxford University Press, recommending the printing of this powerful attack on 'Jesuitical stratagems'.

In 1622 a difficult problem arose at Oxford when William Knight, a controversial young preacher of Broadgate's Hall, began to disseminate the theories of the German scholar, Paraeus, which advocated, in extreme cases, public opposition to a sovereign if all other courses of action had failed. Although these ideas were treated at Oxford largely as a subject for academic disputation, their practical implications to the authority of the monarchy were taken very seriously at court. Pembroke and other members of the Privy Council sent 'a mandatory letter' to the university, ordering the immediate 'suppression of these dangerous and false assertions of Paraeus', along with the confiscation of his books from students, stationers and college libraries. The Vice-Chancellor, aware of James's intense displeasure, instigated the incarceration of Knight and the public burning of the offending volumes.[41]

Pembroke also sought to stem the rise of Arminianism at the university but with markedly less success since, in contrast to the Paraeus issue, he lacked the full weight of court and royal opinion behind him. The English followers of the Dutch theologian, Jacob Arminius (1560-1609), rejected the doctrine of predestination, denying the existence of an elect and insisting that God made a gift of grace to all men. Like Puritanism itself, this doctrine was first formulated and expressed as a systematic code at the universities. Although it met with determined opposition from Puritan and Calvinist scholars, its popularity grew enormously during the 1620s. Pembroke declared himself an implacable opponent of Arminianism, writing to congratulate the Vice-Chancellor, John Prideaux, on his attempts to restrict its spread through the university. Prideaux, Rector of Exeter College and Bishop of Worcester, preached against its doctrines and dedicated his Orationes Novem Inaugurales (1626) to the Chancellor. Sir Benjamin Rudyerd, widely regarded as Pembroke's parliamentary spokesman, also attacked Arminianism in the Commons. Cornelius Burges, later ejected for propounding similar views, dedicated his anti-Arminian tract, The Fire of the Sanctuary (1625) to the Earl. Other writers who held anti-Arminian views and sought Pembroke's patronage included Walter Sweeper, Nathaniel Carpenter and Daniel Featley.[42] However, a royal declaration of 1628, forbidding any further discussion of the questions of predestination and free-will, vetoed an effective opposition to Arminianism at Oxford. Archbishop Laud, its most powerful supporter, confirmed its ascendancy when he was elected Chancellor in succession to Pembroke in 1630.[43]

It is perhaps for his instigation in 1629 of a thorough revision of the university's statutes, completed by the Laudian Code of 1636, that Pembroke deserves most credit as Chancellor of Oxford. His concern for discipline and correct procedure at the university had always been un-wavering. Soon after his election in 1617, he recommended to the Vice-Chancellor and Heads of Houses, 'a great restraint for Scholars haunting of Town-houses, especially in the night', and that 'all Scholars both at Chapel and at the Schools keep their scholastical habits'. Pembroke continued to concern himself with such issues, writing, for example, against the appearance of the Vice-Chancellor and Doctors bareheaded in the Convocation House.[44] But it was not until 1628 that any really significant changes were initiated. Arguments had arisen over the irregular selection of Proctors; and the King himself, at Laud's suggestion, instructed the Chancellor to rectify the situation. He wrote to the university authorities, advising them to regularise their procedures, but when the disputes continued, Pembroke took the matter into his own hands by issuing an order for the immediate election of 'Mr Williamson, Fellow of Magdalen College, and Mr Lloyd, Fellow of Jesus College'.[45] Soon afterwards, again at Laud's urging, Pembroke set in motion an ambitious plan for a complete overhaul of the university's statutes, 'reformed and digested into one entire book'. At his direction, delegates were appointed by the Proctors, including Dr Prideaux, Mr Williamson, Brian Twyne the antiquarian scholar, and Thomas James who had dedicated a theological tract to Pembroke in 1625.[46] Work then began on compiling the regulations which were still in use until the middle of the nineteenth century.

Pembroke's diligence in the performance of his duties as Chancellor of Oxford University greatly enhanced his reputation as a patron of learned men. Sometimes, as in the selection of members of parliament, the Earl's high-handed manner aroused the hostility of the university authorities. But, generally, they recognised him to be their most powerful and direct link with the King and court life. The effectiveness with which Pembroke protected their rights and privileges, along with his extensive personal involvements in the careers of academics and young scholars, earned him widespread respect among men of learning. Thomas Adams stated that the Chancellor's name was recognised as 'a sanctuary of protection to the labours and persons of students', adding that his 'patronage is so generally sought for, not only by private ministers, but even by whole universities'. Just before the death of Pembroke in 1630, Daniel Featley provided a just summary of the Earl's achievements as Chancellor, insisting upon the major contribution he had made to the enhancement of university life:

> Since the Muses of Sion and Helicon chose you their patron, their revenues have been so enlarged, the libraries furnished, the number of professors increased, the buildings raised and beautified ... Yet the rearing of these high and stately buildings doth not erect so lasting a monument of your praise, as the repairing [of] the collapsed discipline, and reviving of our ancient statutes.[47]

'A HAPPY GENIUS FOR ENGLAND'S HONOUR'

By July 1616, when the Earl of Pembroke, as Lord Chamberlain, presided over the arrangements for the King's summer progress, the Herbert brothers were widely recognised as being among James's most intimate advisers and friends. In September, Pembroke and the King stood as godparents to the Earl of Montgomery's first son, a short-lived heir to the Pembroke Earldom. Early in the following year, William and Philip Herbert were expected to join the royal progress to Scotland, lasting from March to September. Their high favour with the King and Queen was also confirmed by their continuing involvement in court masques; Pembroke as the official responsible for their staging, and Montgomery as an enthusiastic peformer in such entertainments as Jonson's The Vision of Delight (1617), Pleasure Reconciled to Virtue (1618) and For the Honour of Wales (1618).

During the same period, Pembroke's erstwhile protégé, George Villiers, was enjoying a meteoric rise to prominence at court. After 4 January 1616, when James made him Master of the Horse, a steady stream of honours came his way: the Order of the Garter in April, the title of Viscount Villiers in August, and the Lord Lieutenancy of Buckingham in September. James's affection for Villiers endured undiminished, and on 6 January 1617 he was created Earl of Buckingham. Montgomery carried his robes at the ceremony and on the next night they both danced with the Queen in Jonson's mumming, Christmas His Masque. Buckingham's skills and grace as a dancer were again on view on Twelfth Night 1618 when he received much acclaim for his lively performance in the Prince of Wales's masque, Pleasure Reconciled to Virtue. And there was every reason for Villiers to play such a prominent role in court entertainments since on the preceding 1 January he had been created, at the King's wish, Marquis of Buckingham. Pembroke, Montgomery and Sir Robert Sidney were among those 'few noblemen' invited to witness his rise to a position within the English nobility which outranked them all.

Villiers had been sent, at the age of ten, to Billesdon School near Leicester under the charge of the local vicar, Anthony Cade, who trained 'young gentlemen of the best sort ... in the learned tongues, mathematical arts, music, and other, both divine and human, learning'. His pupil, however, proved 'by nature little contemplative', and revealed no aptitude for scholarly pursuits.[48] But, inevitably, the pre-eminent royal favourite attracted the attention of aspiring court writers, and between 1616 and 1618 Villiers received printed dedications from, among others, the poets John Dunbar, John Davies of Hereford, Josuah Sylvester and John Taylor; a book on horsemanship by Michael Barret; volumes celebrating James's reign by Captain Thomas Gainsford and Samuel Garey; and religious tracts by Bishop Thomas Morton and Bartholomew Parsons. The stationer, John Budge, went so far as to cancel the dedication to Pembroke which had prefaced the 1615 edition of Sir John Harington's Epigrams, in favour of a new one to Buckingham in the 1618 edition. Similarly, in 1621 William Slatyer openly stated in his History of Great Britanie that he regarded Buckingham's patronage as a more reliable route to royal favour than Pembroke's.

The transformation of George Villiers from a decorative favourite into a figure of political importance came at a time when anti-Spanish and anti-Catholic feelings were rife at the English court. In 1616, for example, the apostate Richard Sheldon, a renegade Jesuit turned Protestant propagandist, dedicated to Pembroke A Survey of the Miracles of the Church of Rome, representing King James as David resolutely opposing the 'Goliath of Rome'. Sheldon also advocated, in the most strident terms, a Protestant military campaign against the growing threat of Catholicism in Europe. James, however, increasingly favoured a policy of appeasement towards Spain. In particular, the execution of Raleigh in October 1618, ostensibly for contravening the King's orders by engaging in hostilities with Spaniards during his last colonisation voyage to Guiana, aroused great public indignation. At the centre of power, the Privy Council, including Pembroke and now Buckingham, resolved to adopt a firm anti-Spanish stance, as rumours spread that Raleigh had been sacrificed largely to placate the complaints of the Spanish Ambassador, Sarmiento. Furthermore, in 1618 the Protestant inhabitants of Bohemia revolted against their Catholic Habsburg ruler, Ferdinand II, and in the following August chose James's son-in-law, Frederick, the Elector Palatine, as their new King. The Catholic powers of Europe, however, were not willing to accept this overt assertion of Protestantism in a nominally Catholic state. As war loomed, Pembroke confided to his close friend, Dudley Carleton, Ambassador at the Hague:

> the King will be very unwilling to be engaged in a war. And yet I am confident, when the necessity of the cause of religion, his son's preservation, and his own honour call upon him, that he will perform whatsoever belongs to the Defender of the Faith, a kind father-in-law, and one careful of that honour which I must confess by a kind of misfortune hath long lain in suspense. [49]

169

The progress of events revealed Pembroke's hopes to have been misplaced. Following the expulsion of Frederick from Bohemia after the battle of the White Mountain in October 1620, it became apparent that neither the cause of Protestantism nor the welfare of his daughter and her husband would deflect James from his dream of bringing peace to Europe and prosperity to his own kingdom through an Anglo-Spanish alliance. As early as 1614, less than a year after the court had been rife with rumours that a Spanish invasion was imminent, James discussed with Sarmiento the possibility of a Spanish marriage for Prince Charles. By 1615 he was seriously interested in a union between his son and the Infanta which might have entailed Catholic succession to the throne of England. During the next three years, negotiations continued over the religious questions raised by this proposal, particularly a Spanish insistence upon toleration for English Catholics. The Protestant revolt in Bohemia led to the temporary suspension of discussion but in 1620 a secret treaty for the marriage of the Infanta to Prince Charles was signed.

Sarmiento, now the Count of Gondomar, recently returned to England to begin his second embassy, had played a leading part in reaching this agreement, and had successfully lured Buckingham over to his side. Nevertheless, there was also considerable opposition to these proposals which found expression in a powerful and persistent propaganda campaign, eliciting an exceptionally severe programme of repression. Dr John Everard, reader at St Martin's-in-the-Fields, found himself imprisoned for sermons hostile to the marriage. Several other preachers who spoke out suffered incarceration, house-arrest and public burnings of their works.[50] One of the most effective anti-Spanish publications was the tract, Vox Populi (1620), by Thomas Scot of Norwich which purported to recount Gondomar's secret missives home, revealing the empire-building ambitions of his Spanish masters. James was outraged and, although warrants were issued for Scot's arrest, he managed to escape abroad where he was given refuge by Prince Maurice of Nassau. He eventually joined the exiled entourage of Elizabeth and Frederick who were then living with Ambassador Carleton. For the rest of James's reign, Scot continued to pen polemical tracts, most notably The Second Part of Vox Populi (1624), attacking the Anglo-Spanish marriage alliance and advocating English military support for the restoration of Frederick.[51]

Captain Thomas Gainsford, a soldier and gazette-maker, compiled a manuscript sequel to Vox Populi, entitled 'Vox Spiritus', in which the ghost of Raleigh appears to condemn Spanish imperialism and the threat which it posed to Anglo-Dutch relations. Gainsford was an ardent supporter of Elizabeth and Frederick, seeing their fortunes as central to the fate of European Protestantism. Probably at about the same time, he produced another manuscript tract, 'Courts and Camp Politiques', dedicated to the Earl of Pembroke, proclaiming him as 'a happy Genius for England's honour'.[52] This treatise, combining an exposition of military tactics with a Machiavellian consideration of statecraft, warned of the dangers of insidious conspiracies, such as the Gunpowder Plot, and the threat posed by foreign powers. Gainsford also called upon Pembroke to acknowledge his position as a national leader and defender of the realm.

By the early 1620s, Pembroke's influence at court and in Parliament was at its height. Following Queen Anne's death in 1619, James himself fell ill and, fearing the worst, recommended the Earl to Charles as one of his most trusted advisers. In 1621 Pembroke was appointed as Lord Lieutenant of both Somerset and Wiltshire, offices of great prestige which provided him with opportunities for exerting influence over local and parliamentary elections, ecclesiastical preferment and the county's militia. It has been calculated that during the Parliament of 1621, Pembroke controlled at least 26 seats in the Commons and could command nine votes in the Lords, making him the only aristocratic courtier capable of effectively countering Buckingham's parliamentary influence.[53]

During 1617, in response to hostility from the Howards, Buckingham had sought friendly relations with Pembroke, acquiescing to his wishes in several matters of preferment, and twice accepting invitations to be godfather to Montgomery's children. However, with the appointment of his mentor, Francis Bacon, as Lord Chancellor in January 1618, followed by the fall of Thomas Howard in July, Buckingham stood supreme at court. In the following year, he experienced his first serious clash with Pembroke, over an apparently inconsequential appointment of a Groom Porter. James had approved one of Buckingham's protégés for the post, much to the irritation of Pembroke who claimed, with some justification, that as Lord Chamberlain, the position fell within his gift. The King himself was obliged to instigate a reconciliation between the two men, assuring them at a private audience 'of his affection to both and of both their noble dispositions'. Their differences, Roger Lockyer remarks, were resolved into 'an uneasy blend of friendliness and suspicion, typical of relations between men of influence and ambition'.[54] At this period, Buckingham was also on intimate terms with Pembroke's brother-in-law, the Earl of Arundel; his brother, Montgomery; and with the latter's friend, James Hay, Viscount Doncaster. The usefulness of preserving these friendly associations may have been in Pembroke's mind when he argued for moderation during Bacon's trial in 1621 on charges of 'corruption and neglect'. After the trial was over, Bacon made notes for a letter to thank the Earl for 'his kind remembrance' and for the 'moderation and affection' which he had shown.[55]

By 1622 James was convinced that a Spanish match, rather than direct military intervention, offered the most likely route to the restitution of the Palatinate. Prince Charles concurred with this thinking and began to take Spanish lessons. Parliament was dissolved in January, partly as a means of limiting the circulation of opposition points of view, and even more severe restrictions were placed upon hostile preachers. Pembroke, however, remained unconvinced and began to adopt openly a more independent line. In April, he appears to have been instrumental in obtaining the release of the outspoken MP, John Pym, from detention in London to a more comfortable house-arrest in the country.[56] Even Buckingham was beginning to feel doubtful about the success of the marriage proposals, particularly since John Digby, Earl of Bristol, sent to Madrid to complete the negotiations, had not been able to bring them to a satisfactory resolution. In February 1623 Buckingham and Charles took matters into their own hands, crossing to Paris incognito, with the intention of bringing the Infanta back with them to England. A Papal dispensation was issued to allow the marriage, but the discussions once again ground to a halt, this time due to Spanish insistence upon unacceptable concessions to Catholicism in England. As though to confirm his approval of Buckingham's firm stance in Madrid, as well as indicating his honorary membership of the royal family, James conferred a Dukedom upon him in May.[57]

By mid-June, hopes were rising that an end was in sight. This placed Pembroke in a difficult position because, although he was now openly hostile to any concession towards Catholicism, as Lord Chamberlain he was obliged to supervise the arrangements being made for the return of Prince Charles with his bride. He joined a group of prominent noblemen, along with Inigo Jones and Edward Alleyn, heading 'towards Southampton', charged with devising 'shows and pageants' to welcome the Infanta. When the swearing to the articles of the marriage treaty took place on 20 July, Pembroke was conveniently (but genuinely) taken ill; his brother, Montgomery, deputising as Lord Chamberlain. On 28 August the English and Spanish representatives at Madrid exchanged oaths to conform to the agreed articles of marriage.[58]

Back in England by early October, Buckingham steadily lost confidence in the Spanish expressions of goodwill which he had received during the marriage negotiations. He was finally obliged to recognise that the imperialist ambitions of the Catholic Habsburgs posed a genuine threat to European peace. He also realised that James's persistent hopes for a constructive Spanish reply to his desires concerning the Palatinate were unfounded.[59] Buckingham therefore proposed that the treaties with Spain should be revoked before the meeting of Parliament but, to the astonishment of many at court, Pembroke resolutely opposed such a move. Already concerned by the Duke's pre-emptory manner, and considering that he now wished to browbeat both the King and the elected legislature, Pembroke was determined that the issue should be fully discussed in Parliament. Wary of the Earl's extensive parliamentary influence, Bacon counselled Buckingham that he should not antagonise Pembroke. Prince Charles also did his utmost to reconcile the two men.[60] Pembroke remained throughout this disagreement a firm advocate of an anti-Habsburg stance. It is understandable why in 1624 an outside observer, the Venetian ambassador, deemed the Earl to be 'one of Buckingham's greatest enemies'.[61]

In January 1624 it was formally decided to break off negotiations with the Spanish. After Buckingham had given Parliament a detailed account of his experiences in Madrid, Pembroke declared his 'complete satisfaction' with his behaviour. By March Rudyerd was arguing in the Commons for the formation of a Council of War; and it seems that Pembroke believed that the only realistic means of supporting an expeditionary force to the Palatinate was through an alliance with France. Preliminary investigations into the possibility of a French match were already in hand.

By the end of September, both Buckingham and Pembroke, whom many now regarded as allies, were confident that Charles would marry Henrietta Maria, the sister of Louis XIV. At this point, Montgomery was at last offered a seat on the Privy Council and was instructed to accompany Buckingham on his journey to France to fetch the Prince's bride. Pembroke had few doubts that war would soon ensue, confiding in Dudley Carleton at the Hague: 'it were better for the general cause that this war be styled by us rather a particular war for the kingdom of Bohemia than a war for religion, though I know in the consequence, these cannot be severed.'[62] Others, however, still hankered after the idea of a Protestant Holy War, as was made clear by the writer who veiled himself behind the anagram or pseudonym, 'I.D. Dralymont'. He dedicated to Pembroke early in 1625 a tract, The Spanish Pilgrim, which according to its sub-title, showed 'how necessary and important it is for the Protestant Kings, Princes and Potentates of Europe; to make war upon the King of Spain's own Country.'[63] Adopting a more temperate tone, Pembroke's political protégé, Sir John Stradling, addressed to him in manuscript, 'A Politike Discourse', advocating support for Princess Elizabeth.[64]

Anti-Spanish and anti-Catholic tracts continued to flood onto the market between 1623 and 1625. By this stage, Pembroke was addressed as a patron who was known to be openly sympathetic to such views. Abraham Darcie dedicated to the Earl a translation of a tract by Pierre Du Moulin, the elder (1568-1658), a French Protestant leader and noted opponent of the Jesuits.[65] Samson Lennard, who had fought with Sidney at Zutphen in 1586, and later became a genealogist, addressed to Pembroke a translation of Jean Paul Perrin's anti-Catholic tract, The Bloody Rage of that Great Anti-Christ of Rome (1624), which purported to trace the roots of Protestantism back to well before Luther. Other propagandist tracts which claimed the Earl's protection included the anonymous A Gag for the Pope and the Jesuits (1624); George Jenney's A Catholic Conference Between a Protestant and a Papist (1626); and Cornelius Burges's The Fire of the Sanctuary (1625), which identified links between the rise of Popery and Arminianism. Official court repression, however, was still being vigorously pursued and the pleas for Pembroke's protection made in these publications were meant as no idle compliments.

John Reynolds of Exeter, who had dedicated the third book of The Triumph of God's Revenge (1623) to Pembroke, was imprisoned in the following year for his attacks on Gondomar's influence in <u>Vox Coeli</u> and <u>Votivae Angliae</u>. Another seeker of Pembroke's protection, Richard Sheldon, was disgraced and dismissed from his post as a royal chaplain for preaching an anti-Catholic sermon at St Paul's Cross in 1622.[66] Pembroke may also have been influential behind the scenes during the controversies occasioned by Thomas Middleton's highly successful, <u>A Game at Chess</u>, staged in August 1624. Drawing on the <u>Vox Populi</u> tracts of Thomas Scot of Norwich, the play represented by means of stylised chess-pieces the machinations of Gondomar, along with other figures involved in the Anglo-Spanish marriage negotiations. After nine days of performances to packed houses, the King responded to the complaints of foreign ambassadors by forbidding its staging and ordering the apprehending and punishment of those responsible. However, neither the dramatist nor the company, the King's Men, seem to have been seriously inconvenienced by this censorship and threat of disciplinary measures. Nor did Sir Henry Herbert, the Master of the Revels, have to do much more than provide the Privy Council with an account of his reasons for licensing the play. In view of this remarkable leniency, there are grounds for suspecting that the Lord Chamberlain may have exerted some influence to protect his cousin and the members of the King's Company from James's wrath.[67]

The impression of Pembroke which has emerged from this account of his political and literary involvements during James's reign, is in sharp contrast to the ineffectual courtier with whom he has sometimes been identified. His determined pursuit of royal favour as a young man, followed in maturity by his tenure of several high offices at court and control of an extensive parliamentary network, mark him out as one of the most effective but underestimated politicians at the Jacobean court. Robert E. Ruigh provides the most accurate assessment of Pembroke's court career, describing him as,'the natural leader of the moderates' and a 'canny' political operator.[68]

The third Earl of Pembroke was, by all accounts, an intelligent and well-educated man, a practising poet who could number Jonson and Donne among his friends. As a patron, he was willing to peruse the compositions not only of writers who were in his service or personally known to him, but also of strangers if he thought that their work merited attention. Sometimes he would use his influence to recommend manuscripts for publication, along with assisting the careers of their authors and protecting them from official repression. For a considerable number of writers he became a political as well as a literary focus; while for others, particularly Oxford academics and their students, he was a powerful and committed patron of scholarship. As Lord Chamberlain, Pembroke had proved himself to be a ready defender of the King's Men's rights, protecting them against cuts in their wardrobe, attempting to prohibit illegal performances of their plays in the provinces, and presumably watching them perform at court. In addressing the First Folio of their friend's plays to Pembroke and Montgomery in 1623, the actors John Heminge and Henry Condell explained that they were seeking to acknowledge 'the many favours we have received from your L.L.':

> But since your L.L. have been pleas'd to think these trifles some-thing, heretofore; and have prosequuted them, and their Author living, with so much favour: we hope, that (they out-living him, and he not having the fate, common with some, to be exequutor to his own writings) you will use the like indulgence toward them, you have done unto their parent.

It is pleasing to think that at some stage during his career, Shakespeare was a beneficiary of the 'indulgence' of William Herbert, 'the greatest Maecenas to learned Men of any Peer of his time'.

THE LORD CHAMBERLAIN AND THE LORD STEWARD

On 22 March 1625, five days before James's death, Pembroke was by the King's side at Theobalds. Earlier in the month, rumours spread that a Scottish courtier, the Marquis of Hamilton, had undergone a death-bed conversion to Roman Catholicism. Troubled by such thoughts, James insisted that Pembroke should not leave him, reputedly saying: 'No, my Lord, you shall stay till my next fit be passed; and if I die, be a witness against those scandals that may be raised of my religion, as they have been of others.'[1] The King's personal reliance upon William Herbert was complemented by his official prominence at court as Lord Chamberlain. At James's funeral on 7 May he processed, staff in hand, immediately in front of the bier; while at Charles's coronation, he carried the crown to the throne. Within a few weeks, one observer was noting that 'after the Duke [Buckingham], the King hears no counsellors so gladly as the Lord Treasurer [Lord Ley] and the Lord Chamberlain.' At about the same time, Charles formed a special commission of privy councillors, including both Buckingham and Pembroke, to consider the 'renewal of foreign alliances, and especially what form should be held with Spain, the proposed league with France, the recovery of the Palatinate, the treaty to be held at the Hague, the arming of the militia, and the employment of the navy.'[2] By the end of April, Pembroke was established as one of Charles's most experienced advisers.

William and Philip Herbert were also closely involved in Charles's marriage to Henrietta Maria, celebrated by proxy in Notre Dame at Paris on 1 May. Buckingham was accompanied by Montgomery on his trip to bring the bride back to

England. This was apparently Philip Herbert's only travel
abroad, an experience marred by his seasickness during the
Channel crossing. On 12 June the combined English and
French party escorting Henrietta Maria arrived at Dover
where Charles came on the next day to meet her.[3] In
recognition of the intimacy which Pembroke and
Montgomery enjoyed with the royal couple, William
Vaughan, a noted colonial pioneer and arch-opponent of
Spain, dedicated to them jointly his Latin poem,
Cambrensium Caroleia (1625), in honour of the marriage.
Pembroke may have been impressed enough with these
efforts to offer him some reward, since in 1626 the sixth
edition of Vaughan's most popular publication, Natural and
Artificial Directions for Health, was hastily re-dedicated to
the Earl. It would seem that during the marriage
celebrations, Pembroke was shrewdly assessing Henrietta
Maria as a potential lever for loosening Buckingham's
influence over Charles, even though he had never really
approved of this match with a practising Catholic. Thomas
Erskine, Earl of Kellie, usually a well-informed observer of
court intrigues, had little doubt that his sentiments were
reciprocated, commenting that the Queen was 'resolved to
take Pembroke by the hand and make a party against
Buckingham'.[4]

In October 1625 Pembroke's obvious hostility towards
Buckingham incurred Charles's displeasure, and he was
deliberately excluded from the royal entourage on a trip to
Plymouth. In retaliation, Pembroke paid an unauthorised
visit to the Earl of Bristol at Sherborne, who was then in
disgrace and under virtual house arrest. To his credit, the
King realised that such tensions were counter-productive
and prudently sought a reconciliation. Both Charles and
Buckingham visited Pembroke at Wilton, a stratagem which
was at least partially successful, eliciting 'a strangeness,
rather than an open dislike' between the Earl and the Duke.[5]
By the summoning of the 1626 Parliament, however, their
relationship had again degenerated into open antagonism;
and with the Earl of Arundel imprisoned, Pembroke was now
regarded as Buckingham's most powerful opponent. The
Earl's parliamentary influence under Charles was extensive,
since over twenty-five members probably owed their seats
directly to his patronage. His followers played a prominent
role in the subsequent impeachment of the Duke, on charges
of corruption, profligacy with the King's estate, and
engrossing offices.[6] In the Commons, Sir Edward Herbert,

Pembroke's kinsman, enlarged upon the formal indictment brought against the Duke. In the Lords, William Herbert himself denounced 'this too great power, gotten with exorbitant ambition into a young and inexperienced hand, for particular profit'.[7] To save his favourite, Charles was obliged in June to dissolve Parliament. A few weeks later, perhaps again because of royal intervention, it was rumoured that Pembroke and Buckingham had resolved finally to settle their differences.[8]

The first tangible sign of this new determination came in August 1626 when marriage articles were signed for the union of Montgomery's eldest son, Charles Lord Herbert, and Buckingham's daughter, Mary, who had once been considered as a bride for the son of the Elector Palatine. The seven years old Charles was the heir to both the Pembroke and Montgomery Earldoms, and it was agreed that Pembroke would give his nephew £10,000 a year, in addition to £2,000 a year from Montgomery. As his part of the bargain, Buckingham promised a dowry of £20,000, although the first half instalment was not due until Mary, then aged five, reached fourteen.[9] The Herberts' finances were thereby made heavily dependent upon future payments from Buckingham, ensuring an effective end of hostilities between the two families. In fact, Pembroke was already intent upon taking full and immediate advantage from this intimacy with the chief royal favourite. During the summer of 1625 he had acted as a temporary Lord Steward to the royal household. In June 1626 he was sworn in as the confirmed holder of this senior post, passing on his Chamberlain's staff to his brother, Philip.[10]

Thoughts of war often preoccupied Pembroke's mind during the first three years of Charles's reign. As a member of the commission which in September 1625 had signed an Anglo-Dutch alliance against Spain, the Earl was recognised as a firm advocate of Protestant opposition to the Imperialist forces on the continent. This stance attracted the dedications of John Roberts's Compendium Belli (1626), a treatise on military discipline; and The Book of Honour (1625) by the old soldier and Herbert family retainer, Francis Markham, who had seen active service in the Low Countries, France and Ireland. But after the disastrous failure of the Cadiz expedition in October 1625, diplomatic relations with France also began to degenerate rapidly, placing England in the impossible position of being in conflict with two major European powers at once. The routing of Buckingham's forces on the Ile de Rhé between July and October 1627, sent to assist the beleaguered Huguenots of La Rochelle, effectively marked the end of the Lord Admiral's and Pembroke's interventionist foreign policy.

Despite these setbacks, Pembroke's position at court was not significantly weakened. By mid-summer 1628 rumours were circulating that he would either be created a Duke or take over the Lord Admiral's duties, leaving the way clear for his brother, Montgomery, to inherit the Stewardship.[11] His position at court was strengthened on 23 August when Buckingham was assassinated at Portsmouth by John Felton, a discontented professional soldier who had held a lieutenancy during the Ile de Rhé expedition. Pembroke joined a committee of five, appointed to 'take such course as is fittest for the foul fact and actor of the bloody murder of the Duke'; and later, along with Montgomery, he was named as a member of the commission delegated to execute the offices of the Lord Admiral. In private, Pembroke made little effort to disguise his pleasure at the unexpected departure of this troublesome royal favourite. Writing to his friend, James Hay, now Earl of Carlisle and Ambassador Extraordinary to Savoy, he remarked that Felton's bloody deed, 'grows every day more admirable unto me'. Without Buckingham, Pembroke observed, 'the King, our master, begins to shine already', prompting the Earl even to hope, 'this next session to see a happy agreement between him and his people'.[12]

The majority of the members elected to Charles's first three parliaments through Pembroke's extensive powers of political patronage were, as Conrad Russell observes, 'above all consistent devotees of unity, wanting amicable relations between the King and his Parliaments'.[13] Although the Earl supported such radical legislation as the Petition of Right (1625), he had no desire to see the King's prerogative threatened. He considered that moderation on both sides was essential if a harmonious and productive relationship was to be established between the Crown and Parliament. Sir Benjamin Rudyerd preached the same message to the Commons, insisting that 'moderation is the virtue of virtues, and wisdom of wisdoms. Let it be our masterpiece so to carry our business, as we may keep parliaments on foot.'[14] Throughout 1627 and 1628, however, Pembroke was plagued by ill health, probably the stone and gout, and it seems that his influence over the King was beginning to weaken. In any case, Charles's decision to dissolve his third Parliament in March 1629 and to govern by 'personal rule' totally shattered the hopes of those, like Pembroke, who envisaged moderation and conciliation as basic tenets of good government.

One of the contributory factors leading to the dissolution of Parliament was the Commons' decision to pass resolutions against Arminianism, enthusiastically embraced by Charles, but now regarded by many at court as a serious threat to the authority of the Church of England. Pembroke shared this concern, particularly since his political ally, George Abbot, Archbishop of Canterbury, had previously been suspended for his overt hostility to the spread of Arminianism.[15] At Oxford, the Chancellor's powers over ecclesiastical conformity were also rapidly being eroded by the doctrine's most influential champion in England, Bishop Laud. So much so, that in 1628 Thomas Jackson, a known Arminian and supporter of Laud, boldly dedicated to Pembroke a section of his ambitious commentary on the apostles' Creed, A Treatise of the Divine Essence and Attributes. Parliamentary opposition came to a head in 1629 when Rudyerd and two other Pembroke men, Sir John Eliot and William Coryton, argued strongly for the restraint of Arminianism, representing it as a danger not only to the English Church but also to Parliament itself.[16]

The threat posed by Arminianism was increasingly equated with that from Roman Catholicism, a connection of considerable interest to anti-Arminian controversialists. In 1628 Charles and Laud vigorously repressed opposition to Arminianism, for example, imprisoning William Coryton for his speeches in Parliament. Attacks on popery, however, could still be interpreted as the worthy labours of patriotic and staunchly Protestant writers, and they circulated with far fewer restrictions. Consequently, we find Daniel Featley (or Fairclough), a known anti-Arminian, dedicating to Pembroke his tract, The Grand Sacrilege of the Church of Rome (1630). This work professed to be a denunciation of 'popish heresy', but also warned darkly of the imminent threat of 'schism' in the English Church, occasioned by 'semi-pelagian alloy'. Featley's choice of phrase was delicately ambiguous. While 'semi-pelagian' was used in the early seventeenth century to refer to the doctrines of the Jesuit, Luis de Molina (1535-1600), it also indirectly recalled the similarly named teachings of the fourth-century British monk, Pelagius. Arguing against the extreme Augustinian view of man's fallen nature and the doctrine of original sin, he maintained that human will was itself capable of good without depending totally on divine grace. His teachings led to the emergence of another more conservative group of theologians, known as 'semi-pelagians', who attempted to follow a middle way between Augustinianism and Pelagianism. Both doctrines were condemned by the Council of Orange (529) and largely died out in the sixth century.[17] However, Arminius's own insistence upon free will afforded an obvious comparison with Pelagius' (he had been accused of Pelagianism by the Dutch authorities in the late 1580s). Featley, therefore, managed to remind his readership of the schismatic influence of Arminianism, while being able to claim, as he did in his dedication to Pembroke, that he was using 'semi-pelagian' only in its anti-Jesuitical sense.

The range of dedications addressed to Pembroke during the last five years of his life emphasise the three main areas of his influence: the court and Parliament, Oxford University, and his own family circle. In 1626 George Jenney, formerly a Gentleman Server of Queen Anne's Chamber in Ordinary, made it clear in a dedication to Pembroke that he was looking for a way back into court service. Cornelius Burges, Henry Leslie, Thomas Jackson and Alexander Udny had all held the position of the King's Chaplain in Ordinary and recognised William and Philip Herbert's authority as successive Lord Chamberlains over appointments to the royal chapel.[18] John Norden (to be differentiated from the famous topographer), was perhaps aware of rumours concerning this succession when in 1626 he addressed his devotional tract, A Pathway to Patience, to Pembroke, also including Montgomery in the dedication. In Parliament, Sir James Perrott affords yet another example of a Pembroke supporter with literary leanings. Recognised as an ardent opponent of Catholicism and the Spanish match, he had once been an admirer of the Elizabethan Earl of Essex, and according to Anthony Wood, wrote 'A Book of the Birth, Education, Life and Death ... of Sir Philip Sidney', now lost. In the 1620s he was a member of the Virginia Company and also served as Deputy Vice-Admiral through Pembroke's patronage. He gratefully acknowledged the assistance which he had received from the Earl by dedicating to him in 1630 a collection of Certain Short Prayers and Meditations upon the Lord's Prayer. At Oxford, Thomas James, Bodley's Librarian, addressed to Pembroke his edition of George Witzell's Methodus Concordiae

Ecclesiasticae (1625). Four years later, Richard Zouche, Regius Professor of Civil Law, and a leading figure in the Laudian codification of the statutes, paid tribute to Pembroke's Chancellorship in the dedication of his acclaimed textbook on Roman Law, Elementa Jurisprudentiae (1629).

Zouche, born at Ansty in Wiltshire, could also claim a local connection with the Earl. Other writers justified their dedications by pointing to time spent in the Herbert family's service. Griffith Williams had been a domestic chaplain to the Earl of Montgomery before becoming a prebendary of Westminster in 1628. He readily acknowledged his debts to the family in his defence of English Protestantism, The True Church (1629), dedicated to Pembroke; and during the 1630s he kept in touch with Philip Herbert's children whom he had tutored a decade earlier.[19] Thomas Adams dedicated the massive 1629 edition of his collected Works to Pembroke, by way of thanks for his prolonged patronage and friendship. In the same year, perhaps wishing to emulate Adams's example, the stationer Abraham Sherman addressed a posthumous edition of Edward Chaloner's sermons to the Earl, in recognition of Pembroke's generosity towards the preacher. However, few writers - except perhaps for the Markham brothers - could hope to rival the claims of John Thornborough, Bishop of Worcester who in 1630 proudly recalled the patronage which he had received from three successive generations of the Herberts:

> I call to mind how your most Noble Grandfather was the first means to plant me in the Church of Christ, by giving me the advowson of Chibmarke, a very good Rectory. Your Noble Father with much grace, watered my growth, then dwelling near his Honour. And Your Honourable Self hath given increase by your many gracious favours in the now period of my days.[20]

Pembroke had suffered from periodic attacks of the stone and gout throughout the 1620s, but early in 1630 his health seemed to be showing signs of improvement. On 8 April he celebrated his fiftieth birthday, perhaps giving some idle thought to a prophecy once made by his childhood tutor, Hugh Sanford, that he would not live beyond two score and ten. On the following evening he dined out with the Countesses of Bedford and Devonshire, returning to his

London house, Baynard's Castle, in good spirits, 'after a full and cheerful supper'. Early the next morning, William Herbert died suddenly of apoplexy. Elegiac tributes to him soon began to circulate in manuscript at court. Several family retainers also penned their own commemorations, including John Earle, the author of <u>Microcosmography</u> and Bishop of Salisbury after the Restoration, whom Philip Herbert employed later as a chaplain.[21] Undoubtedly, the most striking lament for Pembroke was that delivered by his own chaplain, Thomas Chaffinge (or Chafin), at Baynard's Castle, prior to the burial service in the family vault at Salisbury Cathedral. Chaffinge warned his listeners that Pembroke's demise was a serious loss to the whole nation, and lamented the growing tensions between 'court' and 'country' which threatened to provoke 'such intestine wars ... as once did between those two fatal Houses for the mastery of the double Rose'.[22]

'THE SOLE INHERITOR AS OF HIS HONOURS, SO OF HIS FORTUNES'

One of Philip Herbert's first responsibilities on becoming fourth Earl of Pembroke was to look after the welfare of his brother's widow and illegitimate children. William Herbert's brother-in-law, the Earl of Arundel, alleged that the third Earl's widow, Lady Mary, was not mentally competent to manage her own affairs. He sought from the King the authority to exercise control over her considerable inheritance. Arundel's solicitude was heavily influenced by the knowledge that his eldest son was Lady Mary's heir apparent, assuming she did not remarry and have children. Presumably aware of this ulterior motive, the Lady herself much preferred to be placed under Philip Herbert's charge. Charles eventually agreed to this proposal and she was allowed to reside at Wilton and Ramsbury until her death in 1650.[23] According to Sir Thomas Herbert of Tintern (1606-82), who wrote a family history of the Herberts in the mid-seventeenth century, Philip also maintained an interest in his brother's son, William, by Lady Mary Wroth. In 1640 Sir John Leeke informed Sir Edward Verney that he had recently received, 'a most courteous and kind letter from my old mistress, the Lady Mary Wroth ... She wrote me word that by my Lord of Pembroke's good mediation, the King hath given her son a brave living in Ireland.' During the Civil War, William served as an officer

in the royalist forces of Sir Henry Herbert, formerly Master
of the Revels, and later under Prince Maurice, the son of
Frederick V.[24]

In addition to family responsibilities, an expectation
prevailed that the fourth Earl would take over much of his
brother's ecclesiastical patronage. One of his first duties
following William Herbert's death was to confirm the
appointment of his cousin, George Herbert, to the living of
Fugglestone-with-Bemerton, and he assumed authority over
several other local rectories. In view of this succession, the
third Earl's chaplain, Thomas Chaffinge, had little option
but to observe: 'I know none fitter to own any remainder of
a brother, than a brother, the sole inheritor as of his
honours, so of his fortunes.'[25] It does not appear, however,
that Chaffinge was taken into the fourth Earl's service. John
Reynolds of Exeter, who had dedicated his juvenile prose
romance, 'Love's Laurel Garland,' to Philip in about 1605,
addressed to him the fourth book of The Triumphs of God's
Revenge (1635), celebrating his inheritance of William's
reputation as a patron: 'as England, so Europe perfectly
knows, that you are as true an heir to his virtues, as to his
fortunes.' In the same year, Thomas Palmer claimed in a
sermon, entitled Bristol's Military Garden, that Philip
reflected the combination of piety and Protestant militancy
once embodied by Prince Henry.

Although none of these preachers is known to have
received any significant rewards for their dedications, the
fourth Earl proved himself an influential and generous
patron to those already in his personal service. One A.
Kemp, for example, found that employment in the Lord
Chamberlain's own household afforded him in 1633 an
enviable opportunity to preach before the King's household
at Whitehall.[26] On a much grander scale, John Earle was
appointed as chaplain to Philip Herbert, a position which
laid open a route to the highest court patronage. In 1639
Pembroke presented him to the living of Bishopston in
Wiltshire and also brought his considerable academic
attainments to the attention of Charles. The King was
impressed enough to appoint Earle as a tutor to his son,
Prince Charles, following the raising of his former tutor, Dr.
Duppa, to the Bishopric of Salisbury. Further advancement
followed, most likely with Philip Herbert's complicity, when
early in 1643 Earle was elected as Chancellor of Salisbury
Cathedral, within half an hour's ride of Wilton House.

Philip Herbert was keen to succeed his brother as

Chancellor of Oxford University but Archbishop Laud, who had been consolidating his position at Oxford since the mid-1620s, provided him with a determined and highly organised rival for this position. Anthony Wood recounts: 'Dr Laud's friends of divers colleges, especially of St. John's, bestowed themselves in his behalf. These also that were not well-wishers to the Bishop, which were chiefly the Calvinian party, were active for the Earl, and as also were those of the Welsh nation, and of the four Colleges belonging to the Visitation of the Bishop of Lincoln, to the scholars of which, Dr Williams, the Bishop of that place, had sent letters and agents in the Earl's behalf.' After a scrutiny of the votes, Laud was declared the winner, although Pembroke's supporters continued to insist that theirs was the larger party.[27] To a limited extent, Philip Herbert was still able to exert some influence in university matters. It was reported that one of his most ardent supporters, John Prideaux, Professor of Divinity and Rector of Exeter College, retained his chair in 1631 only through Pembroke's influence. As late as 1634, Henry Tozer, a student and later sub-rector of the same college, still considered it worth his while to dedicate a Latin tract, Christus: Sive Dicta & Facta Christi, to Philip Herbert. Elsewhere, the opponents of Laud and Arminianism continued to regard the Earl as a potential patron. It was recorded that the preacher, John Shaw, was protected from the censorship of Archbishop Neile, Laud's mentor, only because he was known to be Pembroke's chaplain.[28] It is noticeable, however, that after Laud's election, the dedication of theological works by Oxford scholars to Philip Herbert dwindled to the thinnest of trickles.[29]

This decline was probably also partly due to the fourth Earl's reputation as one, according to Aubrey, who 'did not delight in books, or poetry: but exceedingly loved painting and building'.[30] There seems little reason to doubt the truth of this observation since the only poetry of any significance dedicated to him after 1630 was a brief panegyrical poem by Robert Herrick, printed in his Hesperides (1648), and some inconsequential verses in Arthur Johnson's 1637 collection of Latin poetry, Delitiae Poetarum Scotorum. To this may be added an acrostic upon his name by Alice Sutcliffe and an epigram by Mary Fage. A few other printed works were addressed to him before 1642, including a posthumous edition of John Preston's sermons on humiliation, and Alexander Read's 1638 'treatise of wounds'.[31]

The dedication to the fourth Earl of translations of two

popular French romances, Jean Desmaret's Ariana (1636) and Gilbert Saulnier's Romant of Romants (1640), can probably be accounted for by his earlier interest in the form, coupled with current fashion for such works set at the English court by Henrietta Maria. In his capacity as Lord Chamberlain, Philip ordered in about 1628 the printing of Captain Robert Le Grys's translation of John Barclay's allegorical-political romance, the Argenis. While awaiting a licence to print, Le Grys suggested that some commendatory verses by the poet and dramatist, Tom May, could be added to the volume. May, the son of a gentleman landowner who had gone bankrupt, had previously dedicated the second book of his translation of Lucan's Pharsalia (1627) to the third Earl of Pembroke. These additions were approved and in 1634 Philip saw fit to recommend him, although unsuccessfully, to the Lord Mayor as Chronicler to the City of London.[32]

Former protégés of the third Earl occasionally turned to his younger brother in the hope that he would maintain their patronage. Sir Thomas Herbert, a descendant of the fifteenth-century Earl of Pembroke, had obtained in 1627 a place on Sir Dodmore Cotton's embassy to Persia, largely through the influence of the third Earl of Pembroke. However, William Herbert's death in 1630 shattered his hopes of preferment at court. The dedication to Philip in 1634 of an exciting but at times fanciful account of his travels in Africa and Asia, A Relation of Some Years' Travel, Begun Anno 1626, along with his compilation of a Herbert family history, seems to have been part of an attempt to revive his connections and prospects. It might be suspected that Philip would have had little sympathy with most of the poets who had sought his brother's interest. However, men like William Browne, who was a salaried or pensioned employee, probably had little difficulty in retaining their positions. As late as 1640, Browne was still cheerfully paying his respects, in a letter to Sir Benjamin Rudyerd, to Philip Herbert.[33] In addressing to the fourth Earl the fourth book of his Emblems (1635), George Wither relied heavily upon recalling the third Earl's generosity to him. Unfortunately, there is no evidence that Philip considered himself under any obligation to assist Wither, who continued to eke out a precarious and unhappy livelihood from his writings.

The fourth Earl's second marriage in 1630 at first boded well for the continuation of the family's literary involvements. Susan Vere, Countess of Montgomery, had died in 1629, and on 1 June of the following year Philip married Lady Anne Clifford, formerly Countess of Dorset. She was already well known to him since they had danced together in Daniel's Tethys' Festival (1610), and in subsequent years she was often in the company of Susan Vere, Lady Mary Wroth, Barbara Sidney and Mary (Talbot) Herbert. She had been tutored as a child by Daniel and remained an avid reader throughout her life of English and foreign literature, particularly historical, philosophical and pietistic works. A well known portrait at Appleby represents her with a collection of works by some of her favourite authors, including Daniel, John Donne and George Herbert. She received a lavish panegyrical verse epistle from her former tutor, listened to Donne's preaching, and corresponded with George Herbert after her arrival at Wilton in 1630. She was, potentially, the ideal figure to maintain the tradition of female literary patronage established at Wilton by her husband's mother and first wife. But the marriage was not a successful one, and she lived with her husband for only about four and a half years. Matters came to a head in 1634 when Philip Herbert sought to force a marriage, for financial reasons, between one of his younger sons and her daughter, Lady Isabella Sackville. Lady Anne was equally determined that such a match would not be instigated, and although her view ultimately prevailed, in December 1634, she agreed with her husband to reside chiefly at Baynard's Castle, Wilton and Ramsbury, while he stayed mostly in his chambers at Whitehall and the Cockpit. From this date onward, she lived a retired existence, as she put it, amidst 'good books and virtuous thoughts'. Inevitably, this withdrawal from court life greatly reduced her personal contact with writers and scholars.[34]

PAINTING AND BUILDING

Aubrey's comment that the fourth Earl of Pembroke, 'exceedingly loved painting and building', merits further investigation, since it draws attention to a distinct shift which took place around 1625 in royal and aristocratic attitudes towards the patronage of the arts. Neither Elizabeth nor James evinced much interest in painting, apart from portraiture, but as a young man, Charles's own artistic tastes, coupled with his growing desire to be seen as a great Renaissance prince, led him to assemble a royal picture collection which at its peak was to outshine even those of Spain, France and the Holy Roman Empire. The King's passion for picture collecting stimulated a healthy interest in continental art among the richer members of the English aristocracy. Predictably, as well-seasoned royal favour-seekers, William and Philip Herbert were in the forefront of this cultural trend. Although the lack of an adequate catalogue makes it virtually impossible to determine which, if any, of the paintings still at Wilton were purchased by the Herberts during Charles's reign, it is clear that the acquisition of a picture collection provided the Herbert brothers with a useful means of maintaining their intimacy with the King.[35] The third Earl, for example, delighted Charles by giving him a small but exquisite painting of St. George by Raphael, which had been brought to England by Castiglione himself as a gift from the Duke of Urbino to Henry VII. In exchange, he received a set of famous men and women at the court of Henry VIII, drawn by Hans Holbein, the younger, in about 1530.[36] There is also at St. James's Palace, a picture by an unknown artist showing Charles and Henrietta Maria in the company of William and Philip Herbert; in the background two of the King's Titians are visible. The painting has rightly been described as 'a sort of monument to the loyalty of the Earls of Pembroke and to the King's connoisseurship'.[37]

Like many of his contemporaries, William Herbert employed the skills of miniaturists, such as Peter Oliver. Another, David des Granges, a friend of Inigo Jones, produced for him a miniature engraving of the Raphael 'St. George', given to Charles. Philip shared his brother's interest in this form of painting. In the 1630s along with the Earl of Suffolk, Arundel and others, he sent some of his own miniatures to a display of small paintings organised at Whitehall. The fourth Earl also utilised the skills of Richard 'Dwarf' Gibson from the early 1630s onward. Like Des Granges, he may have first found employment with the family as a miniature copyist of the paintings in the Pembroke collection. Peter Lely, a life-long friend of Gibson, was another protégé of Philip Herbert and was introduced by him to royal patronage. In the late 1640s, Pembroke commissioned from Lely the Wilton double portrait of Richard and Anne Gibson, and set up an annuity for their future to be paid from his estate. Following the royal example, the fourth Earl employed an agent, one 'Mr Touars', to buy pictures for him from abroad, and generously rewarded him, according to Aubrey, with a pension of £100 a year.[38]

During the 1630s, the fourth Earl also involved himself with ambitious schemes for the redevelopment of Wilton House and its gardens. Generally, there was little rebuilding of 'great houses' at this period, but Pembroke's immense wealth placed him alongside Buckingham and Arundel as one of the few members of the aristocracy who could afford to flatter to the full Charles's ideal of a king and his courtiers working together in the enhancement of their national culture. According to Aubrey, until about 1652 the Pembroke estates brought in £16,000 a year and, 'with his offices and all', Philip's annual income was nearer to £30,000.[39] Although Aubrey's calculations were probably based on hearsay rather than actual financial accounts, there seems little reason to doubt these figures.

It seems that Philip Herbert's decision to undertake an expensive rebuilding programme was directly influenced by Charles's enthusiasm for architectural schemes. Aubrey records:

> King Charles the first did love Wilton above all places, and came thither every summer. It was he that did put Philip first Earl of Pembroke [ie. the fourth Earl] upon making this magnificent garden and grotto, and to new build that side of the house that fronts the garden, with two stately pavilions at each end, all al Italiano. His Majesty intended to have had it all designed by his own architect, Mr Inigo Jones, who being at that time, about 1633, engaged in his Majesty's buildings at Greenwich, could not attend to it; but he recommended it to an ingenious architect, Monsieur Solomon de Caus, a Gascoigne, who performed it very well; but not without the advice of Mr Jones; for which his Lordship settled a pension on him of, I think, a hundred pounds per annum for his life, and lodgings in the house.[40]

In 1635 a traveller through Wiltshire, one Lieutenant Hammond, was given a guided tour of Wilton House and its gardens. It is clear from his account that work was already well advanced on the gardens, including an ingenious mechanical water-works designed by De Caus which was nearing completion. Although he was shown all around the house, Hammond gives no indication that any building had been initiated. In fact, A.A. Tait discovered an entry in Pembroke's warrant-book, preserved in the Public Records Office, which suggests that work commenced on the south front of the house in March 1636, under the direction of Isaac de Caus. He was also commissioned to redesign the gardens, with assistance from Domenic Pile in the planting of 'fruits, herbs and roots'.[41]

Little was known about these plans until 1955 when Howard Colvin gave notice of his discovery in the Library of Worcester College, Oxford, of an illustration of this proposed south front which had been loosely placed in a copy of _Vitruvius Britannicus_. This huge pedimented front, approximately 400 feet in length, would have almost certainly contained two sets of state rooms, one on either side of the central portico which was flanked by six Corinthian columns. Such grandeur suggests that the house was being designed specifically as a suitable location for Philip Herbert's entertainment of royal visitors. It may even have been planned to rebuild the rest of Wilton House on similar proportions. At some stage before 1640, however, this 'Grand Design' was abandoned in favour of a drastically curtailed scheme, less than one half of the size of the original plan. It is clear from the positioning of Wilton House in the mid-seventeenth century that rebuilding work had begun in 1636 on the east side of the house; and it was probably De Caus himself who drew up these revised plans. The attractive Venetian window, which in the 'Grand Design' would have formed the centre of the east wing, became the focal point of the redesigned south front. Two pavilion towers were also added, Howard Colvin explains, 'to give definition to a façade which, designed originally to flank a dominating central feature, had been made instead into an isolated unit which had somehow to be enabled to stand on its own.'[42]

Work began on the revised version of the initial scheme during the late-1630s. Oliver Hill and John Cornforth suggest that De Caus may have submitted his designs to Inigo Jones who then made various amendments based upon Italian models. Even these plans however, were probably not carried out in full because there is a drawing at Worcester College, Oxford, of a proposed chapel which apparently was never built but appears to be in keeping with the designs for the south front. Eventually, most probably during the early-1640s, the rebuilding of this front was completed according to De Caus's revised plans, although the momentous events of the mid-1640s would have presumably prohibited any prolonged building programme.[43]

Like his grandfather, the first Tudor Earl of Pembroke, Philip Herbert regarded building as a means of publicly asserting his own wealth and social position. Similar sentiments appear also to have influenced his patronage of artists, above all in his employment of Van Dyck's skills as a portraitist. The artist returned to England in 1632 and during the next eight years created a whole new ideology for the representation of the English royal family and aristocracy. The Double Cube Room at Wilton provides ample evidence of Van Dyck's impact on the Caroline court. This room, once described as 'perhaps the most distinguished in any country house', was specifically designed to display Pembroke's collection of Van Dycks which had probably been housed at his London residence, Durham House off the Strand. The viewer's eye is constantly focused on the glory of the Herberts and the room is dominated by Van Dyck's renowned 17 feet by 11 feet study of the fourth Earl of Pembroke's family. Begun in about 1634/5 and completed by 1636, it was, Oliver Millar explains, 'the first such picture to have been painted in such magnificent terms in this country. Immensely influential, it was never to be equalled by any of Van Dyck's successors.'[44]

In reality, the fourth Earl's family life bore little resemblance to the idyllic image of domestic unity which Van Dyck sought to propagate. In the mid-1630s, Philip Herbert and his wife, Anne Clifford, decided to live apart, although still on amicable terms, almost certainly before the painting was finished. Similarly, Charles Lord Herbert set out on the Grand Tour within a few days of his marriage in January 1635 and died of smallpox at Florence a few weeks later, again probably before Van Dyck's work was completed. Even the Lord Chamberlain's Staff of Office, held so authoritatively by Pembroke in the picture, would have evoked memories starkly out of keeping with Van Dyck's image of refined dignity. At court in February 1634, Philip Herbert, in a fit of pique, broke his Staff over the shoulders of Tom May, who had accidentally collided with him. This indecorous incident earned Pembroke a royal rebuke and it was reported that he had been obliged to present May with £50 by way of recompense. But just as portrait painters were expected to flatter their sitters by spiriting away unwanted physical blemishes, so Van Dyck had been commissioned to represent in 'The Pembroke Family' not the reality but the myth of aristocratic family life in the Caroline period.

CHARLES'S LORD CHAMBERLAIN

As with the visual arts, an enthusiasm for court theatricals provided prominent aristocrats with a ready access to their King and Queen. Philip Herbert appeared with Charles in one of Jonson's and Jones's last collaborations, Love's Triumphs Through Callipolis, which sought to reflect in the figure of Charles, 'the honour of his court, and the dignity of that heroic love, and regal aspect born by him to his unmatchable lady, and spouse, the Queen's Majesty.' Pembroke was also involved in this production on another level, since as Lord Chamberlain he was responsible for supervising the financing of the King's masques. In the case of Love's Triumphs, his secretary, Edmund Tavener, was paid £600 in two instalments to cover expenses incurred in its design and preparation.[45] A few weeks later, the Queen replied to Love's Triumphs by taking the leading role in her own masque, Chloridia, which proved to be Jonson's last masque at court.

On at least three occasions, Philip Herbert privately commissioned dramatic entertainments from court writers, all of which were given royal performances. In 1633, at his own expense, he held a feast followed by a masque for the King and Queen at Whitehall. The complete text of this masque has been lost, but its Prologue and Epilogue, along with four songs 'by way of Chorus', all by Thomas Carew, have survived. On 6 April 1630, Pembroke, in his capacity as Lord Chamberlain, had approved, 'A warrant to swear Mr Thomas Carew a gent of ye privy Chamber extraordinary'; and he had perhaps maintained an amicable relationship with Carew since then.[46] In January 1635, he sponsored a performance at York House, again attended by Charles and Henrietta Maria, of Henry Killigrew's The Conspiracy, intended, according to its 1638 title-page, 'for the nuptials' of his son Charles and Lady Mary Villiers. Finally, in 1640 Philip Herbert presented as a gift to the King and Queen the play Cleodora. Queen of Aragon, by his kinsman through marriage, William Habington. Its first performance was held at Whitehall, acted according to Sir Henry Herbert, by Pembroke's 'servants out of his own family, and [at] his charge in the clothes and scenes, which were very rich and curious'. The play proved successful enough to be restaged at court and then at Blackfriars, and enjoyed a revival after the Restoration.[47]

As Master of the Revels for as long as the theatres remained open during Charles's reign, Sir Henry Herbert exercised a powerful influence over most forms of dramatic entertainments and public shows. He charged £1 for licensing a play, £2 if any alterations or censorship were required, and in 1632 doubled his fees. The King's Men were expected to hand over to him each year the takings from two separate performances of his choice. Herbert did his best to ensure that these were money-spinners, selecting works by Shakespeare, Jonson and Fletcher. He received numerous other miscellaneous payments, including living expenses from the Treasury whenever he was obliged to lodge out of court.[48]

The holder of such a lucrative post required powerful friends to enable him to keep a firm hold on it. Sir Henry was particularly fortunate in having his cousin, Philip, as Lord Chamberlain until 1641. There seems little doubt that they were often aware of each other's interests. In 1627 the Earl of Montgomery wrote directly to Sir William Uvedale, the Treasurer of the King's Chamber, demanding immediate payment of £52 to Sir Henry Herbert for his 'lodging out of court'. In 1636 he reminded the King's Auditors that, his cousin was owed £12 for 'unusual attendance' between October 1632 and October 1635. In return, in May 1633 Sir Henry excised a whole part from the play, The Tale of the Tub, 'by command from my lord chamberlain; exceptions being taken against it by Inigo Jones, surveyor of the King's Works, as a personal injury to him'. From this statement, it would seem that Jones had complained to Philip Herbert, knowing that, as Lord Chamberlain, he could pull strings on his behalf. Sir Henry appears to have been glad to help, particularly since such censorship entailed an automatic doubling of his fee. During the 1640s, his brother, Edward, Lord Herbert of Cherbury, rightly observed that Sir Henry 'attained to a great fortune' and grew 'dextrous in the ways of the Court, as having gotten much by it'.[49]

The Lord Chamberlain and the Master of the Revels were also of crucial importance to the King's Men during Charles's reign. In 1626 John Heminge paid Sir Henry Herbert £3, 'for a courtesy done him about the Blackfriars House'; and in the following year he received £5 from the same actor, 'to forbid the playing of Shakespeare's plays to the Red Bull Company'. In 1631 the King's Men were obliged to pay a fee of £3.10s to Sir Henry for a licence to re-commence performing after an outbreak of the plague. In view of the close working relationship between the Lord Chamberlain and the Master of the Revels, it was also sometimes possible for the King's Men to appeal directly to Philip Herbert for assistance. In 1631 he defended their interests by writing to Sir William Uvedale, concerning outstanding payments due to them.[50] Four years later, Philip was sent a petition by three members of the Company who resented not being able to buy shares in the Globe and the Blackfriars Theatres.[51]

In 1637 Pembroke's close links with the actors occasioned a direct confrontation with Laud. The Archbishop had recommended the closure of the theatres, supposedly because of the plague and it being Lent. Possibly suspecting Laud's motives, or perhaps mindful of the financial losses which the actors would suffer, Philip Herbert argued that they should be kept open. The King, however, overruled Pembroke and accepted Laud's advice.[52] In the same year, the King's Men complained to the Lord Chamberlain that some of their plays were being printed without permission. Pembroke sympathised with the view that, 'not only they themselves had much prejudice, but the books much corruption, to the injury and disgrace of the authors'. He responded by issuing an order forbidding all such publications. In 1639 he was obliged to issue another forceful mandate to unscrupulous actors; this time ordering them not to 'intermeddle' with William Beeston's repertory at the Cockpit or Phoenix. Beeston himself, however, was to fall foul of the Lord Chamberlain in the following year. According to Sir Henry Herbert's records, a play was performed at this theatre at the end of April or the beginning of May 1640 which 'had relation to the passages of the K[ing's] journey into the North' in 1639. This was a reference to Charles's abortive attempts, leading to 'The Bishops' Wars', to establish religious uniformity between England and Scotland. The King ordered Sir Henry's officers to apprehend the offenders. 'By my Lord Chamberlain's warrant', the play was banned, and Beeston, along with some of his actors, was committed to the Marshalsea. Only after four days did they regain their freedom, again 'at my Lord Chamberlain's entreaty'.[53]

Suggestions that, as Lord Chamberlain, Philip Herbert may have occasionally used his influence over drama for his own political purposes are as intriguing as they are difficult to prove. In her challenging study, Puritanism & Theatre, Margot Heinemann speculated over the incidents at the Phoenix: 'There seems a distinct possibility that Pembroke may have indirectly patronised or sponsored a popular political play on the Scottish business.'[54] Whatever the truth of the matter, it does indeed seem curious that, within one year, the Lord Chamberlain had protected Beeston's repertory, only to have him imprisoned, and then, just as quickly, released.

Philip Massinger has also been viewed as a dramatist whose plays sometimes complemented the Herberts' political views. John Aubrey observed that he 'was a servant to his Lordship, and had a pension of twenty or thirty pounds per annum, which was paid to his wife after his decease'.[55] In 1624 Massinger dedicated his play, The Bond-man, to Philip Herbert, implying that he had in some way assisted in its production: 'When it was first acted, your Lordship's liberal suffrage taught others to allow it for current.' However, the rest of the dedication, along with that of A New Way to Pay Old Debts (1635), to Pembroke's son-in-law, Robert Dormer, Earl of Carnarvon, made clear that as late as 1633, Massinger could still not claim any personal familiarity with Philip Herbert. Two or three years later, he penned an elegy, 'Sero, Sed Serio', on the death of his son, Charles Lord Herbert. But once again, he made no clear reference to any personal patronage from the Herberts. In 1638 he was still seeking to earn a living from the stage. It would seem, therefore, that if Massinger did express in these plays his sympathies with the political stance of the Herberts, a view that has also recently been put forward in the case of The Bashful Lover (1636), then he was probably doing so only as an informed outsider rather than as a manipulated family protégé.[56]

There seems much less doubt surrounding Pembroke's gift to the King and Queen of Habington's Cleodora, one of the most interesting court plays of the reign. Philip Herbert went to considerable lengths in April 1640 to have it staged twice at Whitehall in a remarkably sumptuous production. The play itself, Martin Butler explains, 'confronts the courtly complacency about rank and obedience most forcefully'; and argues 'a radically new, and potentially revolutionary, understanding of the basis of government which anticipates (astonishingly) that distinction between power and authority which would enter the literature of political controversy only for the first time in the 1640s.[57] Of course, these should be regarded as Habington's rather than Pembroke's views, but the Earl could hardly have failed to appreciate their significance.

Philip Herbert's relationship with the King and Parliament began to take a new turn from 1640 onward. In 1639 he had joined the Scottish expedition, but after Charles's defeat in the Second Bishops' War, in the autumn of 1640, he was a firm advocate for peace, recommending acceptance of the Scottish terms. When, however, a council of Peers, including Pembroke, met with the King at York, Charles chose to reject this advice. Already a firm opponent of Laud, actively disliked by the Queen, and disturbed by Charles's summary treatment of the Short Parliament (April-May 1640), Philip Herbert began to distance himself from royal decision-making. In 1640 the parliamentary leaders impeached both Laud and Thomas Wentworth, Earl of Strafford, whom Charles had summoned from Ireland to help him against the Scots. Laud, now an old and sick man, was left to linger in prison until he was finally executed in 1645. Strafford, however, was rapidly tried before the House of Lords in March and April 1641. With Pembroke as one of those voting against him, he was executed by Act of Attainder in May.

In the same year, Charles was provided with an opportunity to reduce greatly Philip Herbert's influence at court. In a committee of the House of Lords, Pembroke clashed verbally and then physically with the Earl of Arundel's son, Lord Maltravers. Herbert struck him over the head with his Lord Chamberlain's Staff, while Maltravers retaliated by hurling an inkstand at the Earl. A complaint was lodged with the King who committed both of them to the Tower. According to Clarendon, Charles was intent upon 'taking advantage of this miscarriage', and having become increasingly annoyed by Pembroke's 'passionate, indiscreet, and insolent carriage', dismissed him in July from his post as Lord Chamberlain. Rumours circulated that it was really the Queen who had insisted upon this action.

Backed by many of those whom he had eased into seats in the Long Parliament, the Commons unsuccessfully petitioned the King in December to have Pembroke appointed Lord Steward. The London theatres had been closed on account of the plague from August to late November 1641, and although they then briefly reopened, by February 1642 Parliament was already discussing their total suppression. Following his rejection of the parliamentary leaders' 'Nineteen Propositions' made in June, Charles raised his standard at Nottingham on 22 August. One of the most rapid responses from Parliament was an order on 2 September closing the theatres, 'while these sad causes and set times of humiliation do continue'.[58] Sir Henry Herbert shut up the Revels Office and took up arms in the service of the King. His brother, Edward, Lord Herbert of Cherbury, resolved to remain neutral, although his sons became zealous royalists. Philip Herbert, Earl of Pembroke and Montgomery, looked to himself.

THE KING OR WILTON

Looking back over the events of the 1640s, Edward Hyde, Earl of Clarendon, implied that an overwhelming concern to preserve their estates and wealth had been the main reason why some aristocratic members of Charles's court joined the parliamentary side. He observed of the Earl of Pembroke and William Cecil, Earl of Salisbury: 'though they wished they might rather be destroyed than the King, they had rather the King and his posterity should be destroyed than that Wilton should be taken from the one of them or Hatfield from the other.' Hyde was well placed to pass comment. He was born at Dunton, near Salisbury; and by 1630 could count among his friends Sir Charles Morgan, a kinsman of the third Earl of Pembroke, and his personal chaplain, Thomas Chaffinge. On 4 December 1634 the fourth Earl helped him to secure the reversion of the office of Custos Brevium in Common pleas. Soon afterwards, Hyde entered Parliament as a Pembroke nominee for Coventry.[59]

Following the loss of his lucrative post as Lord Chamberlain, John Morrill explains, Philip Herbert 'was forced into an ever-closer liaison with the opposition as the only way back to office'.[60] This realignment was most probably the cause of his alienation from the staunchly royalist Hyde who dismissed him as an unprincipled time-server, 'totally without credit or interest in the Parliament or country'. Taking a more sympathetic view, Sidney Lee compounded this impression of a political lightweight by suggesting that 'the flattery of his new allies doubtless carried him further in opposition to the king than he at first intended'.[61] The surviving evidence, however, provides a rather different picture of Pembroke as a man whose judgement and ability to perform difficult missions was valued highly by his fellow parliamentarians.

Throughout 1642, Pembroke was carefully weighing up the prospects of either side. In the spring he voted for the Militia Ordinance which effectively transferred to Parliament the sovereign's authority over the militia. Charles responded with a counter-proclamation. Hyde began to correspond with known moderates in the Lords and Commons, including Pembroke, in an attempt to regain support for the King. Perhaps genuinely seeking some sort of rapprochement, Philip Herbert insisted in June that Charles could still count on his friendship: 'wheresoever I am there is a heart full of loyalty and a tongue that speaks nothing but duty'. At the same time, however, his prestige among parliamentarians was steadily rising. In August he was appointed as Governor of the Isle of Wight by a Parliamentary Ordinance, replacing the King's own choice, Jerome Weston, Earl of Portland. Following the indecisive battle of Edgehill in October, he again became a leading advocate for peace. In November he joined a delegation which sought to persuade Charles to come to an understanding with Parliament. In the following month, he made a powerful speech in the Lords, warning of the social chaos which would be the inevitable consequence of civil war.

During the next three years, Pembroke was active in committee work and a persistent advocate for peace. He also saw military action in October 1642 against Lord Coventry in Wiltshire; and again in February 1643 when an unruly multitude rioted on his lands at Aldbourne. Nevertheless, he remained one of Parliament's most prominent negotiators for peace. In January 1643, he tried unsuccessfully to persuade the King at Oxford to accept parliamentary proposals for the cessation of hostilities. Two years later, he was in attendance at the Uxbridge negotiations between Charles's commissioners and those appointed by Parliament and the Scots.[62] At these discussions, Pembroke urged Hyde to support the new peace proposals, even though, according to The History, in private conversation he dismissively termed those 'who now governed in Parliament' as 'a pack of knaves and villains'.[63] Following the failure of these negotiations, Pembroke lent his support in the Lords to the formation in February 1645 by Parliamentary Ordinance of the New Model Army, which drew together the various parliamentary forces under the command of Sir Thomas Fairfax. The Battle of Naseby in the following June proved the decisive conflict. Charles's young nephew, Prince

Rupert, Elizabeth of Bohemia's younger son, brilliantly routed the left wing of the parliamentary forces. But Cromwell's forces, on the other flank, smashed through the royalist cavalry and then overwhelmed the King's infantry. By May 1646, Charles realised that he could no longer maintain the struggle and gave himself up at the Scottish camp outside Newark. It is interesting to note how the King's surrender affected Pembroke and Sir Henry Herbert. Early in 1646 rumours circulated that Philip Herbert was to be made a Duke; and in July he resumed his duties as a Commissioner for Peace. His cousin, on the other hand, had his estates sequestrated and over £400 of plate confiscated.

As late as 1647, however, suspicions lingered that Pembroke had continued to hedge his bets while the outcome of the struggle between King and Parliament remained uncertain. Only in January of that year were charges finally dismissed that, as an insurance, he had previously sent to Charles a considerable amount of gold. With his name cleared, even if his reputation remained somewhat tarnished, Philip Herbert was appointed as one of the parliamentary commissioners to receive the King's person from the Scots. Soon afterwards, Pembroke was honoured by the actors of the King's Company in their dedication of an impressive folio collection of Comedies and Tragedies by Beaumont and Fletcher. After proudly recalling how their fellows had previously addressed Shakespeare's dramas to the Herbert brothers, the actors thanked Philip Herbert for his 'most constant and diffusive goodness, from which, we did for many calm years derive a subsistence to ourselves, and protection to the scene (now withered, and condemn'd as we fear, to a long winter and sterility).' The stationer responsible for this volume was Humphrey Moseley, an ardent royalist. Its dedication, backed by a long series of commendatory verses by, among many others, Pembroke's kinsman, William Habington, may have been conciliatory in intention, with the design of persuading the Earl to support the actors' pleas for the reopening of the theatres. If so, it was a gesture which met with little success, since on 17 July 1648 Philip Herbert was one of six Peers who voted not for a limited closure of theatres but rather for the total suppression of plays indefinitely.[64]

At about this time, disaster struck at Wilton House. Aubrey recorded how, 'the south side of this stately house, that was built by Monsieur de Caus, was burnt ann. 1647 or 1648, by airing of the rooms.' Although it was once thought that the whole range had been razed to the ground, it now seems, as Howard Colvin explains, that 'the existing south front is substantially the work of 1635-40, damaged but not destroyed by the fire of 1647/8 and with its interior rebuilt in all its pristine splendour in 1648-50.' During the Civil War, Pembroke had managed to maintain his estates virtually intact and it appears that he was able to instigate repair work almost immediately. According to Aubrey - there seems to be no other account of this fire - Inigo Jones was commissioned to undertake the restoration of the interior. Most of the work, however, was probably performed by his skilled protégé, John Webb, who was also involved in architectural schemes for Durham House. Work was well under way by 1649, from which date survive a series of ceiling designs from the house. The fourth Earl died in 1650 but his son carried on the restoration. In 1652 a Dutch visitor, Lodewyk Huygens, was given a tour of the completed state rooms.[65]

In view of this unexpected expenditure, along with the effective disbanding of the royal court in 1645, it is hardly surprising that Philip Herbert attracted relatively little attention from writers during the late 1640s. And, if we lay aside the Beaumont and Fletcher First Folio, those who did choose to address their works to him were, for the most part, distinctly unimpressive. Between 1646 and 1648 he received the dedications of a posthumous edition of Sir George Buc's (d.1623) long-winded, History of Richard III; William Mercer's Angliae Speculum; a translation by William Browne (not the pastoral poet) of a French romance, Polexader; and an unremarkable manual for the domestic instruction of young girls, Herbert's Careful Father, by one William Herbert, perhaps a kinsman. John Donne, junior, also sought to maintain a friendly contact with the Herberts, addressing in 1644 a printed version of his father's treatise on suicide, Biathanatos, to Pembroke's eldest surviving son, Philip Lord Herbert. During the Civil War, Donne was driven to seek the personal protection of the Earl, once complaining to him in a letter that, since the commencement of military conflicts; 'my study has been often searched, all my books, and almost my brains, by their continual alarms, sequestered for the use of the Committee.'[66] From this motley assembly of writers, it would seem that by the 1640s the once flourishing tradition of literary patronage in the Herbert family had all but withered away in the hands of Philip Herbert.

In sharp contrast, Pembroke's aptitude for the intimidation and repression of scholars was of an entirely different order. By June 1641, Laud was in the Tower and had resigned from the Chancellorship of Oxford University. Philip Herbert was named as his successor, the appointment being commemorated by William Cartwright in a broadside containing a verse panegyric and a portrait.[67] At the same time, the satirist, Thomas Herbert, an opponent of Laud and perhaps yet another of Pembroke's distant kinsmen, published Vox Secunda Populi, or, The Commons Gratitude to ... Philip, Earl of Pembroke, with a crude woodcut portrait of the Earl on its title-page. In August 1642 a small band of royalists entered Oxford. In view of the proximity to the city of the parliamentary forces, the Pro-Vice-Chancellor wrote to Pembroke, urgently requesting his protection against having, 'our Libraries fired, our Colleges pillaged, and our throats cut'. The Earl's response, rushed into print, was unequivocal:

> The best council I can now give you, is, that you presently dismiss the Cavaliers, and yield up unto the Parliament such delinquents as are amongst you, and then the cause being taken away, the effect will follow. When you have put yourselves in the right posture of an university, I will be a faithful servant to you.[68]

By 1643 Philip Herbert's allegiance to the parliamentary side had so alienated the royalists at Oxford that the Marquis of Hertford was appointed as Chancellor in his place. Four years later, however, he was reinstated to preside over the instigation of a Parliamentary Ordinance for the reformation of the whole university. A committee of 26 peers and 52 members of the Commons, chaired by Pembroke, instructed the Visitors to enforce the solemn league and covenant. When some heads of houses objected, they were summoned to London in November to appear in person before the Chancellor. In February 1648, bypassing the established procedures, Pembroke replaced the Vice-Chancellor with one of his own men, Dr Reynolds, and instigated the appointment of several new heads of houses, university proctors and bedels. On 11 April he appeared in Oxford in person and went from college to college, witnessing the ejection of those heads of houses who had still refused to fall into line. The literary outcry against

Pembroke's behaviour was intense, instigating a series of satiric attacks on his parliamentary allegiances, choleric nature and foul language, which continued unabated until his death in 1650.[69] Clarendon suggested that Philip Herbert's actions indicated, 'the extreme weakness of his understanding and the miserable compliance of his nature'. But his post as Chancellor obliged him to carry out the Parliamentary Ordinance; and his personal presence at the removal of recalcitrant heads of houses had at least ensured that violence was kept to a minimum. Undaunted, in May his Committee of Lords and Commons began to summon virtually all fellows, students and servants from the colleges to establish their willingness or not to accept the absolute authority of Parliament.[70]

In November 1647 the King, fearing assassination, had escaped from captivity at Hampton Court and fled to the Isle of Wight, from where he managed to fashion an agreement with the Scots. The Second Civil War began in April and by July Scottish forces had invaded England on his behalf. Cromwell, however, routed them at Preston in August and the Treaty of Newport in the following month effectively ended military hostilities by the royalists towards Parliament. Pembroke, despite his by now recurrent bouts of ill health, acted as one of the Parliament's chief negotiators at Newport.[71]

Severe restrictions were placed upon Charles's personal freedom and four trusted members of his household were ordered to remain in his presence, in pairs, throughout his waking hours. One of these men was Sir Thomas Herbert, a protégé of the third Earl of Pembroke. After his brother's death, Philip Herbert had taken an interest in Sir Thomas's career, supporting in 1632 his appointment, awaiting a vacancy, as an esquire of the King's body. In 1644 Sir Thomas became a Parliamentary Commissioner for the army; and in 1646 was one of those delegated to accept the surrender of Oxford. In 1647, again through Pembroke's influence, he joined Charles's household and appears to have gained the King's trust. However, according to Norman MacKenzie, at the same time, Sir Thomas was almost certainly sending secret reports on the King's plans to his parliamentary masters, perhaps even to Pembroke himself. Herbert later wrote his Memoirs of the Two Last Years of the Reign of ... King Charles I, which unashamedly tried to assert his own and Pembroke's undying loyalty to the King. There is also the strong possibility that after Charles's execution, he helped himself to some of his personal possessions, including his annotated copy of the Shakespeare Second Folio, into which he quietly inserted the inscription: 'Ex dono serenissimi Regis Car. servo suo humiliss. T. Herbert.' Although he avoided attending the royal execution on 30 January 1649, Sir Henry was chiefly responsible for the organisation of the King's funeral. He then returned to his duties as a Parliamentary Commissioner for the army in Ireland. At the Restoration, he rushed to England to welcome Charles II, received a royal pardon, and was created a baronet on 3 July 1660.[72]

The Rump Parliament, brought into being by Colonel Pride's Purge of all those who did not support the army, decided in March 1649 to abolish the Monarchy and the House of Lords, setting up a Council of State with Cromwell as its first Chairman. Pembroke, who in 1604 had risen to the peerage through royal favour, joined the Council in February, and took advantage of the Rump's decision to allow men of his rank to sit as commoners, by accepting the member's seat for Berkshire in April. This move created a serious split in his own family. Although his eldest surviving son, Philip, sat in the Rump, along with his secretary, Michael Oldisworth, another had already been expelled as a royalist, and two more were included by the Purge. Royalist pamphleteers gleefully seized upon this 'ascent downwards' by Philip Herbert, and a flurry of satiric attacks followed. Pembroke's credit in Parliament was by this stage extremely low and the satirists delighted in suggesting that Michael Oldisworth had to write all his speeches for him. Another tract of July 1649, The Earl of Pembroke's Speech to Nol-Cromwell, Lord Deputy of Ireland, with his Royal Entertainment of him at his Manor of Ramsbury in Wiltshire, violently castigated Philip Herbert's ready compliance with the regicides.[73]

Pembroke's death on 23 January 1650 at his lodgings in the Cockpit, elicited a respectful response from his fellow members of the Council of State, who decreed that all members of Parliament were to accompany his coffin two or three miles out of London on the way to its interment in Salisbury Cathedral. In contrast to these solemnities, the royalist pamphleteers launched a final venomous attack on his name, typified by a tract of February 1650, The Life and Death of Philip Herbert ... Once Earl of Pembroke, Montgomery, which in a mock-play traced Philip Herbert's recent political career, 'having by a degenerate baseness, betrayed his Nobility; and entered himself a Commoner, amongst the very scum of the Kingdom.' Depicting him as a Judas who 'did betray his Master, by whose grace / Hee had his Titles, and enjoy'd his Place', it recounted his committal to Hell, and concluded with a dismissive epitaph:

He lies the mirror of our age for treason,
Who in his life was void of sense and reason;
The Commons' fool, a knave in everything;
A traitor to his Master, Lord and King;
A man whose virtues were to whore and swear;
God damn him was his constant daily prayer.[74]

History has not been kind to the memory of Philip Herbert; perhaps partly because of his unfavourable image in contemporary royalist satires, along with the reservations over his character expressed by Clarendon and Aubrey. More recently, estimates have ranged from Conrad Russell's observation that Philip was 'much less able than his predecessor', the third Earl of Pembroke; to John Morrill's description of 'a profligate who had run through the family fortune and was only semi-literate'. Tresham Lever searched for some good qualities but was obliged to conclude that 'he was ill-educated. He was foul-tempered and foul-mouthed, with a nasty streak of malice.' George Williamson, the biographer of his second wife, Lady Anne Clifford, had no doubts whatsoever, condemning him as, 'violent and contemptible, indeed almost crazy, contemptuous of all culture, careless and cross, false, cruel and cowardly ... a man of violent passion and foul-mouthed ... a weak and almost fraudulent turncoat.'[75]

Against this catalogue of accusations may be held Philip Herbert's undoubted skills as a courtier. As a youth, he impressed his contemporaries with his speed in obtaining James's affections; and, just as importantly, in not losing them when he was superseded by Robert Carr. It was reported that James always retained a respect for Philip's judgements, recommending him to Prince Charles as a trusted adviser. Aubrey noted: 'when he was young, he had a wonderful sagacity or faculty of discerning men: ie. to espy the reality or deceit of Ambassadors and Ministers of Estate.' During Charles's reign, his diplomatic skills were in evidence when he forged a reconciliation with the Duke of Buckingham in 1626. Over twenty years later, 'Pembroke the Foole', as the royalists termed him, exhibited considerable political suppleness in his transference of allegiance from King to Parliament, leading to seats in the Rump and on the Council of State. Like his grandfather, the first Tudor Earl of Pembroke, he had a remarkable knack of almost always managing to be on the right side at the right time. Lady Anne Clifford provided possibly the shrewdest sketch of Philip Herbert when she wrote after his death: 'he was of a very quick apprehension, a sharp understanding, very crafty withal, and of a discerning spirit, but extremely choleric by nature.'[76]

The death of the fourth Earl of Pembroke effectively ended an unbroken line of cultural patronage, inherited from his brother, father, mother, grandfather and uncle, Sir Philip Sidney. His heir, Philip, the fifth Earl, had 'an admirable wit', Aubrey tells us, 'but did not much care for reading. His chiefest diversion was Chemistry, which his Lordship did understand very well and he made medicines, that did great cures.' He also completed the restoration of Wilton House, although these expenses presumably played a significant part in the fifth Earl's decision in the early 1650s to sell off many of the collections built up by his predecessors. Furthermore, his father's debts when he died had been calculated at over £44,700, and his funeral alone cost £2,667. At Hatfield House there is a folio volume of 111 pages, dating from 1650 to 1655, of the accounts of the fourth Earl's executors. It records numerous sales of paintings to members of the aristocracy, gentry and purchasers from abroad, particularly Spain. In all, the sales amounted to nearly £2,000 although it is not possible to determine which pictures were sold since references were made only to 'the particulars in the picture book' which is now lost.[77] These sales marked the end of the Pembrokes' dominant position as patrons of the arts until the time of Thomas, the eighth Earl (c. 1656-1733), a distinguished collector of books, paintings and sculpture.

Postscript

On 24 July 1652, Lady Anne Clifford, the widow of the fourth Earl of Pembroke, recorded in her diary that Mr George Sedgwick had travelled from London to her estates in Yorkshire to become her personal secretary. Thanks to an account of his career which Sedgwick later compiled, it is possible to trace the steps which led to this comfortable appointment. After completing his studies at St John's College, Cambridge, the young George had returned home and given serious thought to seeking employment. Fortunately, his father had carefully preserved a letter written many years previously by the Countess of Cumberland (Lady Anne's mother), thanking his grandfather, Mr Jeffrey Sedgwick, 'for his upright dealing as a juror at York', during a legal case between Lady Anne and her uncle, Francis, then Earl of Cumberland. Father and son, therefore, set out 'to the court at Whitehall' to seek an interview with Lady Anne. As soon as she had read her mother's letter, 'she sent forthwith for one of her Lord's secretaries, whom she called cousin, who was then destitute of a young clerk, and immediately preferred me to him.' Sedgwick worked in this capacity for five or six years before himself becoming a secretary to both the fourth and fifth Earls of Pembroke. When this employment came to an end in 1652, he was summoned by Lady Anne, as previously noted, to Skipton Castle. Four years later, she sent him 'into France, Flanders and the Low Countries' with her grandson, Mr John Tufton (d. 1680), later Earl of Thanet. By now a valued and trusted servant, Sedgwick received from Lady Anne before his departure: 'a rent charge of £20 a year for 21 years, and £50 in gold. At our return also £100 in money, and another rent charge of £20 a year, both of which I enjoyed till the expiration of those terms.'[1]

Sedgwick's successive appointments as a junior clerk, personal secretary, travelling tutor and pensioned employee demonstrate the effectiveness of being able to claim - even through something as simple as an old letter of thanks - a personal association with a prospective noble patron. Time and time again, we have seen how men of letters sought to bolster their panegyrics of members of the Herbert family with assertions of varying levels of intimacy. Some, usually the most privileged, took full advantage of being already regarded as a friend or employee and, if possible, tactfully made it clear that they valued their dedicatee's literary discernment just as much as their influence. Others pointedly recalled that a brother, father or grandfather had previously benefited from the Herberts' generosity, presumably hoping, half-seriously, for some form of 'hereditary patronage'. Those without such immediate family associations had to be more inventive, perhaps claiming a deep veneration for the name of Herbert or, almost as commonly, a fond remembrance of Sir Philip Sidney. Alternatively, beneath the traditionally fulsome language of dedicatory addresses, we sometimes find a frank admission that the recipient's influence over political, ecclesiastical, dramatic, publishing or academic affairs was the real motivating factor behind a literary tribute. More often than not, a writer assumed that his prospective patron would immediately appreciate the practical purpose of a dedication -- the skill lay in making it eye-catching, elegant and persuasive.

Of course, personal associations with the family of a patron were no guarantee that practical benefits could invariably be reaped from dedicatory panegyrics. Michael and John Florio, Samuel Daniel, Thomas Churchyard, Philip Massinger, John Davies of Hereford and Nathaniel Baxter all indicated in literary tributes to the Herberts that their expectations of reward or favour had not been totally fulfilled. Nevertheless, the general outlook was distinctly bleaker for those who, lacking any specific contacts with influential patrons, were obliged to cast their net more widely. By the end of Elizabeth's reign, with ever more writers pursuing the limited number of patrons known to be sympathetic towards literary endeavour, both the morality and effectiveness of dedicatory panegyrics were being seriously questioned. Even one of the most enthusiastic exponents of multiple printed dedications, Thomas Churchyard, realised that he was laying himself open to the charge of deceitful insincerity. His defence of the practice carried little conviction:

> and if the world say ... I show a kind of adulation to fawn for favour on those that are happy, I answer that is a point of wisdom, which my betters have taught me ... I take an example from the fish that follow the stream.

Other late-Elizabethan writers openly considered the whole process of dedicatory tributes a demeaning farce. In one of the satirical Parnassus plays (c.1600), the poet expresses his willingness to repay any patron who keeps him in beer-money with 'such an encomium on him, that shall immortalise him as long as there is ever a bookbinder in England.' Understandably, John Marston was not alone in eschewing the conventions by dedicating his play Antonio and Mellida (1602) to 'the only rewarder and most just poiser of virtuous merits, the most honourably renowned Nobody, bounteous Maecenas of poetry and Lord Protector of oppressed innocence.'[2]

After 1600 this kind of forthright rejection of traditional dedicatory panegyrics became virtually a convention in itself, utilised by Ben Jonson, Francis Bacon and George Wither; although each remained willing to confound their proclamation of independence by occasionally showering favoured patrons with lavish words of praise. But there is no denying that frequent disappointments and constant insecurity nurtured a growing pessimism over the long-standing association between the English aristocracy and literary endeavour. The diversely talented Henry Peacham, for example, a scholar, poet, artist, traveller, botanist, linguist and musician, had enjoyed during James's reign the special favour of the Earl of Dorset (Lady Anne's first husband), as well as addressing numerous literary tributes to other members of the court nobility, including the Earl of Pembroke. By 1638, however, reduced to extreme poverty and plagued by fits of melancholy, he was minded to offer only a bitter and retrospective condemnation of the system of patronage within which he had sought to earn a living from his pen. He counselled an imaginary young author that, generally, there was little likelihood of a speculative dedication winning 'the favour and support of some great personage for thy preferment'. He then vividly described the demeaning farce through which an author could be led by a potential patron:

> But then you may say, the dedication will be worth
> a great matter, either in present reward of money,
> or preferment by your patron's letter, or other
> means. And for this purpose you prefix a learned
> and as panegyrical epistle as you can, and bestow
> great cost of the binding of your book; gilding and
> stringing of it in the best and finest manner: let me

tell thee ... if nowadays (such are these times) thou gettest but as much as will pay for the binding and strings, thou art well enough, the rest thou shall have in promises of great matters; perhaps you shall be willed to come another time, but one occasion or other will so fall out, that come never so often, you loose but your labour, your great patron is not stirring, he is abroad at dinner, he is busy with such a lord; to be short, you and your labour are forgotten: some of his pages in the meantime having made himself of your book.[3]

The respective careers of George Sedgwick and Henry Peacham serve as a final reminder that men of education and literary talent who sought to derive some sort of livelihood from aristocratic patronage before 1650 could expect to receive, at one extreme, material security, prestige and rewarding employment commensurate with their abilities, or, at the other, neglect, disappointment and destitution.

Notes

CHAPTER ONE

1. P. Thomson, 'The literature of patronage, 1580-1630', Essays in Criticism, 2 (1952), p. 274.

2. The Letters of John Chamberlain, ed. N.E. McClure (2 vols, Philadelphia, 1939), I. 156.

3. John Donne. The Complete English Poems, ed. A.J. Smith (Harmondsworth, 1971; rpt. 1983), p. 155, 'Satire 1'.

4. The Translation of Certain Psalms (1625), STC 1174, dedication to George Herbert. HMC 4th Report, p. 372b, notes a letter, then at Crowcombe Court, Somerset: 'No date. Fynes Moryson to Wm. Earl of Pembroke, asking him to be patron of his work'. Moryson's Itinerary (1617), STC 18205, was dedicated to the Earl.

5. F.B. Williams, Jr., 'An index of dedications and commendatory verses', The Library, 5 ser., 12 (1957), p. 21, illustrates A. Darcie's The Honour of Ladies (1622), with a blank space left in the Lambeth Library copy and the name of Lady Anne Herbert added in the BL copy. My study is much indebted to Williams's Index of Dedications and Commendatory Verses in English Books Before 1641 (London, 1962), and Supplement, The Library (London, 1975).

6. Francis Bacon. The Essays, ed. J. Pitcher (Harmondsworth, 1985), p. 237.

7. An Antidote Against the Plague (1625), STC 12390, sig. A2^a.

8. The History of Great Britanie (1621), STC 22634, sig. Cc4^b.

9. In preparing a copy of his Ecclesiastes for the Archbishop of Canterbury, Lok cancelled all the other commendatory verses and had the pertinent sonnet printed on a special leaf facing the title-page; see STC 16696.

10. Donne, Poems, p. 139, 'Eclogue 1613. December 26'.

11. Spenser, Poetical Works, ed. J.C. Smith and E. de Selincourt (Oxford, 1912; rpt. 1983), p. 501, 'Mother Hubberd's Tale', ll. 608-10, 614.

12. A Collection of Emblems (1635), STC 25900, Bk. 4, dedication to the fourth Earl of Pembroke.

13. Cited in P. Beal, Index of English Literary Manuscripts, Volume 1, 1450-1625, Part 2 (London, 1980), p. 122.

14. It is a common misapprehension that courtier-writers expected the sovereign to reward them personally; see, for example, B. B. Gamzue, 'Elizabeth and literary patronage', PMLA, 49 (1934), p. 1049.

15. Donne, Poems, p. 140, 'Eclogue 1613. December 26'.

16. (New York, 1955; rpt. 1958), pp. xvi, 9.

17. 'Court patronage and government policy: the Jacobean dilemma', in G.F. Lytle and S. Orgel (eds), Patronage in the Renaissance (Princeton, N.J., 1981), p. 27.

18. Donne, Poems, p. 141, 'Eclogue 1613. December 26'.

19. Spenser, Poems, p. 411, dedicatory sonnet to the Earl of Northumberland.

20. G.K. Hunter, John Lyly. The Humanist as Courtier (London, 1962), p. 73.

21. Osorio da Fonseca, The Five Books ... of Civil and Christian Nobility. Tr. W. Blandie (1576), STC 18886; quoted in Rosenberg, Leicester, p. 3.

22. P. Sheavyn, The Literary Profession in the Elizabethan Age (1909), revised by J.W. Saunders (Manchester, 1967), pp. 101-26. J.W. Saunders, The Profession of English Letters (London and Toronto, 1964), pp. 35-6, 42-3.

23. G. C. Moore Smith, 'Taking lodgings in 1591', RES, 8 (1932), pp. 447-50. CSPD. 1590, vol. 234, p. 697.

24. Vaughan, Most Approved ... Water-works (1610), STC 24603, sigs. D4^b -E1^b. Dowle, The True Friend (1630), STC, 7101, sig. A2^b. R.C. Bald, John Donne. A Life, completed by W. Milgate (Oxford, 1970), pp. 21, 251.

25. Verses appended to the engraving, 'Musar: Hercul: Colum:'. Saunders, English Letters, pp. 50-2.

26. BL Royal MS 18 A.lxvi; pr. in extenso, in G.M. Vogt, 'Richard Robinson's Eupolemia (1603)', SP, 21 (1924), pp. 629-48. H.S. Bennett, English Books and Readers. Volume 2. 1558-1603 (Cambridge, 1965), pp. 47ff.

27. Spenser, Poetical Works, p. 504, 11. 892-908. Donne, Poems, p. 171; p. 101, 'Elegy 6'; p. 158, 'Satire 1'. The Poems of Sir Walter Raleigh, ed. A.M.C. Latham (London, 1929), p. 145, 'The Lie'.

CHAPTER TWO

1. Ed. O.L. Dick (Harmondsworth, 1972; rpt. 1982), p. 221.

2. D. Lloyd, State-worthies (1670), Wing, L2646, p. 552.

3. See my 'Philip Sidney's "Astrophil and Stella 75" and King Edward IV', <u>RES</u> (forthcoming).
4. <u>Brief Lives</u>, p. 222.
5. <u>CSP For. and Dom. Henry VIII</u>, vol. 4, pt. i, p. 871, item 1939 (11); cited in N.P. Sil, 'Sir William Herbert, Earl of Pembroke (c. 1507-70): in search of a personality', <u>Welsh History Review</u>, 11 (1982), pp. 92-107, 98.
6. <u>Brief Lives</u>, p. 222. I have not been able to corroborate this account from French sources.
7. <u>The Book of the Courtier</u>, tr. G. Bull (Harmondsworth, 1967; rpt. 1976), p. 88. R.J. Knecht, <u>Francis I</u> (Cambridge, 1982), pp. 253-73.
8. <u>CSP For. and Dom. Henry VIII</u>, vol. 8, p. 47, item 149 (8, 9).
9. T. Lever, <u>The Herberts of Wilton</u> (London, 1967), pp. 3-4.
10. <u>Survey of the Lands of William, First Earl of Pembroke</u>, ed. C.B. Straton (2 vols, Oxford, Roxburghe Club, 1909), pp. xxviii, xlvi. <u>The Victoria History of the Counties of England. A History of Wiltshire</u> (12 vols, London, 1957-83), VI. 2.
11. N. Pevsner, <u>The Buildings of England. Wiltshire</u>, revised B. Cherry (Harmondsworth, 1981), pp. 35, 580.
12. <u>Acts and Monuments</u>, ed. Pratt, V.556; cited in J.K. McConica, <u>English Humanists and Reformation Politics Under Henry VIII and Edward VI</u> (Oxford, 1965), pp. 224-7.
13. <u>STC</u> 24023², sig. A2ᵃ.
14. <u>CSPD. 1547-80</u>, vol. 9, pp. 23-5, nos 5-9, 23, 25. J. Cornwall, <u>Revolt of the Peasantry, 1549</u> (London, 1977), pp. 125, 134-5, 192, 197-200, 228-9.
15. <u>CSP Sp. 1551</u>, p. 216.
16. <u>STC</u> 4343, sig. A2ᵃ. <u>The Works of John Caius</u>, ed. E. S. Roberts, with a memoir by J. Venn (Cambridge, 1912).
17. (c. 1552), <u>STC</u> 26066. G.B. Parks, 'William Barker, Tudor translator', <u>PBSA</u>, 51 (1957), pp. 126-40.
18. See, for example, A.G. Smith, <u>William Cecil, the Power Behind Elizabeth</u> (London, 1934), p. 53. C. Russell, <u>The Crisis of Parliaments</u> (Oxford, 1971), p. 162.
19. <u>CSP Sp. 1550</u>, pp. 18-19. Churchyard, <u>The Epitaph of the ... Earl of Pembroke</u> (1570), <u>STC</u> 5227. Camden, <u>The History of the ... Princess Elizabeth</u>, ed. and tr. W.T. MacCaffrey (Chicago and London, 1970), p. 11. Aubrey, <u>Brief Lives</u>, pp. 222-3. D. Cressy, <u>Literacy and the Social Order</u> (Cambridge, 1980), pp. 55-6. Sil, 'Sir William Herbert', pp. 95-7.

20. CSP Sp. 1551, p. 425; ibid, 1552, pp. 565-6, 579; ibid, 1553, pp. 13, 40.

21. C.S.L. Davies, Peace, Print & Protestantism, 1450-1558 (St Albans, 1977), p. 290.

22. Cambridge University Library MS Dd. xi.46.

23. F.A. Yates, John Florio (Cambridge, 1934), pp. 5-13. CSP Sp. 1553, p. 169.

24. CSPD. 1554, vol. 4, p. 62. CSP Sp. 1554, vol. 13, p. 12.

25. CSP Sp. 1553, pp. 120, 335. Calendar of Patent Rolls, Philip and Mary (4 vols, London, 1937-9), III.360. Aubrey's account, in Brief Lives, p. 222, of Pembroke pleading for forgiveness from the nuns of Wilton during Mary's reign and then driving them out at the beginning of Elizabeth's is almost certainly fictitious.

26. CSP For. and Dom. Henry VIII, vol. 13, pt. ii, p. 134, item 345.

27. F.S. Ellis, Horae Pembrochianae (New York, 1880). S. De Ricci and W.J. Wilson, Census of Medieval and Renaissance Manuscripts in the United States and Canada (2 vols, New York, 1937), pp. 1654-5, and Supplement (New York, 1962), p. 471.

28. STC 24361, fols 33-4. Turner was probably in Germany by 1555 and the colophon, 'imprinted at Rome', was clearly a blind. It was almost certainly printed by one of the continental Protestant groups which published a steady supply of propaganda during Mary's reign.

29. Foxe, Acts and Monuments, ed. Pratt, VIII. 127-8. C. Hughes, 'Two sixteenth-century northern Protestants: John Bradford and William Turner', Bulletin of the John Rylands Library, 66 (1983-4), pp. 122-38.

30. STC 3504.5. D.M. Loades, 'The authorship and publication of The Copye of a Letter ...', TCBS, 3 (1960), pp. 155-60, 156.

31. Hunnis is described as, 'servant to the right honourable sir William Harberde Knight', on the title-page of his Certain Psalms (1550), STC 2727.

32. See, for example, CSP For. 1551, p. 146, Sir John Mason from Nantes; ibid, 1566, p. 62, Edward Herbert from Eisenberg.

33. CSP Ven. 1558, vol. 7, p. 18. CSP Sp. 1558, p. 11.

34. Printed, in extenso, in A Collection of Scarce and Valuable Tracts, ed. W. Scott (13 vols, London, 1809), 161-75. C. Read, Mr Secretary Cecil and Queen Elizabeth (London, 1955; rpt. 1965), p. 128.

35. Lever, Herberts of Wilton, pp. 28-32.
36. The Dictionary of National Biography mistakenly states that it was Henry who went to Peterhouse. I am grateful to Dr. R. Lovatt for clarifying this confusion.
37. STC 22223, sig. A2ª. Heywood's mother was a daughter of the printer, John Rastell, and his sister, Elizabeth, the mother of John Donne.
38. The Works of Francis Osborn Esq. (1689), p.8; quoted in Sil, 'Sir William Herbert', p. 96. Prise, Historiae Brytannicae Defensio (1573), STC 20309, published posthumously by his son, Richard.
39. Noted in A. Wood, Athenae Oxonienses (4 vols, Oxford, 1813-20), I.167, 216.
40. Listed in Sotheby's Historical Manuscripts Catalogue, 28 March 1983, lot 25.
41. Robert (1567), STC 21076. CSP Sp. 1567, p. 686.
42. CSP Sp. 1566, p. 591.
43. The Nobility of Women by William Bercher 1559, ed. R.W. Bond (London, Roxburghe Club, 1904), p. 34.
44. Quoted in Read, Mr Secretary Cecil, p. 441.
45. Holinshed, Chronicles (1587), STC 13569, III.1213. Churchyard (1570), STC 5227. 'The Pembroke Dragon', in Coryat's Crudities (1611), STC 5808, sig. 3B5ᵇ. Other elegies are in Inner Temple MS 53, 810, fols 1-3; Huntington Library MS 31,118, f. 85; and recorded in A Transcript of the Register of the Company of Stationers of London; 1554-1640, ed. E. Arber (5 vols, London, 1875-94), I.411-13.
46. CSPD. 1567, vol. 42, p. 288, P.J. French, John Dee. The World of an Elizabethan Magus (London, 1972), pp. 32-3.

CHAPTER THREE

1. E.M.J. Buxton, Sir Philip Sidney and the English Renaissance (London, 1954; rpt. 1964), p. 255. J. van Dorsten, 'Literary patronage in Elizabethan England', in Lytle and Orgel (eds), Patronage, p. 200.
2. The Prose Works of Fulke Greville, Lord Brooke, ed. J. Gouws (Oxford, 1985), p. 21.
3. A. Collins (ed.), Letters and Memorials of State (2 vols, London, 1746), I.9.
4. Miscellaneous Prose of Sir Philip Sidney, ed. K. Duncan-Jones and J. van Dorsten (Oxford, 1973), p. 134.
5. Quoted in J.M. Osborn, Young Philip Sidney 1572-1577 (New Haven and London, 1972), pp. 11-12.
6. HMC De L'Isle and Dudley, II.21. M.W. Wallace, The

Life of Sir Philip Sidney (Cambridge, 1915), p. 149. M. McKisack, Medieval History in the Tudor Age (Oxford, 1971), pp. 18-19, 58-9.

7. F.J. Levy, 'Philip Sidney reconsidered', ELR, 2 (1972), pp. 3-6.

8. Greville, Prose Works, ed. Gouws, p. 12.

9. Osborn, Sidney, pp. 36-152.

10. J. van Dorsten, 'Sidney and Languet', HLQ, 29 (1966), pp. 215-22.

11. Greville, Prose Works, ed. Gouws, pp. 17, 25.

12. Henry Herbert's marriage to Lady Catherine Grey had been dissolved in 1554. On 17 February 1563 he married Catherine Talbot (d. 1575), daughter of the Earl of Shrewsbury. An elegy in Welsh for Catherine is printed in MS Gwyneddon 3, ed. I. Williams (1931); see Buxton, Sidney, pp. 95, 266.

13. CSP Sp. 1558-67, pp. 248, 530, 631. Hatfield House MSS, II.154, III.137. Collins, I.88-9. HMC De L'Isle and Dudley, I.249-50. HMC Leeds, p. 146.

14. Collins, I.191, 209. HMC Salisbury, II.154. The Countess of Pembroke's Arcadia (The Old Arcadia), ed. J. Robertson (Oxford, 1973), p. xvi. CSPD. Add. 1566-79, vol. 25, pp. 523-4.

15. Queen Elizabeth and Her Times, ed. T. Wright (2 vols, London, 1838), II.95.

16. R. Howell, Sir Philip Sidney. The Shepherd Knight (London, 1968), pp. 61-2, 64-7. John Stubbs's Gaping Gulf with Letters and Other Relevant Documents, ed. L.E. Berry (Charlottesville, 1968), pp. xlvi-lvi. CSP Sp. 1568-79, p. 693.

17. C. Read, Lord Burghley and Queen Elizabeth (London, 1960; rpt. 1965), p. 217.

18. Collins, I.274. HMC Laing, I.32. CSP Sp. 1580-86, p. 92.

19. Old Arcadia, ed. Robertson, p. xvii. A.C. Hamilton, Sir Philip Sidney. A Study of His Life and Works (Cambridge, 1977), p.41.

20. F.B. Young, Mary Sidney Countess of Pembroke (London, 1912), pp. 27-8. Osborn, Sidney, pp. 324, 328. J.W. Cunliffe, 'The Queenes majesties entertainment at Woodstock', PMLA, 26 (1911), p. 100.

21. Brief Lives, p. 220.

22. The Poems of Sir Philip Sidney, ed. W.A. Ringler, Jr., (Oxford, 1962), pp. 149, 343, 517.

23. The Correspondence of Sir Philip Sidney and Hubert Languet, tr. S.A. Pears (London, 1845; rpt. New York, 1971),

pp. 155, 187.

24. E.M.J. Buxton, 'An Elizabethan reading-list ...', TLS, 24 March 1972, pp. 343-4. Osborn, Sidney, p. 537. Levy, 'Philip Sidney reconsidered', pp. 12-23.

25. Correspondence, ed. Pears, p. 183. The Complete Works of Sir Philip Sidney, ed. A. Feuillerat (4 vols, Cambridge, 1922-6), III.132.

26. Correspondence, ed. Pears, p. 146.

27. Hamilton, Sidney, pp. 2-3. Sidney, Poems, ed. Ringler, pp. 175, 438-42. K. Duncan-Jones, 'Sidney, Stella and Lady Rich', in J. van Dorsten, D. Baker-Smith and A.F. Kinney (eds), Sir Philip Sidney. 1586 and the Creation of a Legend (Leiden, 1986), pp. 170-92.

28. Howell, Sidney, pp. 75-85, 99-107.

29. Stradling Correspondence, ed. J.M. Traherne (London, 1840), p. 29. P. Williams, The Council in the Marches of Wales Under Elizabeth I (Cardiff, 1958), pp. 243-5. Robson (1585), STC 21131.5, sig. A2^a.

30. Miscellaneous Prose, ed. Duncan-Jones and Dorsten, p. 73. Hamilton, Sidney, p. 17.

31. Buxton, Sidney, pp. 56, 89-91. Sidney, Old Arcadia. This tribute was not printed until 1586.

32. J.W. Saunders, 'The stigma of print. A note on the social bases of Tudor poetry', Essays in Criticism, 1 (1951), pp. 139-64.

33. Howell, Sidney, pp. 84, 236-7.

34. Ibid, p. 264. Buxton, Sidney, pp. 171, 175-7, 272. Lloyd (ed.), Peplus (1587), STC 22552.

35. The Works of Thomas Nashe, ed. R.B. McKerrow; rev. F.P. Wilson (5 vols, Oxford, 1958), Pierce Penniless, I.159.

36. Howell, Sidney, pp. 92-3.

37. A Work Concerning the Trueness of the Christian Religion (1587), STC 18149, sig. x3^b.

CHAPTER FOUR

1. Old Arcadia, ed. Robertson, p. 3. Greville, Prose Works, ed. Gouws, p. 11.

2. Arber, II.496. See my 'William Ponsonby: Elizabethan Stationer', Analytical & Enumerative Bibliography, 7 (1983), pp. 91-100.

3. Williams, Wales, pp. 160-1. R. Rebholz, The Life of Fulke Greville First Lord Brooke (Oxford, 1971), p. 175.

4. STC 22536, sig. A4^a. Lord Burghley ordered the

immediate 'taking in' of the volume; see Sidney, Poems, ed. Ringler, p. 545.

5. The Faerie Queene (1590), STC 23080. Complaints (1591), STC 23078. T. Watson, The Lamentations of Amyntas. Tr. A. Fraunce (1587), STC 25118.4. The Arcadian Rhetoric (1588), STC 11338. The Lawyer's Logic (1588), STC 11343. The Countess of Pembroke's Emanuel and Ivychurch (1591), STC 11339-40. The Third Part of ... Ivychurch (1592), STC 11341. T. Watson, Amintae Gaudiae (1592), STC 25117, dedicatory epistle signed, 'C[hristopher?] M[arlowe?]'.

6. Miscellaneous Prose, ed. Duncan-Jones and Dorsten, pp. 65-7.

7. The Harvard Widener Collection contains a copy of a 1613 edition of the Arcadia which bears the following inscription on its title-page: 'This was the Countess of pembrokes owne booke given me by the Countess of Montgomery her daughter 1635'. Sidney, Poems, ed. Ringler, p. 537, concludes that it is 'probably a fabrication'.

8. Ponsonby published Spenser's The Faerie Queene (1590, 96), Complaints, Daphnaida, Amoretti, Epithalamion, Colin Clouts, Astrophel elegies, Four Hymns and Prothalamion.

9. Delia and Rosamond Augmented. Cleopatra (1594), STC 6243.4, sigs. E2^a-4^b. The Harvard Widener Collection contains a copy of Delia with 'M.P.' inscribed on each side of the cover, probably also a fabrication.

10. STC 13569, III.1554.

11. The Countess may have met Duplessis-Mornay during his stay in England as Henry of Navarre's ambassador from the summer of 1577 until June 1578. Another ars moriendi work, Pope Innocent III, The Mirror of Man's Life, tr. H. Kerton (1576), STC 14092, had been dedicated to Lady Anne Herbert, the widow of the first Earl of Pembroke.

12. Sig. C2^b. I.A. Newcomb, 'The Countess of Pembroke's circle', unpublished D.Phil. thesis, University of Wisconsin, 1937, p.122. G.F. Waller, Mary Sidney, Countess of Pembroke. A Critical Study of her Writings and Literary Milieu (Salzburg, 1979), p.137.

13. The Triumph of Death and Other Unpublished and Uncollected Poems by Mary Sidney, Countess of Pembroke (1561-1621), ed. G.F. Waller (Salzburg, 1977), pp. 69, 95.

14. Sidney, Poems, ed. Ringler, p. 545, speculates that 'possibly at the suggestion of the Countess, the sonnets to

Stella were interpreted as having been addressed to the lady who became Sidney's wife'.

15. See Pembroke, Poems, ed. Waller, pp. 53-60.

16. The Works of Edmund Spenser, A Variorum Edition, ed. E. Greenlaw, C.G. Osgood and F.M. Padelford (10 vols, Baltimore, 1932-57), VIII.500-7.

17. Churchyard, Pleasant Conceit (1593), STC 5248, sig. B1b. Fraunce, Ivychurch. 3rd Part (1592), dedication. Moffet, The Silkworms and Their Flies (1599), STC 17994, sig. A2a. Meres, Palladis Tamia, ed. N. Ling (1598), STC 17834, p. 284.

18. The Works of Michael Drayton, ed. J.W. Hebel, K. Tillotson and B. Newdigate (5 vols, Oxford, 1961), I.73-4, II.561. J. Robertson, 'Drayton and the Countess of Pembroke', RES, ns 16 (1965), p. 49.

19. Barnes, Parthenophil and Parthenophe (1593), STC 1469, p. 148. Lok, Ecclesiastes (1597), STC 16696, no. 44.

20. Philip translated the first 43 psalms and his sister completed the rest (44-150). Waller, Countess of Pembroke, pp. 187-9.

21. See my 'Licensing the Sidney Psalms for the press in the 1640s', N&Q, 229 (1984), pp. 304-5. Donne, Poems, 'Upon the translation of the Psalms by Sir Philip Sidney, and the Countess of Pembroke his sister', pp. 332-4.

22. See my 'Nicholas Breton's The Passions of the Spirit and the Countess of Pembroke', RES, ns 38 (1987), pp. 221-5.

23. B.K. Lewalski, 'Of God and good women: the poems of Aemilia Lanyer', in M.P. Hannay (ed.), Silent But for the Word. Tudor Women as Patrons, Translators, and Writers of Religious Works (Kent, Ohio, 1985), pp. 203-24.

24. See also The Countess of Pembroke's Translation of Philip de Mornay's Discourse of Life and Death, ed. D. Bornstein (Detroit, 1983); and her essay in Silent But for the Word, pp. 126-34.

25. D.G. Rees, 'Petrarch's "Trionfo Della Morte" in English', Italian Studies, 7 (1952), pp. 82-96. R. Coogan, 'Petrarch's Trionfi and the English Renaissance', SP, 67 (1970), pp. 306-27.

26. The Psalms of Sir Philip Sidney and the Countess of Pembroke, ed. J.C.A. Rathmell (New York, 1963), p. xiv. Sidney, Poems, ed. Ringler, p. 502.

27. L.L. Martz, The Poetry of Meditation (New Haven, Conn., 1954; rpt. 1967), p. 278.

28. 'Shakespeare's sister', in A Room of One's Own.

29. C. Kohler, 'The Elizabethan woman of letters: the

extent of her literary activities', unpublished Ph.D. thesis, University of Virginia (1936), p. 118. E. Hageman and J.A. Roberts, 'Recent studies in women writers of Tudor England', ELR 14 (1984), pp. 409-39.

30. Quoted in L.B. Wright, 'The reading of Renaissance English women', SP, 28 (1931), p. 139.

31. F.B. Williams, Jr., 'The literary patronesses of Renaissance England', N&Q, 207 (1962), pp. 364-6.

32. L. Stone, The Family, Sex and Marriage in England 1500-1800 (London, 1977), p. 203.

33. See Aubrey, Brief Lives, p. 220, and Natural History of Wiltshire (1847; rpt. with introduction by K.G. Ponting, Newton Abbot, 1969), pp. 89-90, for details of the Countess's scientific interests.

34. W. Sweeper, The True Nobleman, and the Base Worldling (1612), STC 23526, sig. A3ᵃ.

35. STC 3173; rpt. in The Works in Verse and Prose of Nicholas Breton, ed. A.B. Grosart (2 vols, 1879; rpt. New York, 1966), I.xxvi-viii.

36. HMC Bath Longleat, V.198. HMC Salisbury, VII.405.

37. BL Additional MS, 15,232. Collins, II.81, 93. HMC De L'Isle and Dudley, II.319. BL Additional MS, 12,503; 12,506, fols 221, 235, 384. HMC Salisbury, XIV.160. Sotheby's Sale Catalogue, 21-22 July 1983, lot 7. M. Hannay, 'Unpublished letters by Mary Sidney, Countess of Pembroke', Spenser Studies 6 (1986), pp. 165-90.

38. Lambeth Palace MS Bacon Papers, 650, no 231. A Collection of Letters, ed. J. Donne, Jr., (1660), Wing M1319, pp. 85, 89, 91.

39. HMC Salisbury, IX.141-3, X.408. H. Kelliher and K. Duncan-Jones, 'A manuscript of poems by Robert Sidney: some early impressions', British Library Journal, 1 (1975), p. 113.

40. Rpt. in The Letters and Epigrams of Sir John Harington, ed. N.E. McClure (Philadelphia, 1930), pp. 389-90. See my 'Sir Robert Sidney and Sir John Harington of Kelston', N&Q, 232 (1987), pp. 232-7.

41. The Arundel Harington Manuscript of Tudor Poetry, ed. R. Hughey (Columbus, Ohio, 1960), I. no 288, II.360. See also Letters and Epigrams, ed. McClure, p. 310, 'In prayse of two worthy translations, made by two great ladies', possibly addressed to the Countess of Pembroke.

42. STC 1081, 1090, 1095.

43. Rpt. in Howell's Devises 1581, ed. W. Raleigh (Oxford, 1906), p. 16.

44. See my 'The date of the death of Abraham Fraunce', The Library, 6 ser., 5 (1983), pp. 391-2.

45. STC 11338-41, 11343, 25118.4. Ben Jonson, ed. C.H. Herford and E. Simpson (11 vols, Oxford, 1925-52), I.113.

46. The once popular theory that Daniel intended to represent the Countess as his Delia has been discounted by J. Rees, Samuel Daniel. A Critical and Biographical Study (Liverpool, 1964), pp. 16-17.

47. Aubrey, Brief Lives, ed. A. Clark (2 vols, Oxford, 1898), II. 89-90.

48. Nobilis or a View of the Life and Death of a Sidney and Lessus Lugubris by Thomas Moffet, ed. and tr. by V.B. Heltzel and H.H. Hudson (San Marino, 1940).

49. Parry, Victoria Christiana (1594), STC 19336, sig. A2ª. See my, 'The date of the Countess of Pembroke's translation of the Psalms', RES, ns 33 (1982), pp. 434-6. Parry dedicated a translation of a work by Zacharias Ursinus, STC 24532, to the second Earl of Pembroke in 1587.

50. Churchyard, Pleasant Conceit (1593). Baxter, Sir Philip Sidney's Ourania (1606), STC 1598.

51. M.E. Lamb, 'The Countess of Pembroke's patronage', ELR, 12 (1982), p. 162.

52. 'Seneca in Elizabethan translation', Selected Essays (London, 1932), pp. 92-4. M.E. Lamb, 'The myth of the Countess of Pembroke: the dramatic circle', Yearbook of English Studies, 11 (1981), p. 195.

53. Brandon may have had access to a manuscript of Daniel's epistle.

54. D.M. Bergeron, 'Woman as patrons of English renaissance drama', in Lytle and Orgel (eds), Patronage, pp. 274-90.

55. BL Additional MS, 35,186; pr. in The Poems of William Smith, ed. L.A. Sasek (Baton Rouge, 1970), pp. 89-96.

56. Gager, Ulysses Redux (1592), STC 11516; the Huntington Library copy contains a printed address to the Countess. Fitzgeoffrey, Affaniae (1601), STC 10934, sig. G7ª. Davison, A Poetical Rhapsody (1602), STC 6373, dedication to William, third Earl of Pembroke.

57. Morley, Canzonets (1593), STC 18121. V. Stern, Gabriel Harvey. His Life, Marginalia and Library (Cambridge, 1979), pp. 89, 106-8. Nashe, Works, ed. Wilson, III.89-90.

58. P. Hogrefe, Tudor Women: Commoners and Queens (Ames, Iowa, 1975), p. 124.

59. The Poetical Works of William Basse (1602-1653), ed. R. Warwick Bond (London, 1893), pp. 182-3, 189-93, 209-18.

CHAPTER FIVE

1. Nashe, Works, ed. Wilson, I.159.
2. Sidney, Poems, ed. Ringler, p. 260. Collins, I.246-7.
3. Miscellaneous Prose, ed. Duncan-Jones and Dorsten, p. 152. Sidney, Poems, ed. Ringler, p. 436. Levy, 'Philip Sidney reconsidered', p. 16.
4. D.H. Horne, The Life and Minor Works of George Peele (New Haven, 1952), pp. 235-6.
5. Levy, 'Philip Sidney reconsidered', pp. 16-17. R. Heffner, 'Essex the ideal courtier', ELH, 1 (1934), pp. 16-17. M.V. Hay, The Life of Robert Sidney, Earl of Leicester (1563-1626) (Washington, D.C., 1985), pp. 137-8, 144, 163, 180.
6. The Poems of Edward de Vere, Seventeenth Earl of Oxford and of Robert Devereux, Second Earl of Essex, ed. S.W. May, SP, 77, no. 5 (1980), pp. 18-21.
7. Spenser, Poems, p. 554.
8. The Crisis of Parliaments. English History 1509-1660 (Oxford, 1971; rpt. 1981), p. 251.
9. Poems, ed. May, p. 19.
10. Rosenberg, Leicester, pp. 186-7. L.A. Knafla, 'The "Country" Chancellor: the patronage of Sir Thomas Egerton, Baron Ellesmere', in Patronage in Late Renaissance England. Papers read at a Clark Library seminar, 14 May 1977 (Los Angeles, 1983), p. 41. I am grateful to Professor J. Barnard for drawing my attention to this paper.
11. The Dictionary of Welsh Biography Down to 1940 (London, 1959), p. 351. Williams, Wales, pp. 85-99.
12. STC 19605, pp. 3, 30, 38. D.J. McGinn, John Penry and the Marprelate Controversy (New Brunswick, 1966), pp. 60-5, 150-1.
13. STC 1095, sig. 2x2^a-3^b, 2x8^b, Dd6^a. See also W. Darrell, A Short Discourse of the Life of Servingmen (1578), STC 6274.
14. A Sermon Preached at the Court at Greenwich (1591), STC 1094.
15. The Antient History ... of the City of Exeter (n.p.d.), pp. 286-7. Bodley MS Tanner 306, f.191. CSPD. 1603-10, vol. 35, p. 448.
16. E.K. Chambers, The Elizabethan Stage (4 vols,

Oxford, 1923), I.279-83. A. Gurr, The Shakespearean Stage, 1574-1642 (Cambridge, 1980), pp. 28, 30-3.

17. S. Schoenbaum, William Shakespeare: A Documentary Life (New York and London, 1975), p. 90.

18. Gurr, p. 85.

19. Chambers, II.92, 100, 127.

20. Ibid, II.89, 111. Gurr, pp. 117, 121, 144, 150, 200.

21. See p. 140. K.P. Wentersdorf, 'The origin and personnel of the Pembroke Company', Theatre Research International, nos 5-6 (1979-81), pp. 45-68.

22. J.T. Murray, English Dramatic Companies 1558-1642 (2 vols, London, 1910), I.59; II.122-7. Chambers, II.128-34. Henslowe's Diary, ed. R.A. Foakes and R.T. Rickert (Cambridge, 1961), p. 280. A. Harbage, Annals of English Drama 975-1700, revised S. Schoenbaum (London, 1964), pp. 64, 72-4.

23. Chambers, II.130. 3. Henry VI, Cambridge Shakespeare (1964), pp. xlv, xlvii. R.E. Burkhart, 'Finding Shakespeare's "Lost Years"', Shakespeare Quarterly, 29 (1978), pp. 77-9. E.A.J. Honigmann, Shakespeare: the Lost Years (Manchester, 1985).

24. Gurr, p. 194. Schoenbaum, Life, p. 125. The Taming of the Shrew, Arden Shakespeare, ed. B. Morris (London, 1981), p. 52.

25. Sidney, Poems, ed. Ringler, p. 547. Countess of Pembroke, Poems, ed. Waller, pp. 88-91.

26. Williams, Wales, pp. 124, 276-88. Rebholz, Greville, pp. 89-90.

27. Poems, ed. Croft, pp. 95-102. HMC Salisbury, IX.141.

28. STC 11515. J.W. Binns, 'William Gager's Meleager and Ulysses Redux', in E.M. Blistein (ed.), The Drama of the Renaissance: Essays for Leicester Bradner (Providence, Rhode Island, 1970), pp. 27-41. See chapter 4, note 56.

29. Grammatica Britannica (1593), STC 21611. In 1572 the Welsh doctor, John Jones, dedicated to Pembroke his The Baths of Bath's Aid (1572), STC 14724a.3.

30. Lansdowne MS 708. Owen's son, George, presented to the third Earl, 'A catalogue of all the Earls of Pembroke' (c. 1630), Wilton House Archive Room.

31. Honigmann, pp. 91-3.

32. Recorded in J. Sanford, Apollinis et Musarum (1592), STC 21733, sig. C1.

33. STC 24042. Three of the elegists from the Peplus collection, John Gifford, Charles Rives and Matthew Davis,

contributed commendatory verses to Thorne's work.
34. HMC De L'Isle and Dudley, II.422.
35. STC 1500. In All's Well That Ends Well, 'the gallant militarist', Parolles, has 'the whole theorie of war in the knot of his scarf' (IV.iii.137-40).
36. Collins, II.120, 122, 182. HMC Salisbury, XIV.160. This letter is endorsed '1601' in a hand other than the Countess's but clearly refers to this interview.
37. Collins, I.372; II.211.
38. The Sonnets, New Cambridge Shakespeare, ed. J. Dover Wilson (1966), pp. xcix-cviii; and J. Padel, New Poems by Shakespeare. Order and Meaning Restored to the Sonnets (London, 1981).
39. Huntington Library MS, HA 6722.
40. Collins, II.120-3, 146. HMC Salisbury, IX.141-3; X.408; XI.9.
41. HMC Salisbury, IX.3, 13-14. The first and second Earls were commemorated, with woodcut portraits, in H. Holland, Herwologia Anglica (1602), STC 13582, pp. 56-7, 115-16.
42. HMC Salisbury, IX.40.
43. CSP Carew 1601, p. 20. HMC Salisbury, XI.239-40, 340. Chamberlain, Letters, I.179.

CHAPTER SIX

1. STC 6258, rpt. in The Complete Works ... of Samuel Daniel, ed. A.B. Grosart (4 vols, London, 1885-96), I.143, 165. The Pierpont Morgan Library copy of A Panegyric contains the signature, 'Mary Pembroke' in the imprint panel and 'Lady Pembroke' in ink on the vellum cover; both may be Collier forgeries.
2. Chambers, I.54.
3. STC 6333, rpt. in The Complete Works of John Davies of Hereford, ed. A.B. Grosart (2 vols, London, 1878), I.14. Pembroke had earlier received tributes in R. Johnson, Essays (1601), STC 14695, and J. Davies, Mirum in Modum (1602), STC 6336.
4. HMC Salisbury, XV.58, 385. CSP Ven. 1603, pp. 76-7.
5. J. Nichols, The Progresses ... of King James the First (4 vols, London, 1828), I.250, 254; IV.1059-60. CSP Ven. 1603, p. 116. See my, ' "We have the man Shakespeare with us": Wilton House and As You Like It', Wiltshire Archaeological Magazine, 80 (1986), pp. 225-7.

6. Nichols, Progresses of James, I.221, 247, 281. T. Birch, Court and Times of James Ist (2 vols, London, 1849), I.26.

7. STC 6344, sig. A3ᵃ.

8. STC 12752, sigs. A2ᵃ, 11ᵃ. HMC Salisbury, XVII.35, 71, 75, 84; cited in J.R. Briley, 'A biography of William Herbert third Earl of Pembroke 1580-1630', unpublished Ph.D thesis, University of Birmingham, 1961, pp. 518-19.

9. The History of the Rebellion, ed. W.D. Macray (6 vols, Oxford, 1888), I.72. E. Lodge, Illustrations of British History (3 vols, London, 1791), III.238-9, 254. Briley, pp. 441-9, 461-3. J. Owen, Epigrammatum Liber Secundus (1606), STC 18984.5, no. 29, celebrates Pembroke's marriage.

10. Microcosmos (1603), sig. 2M1ᵇ. Cadwallader (1604), sig. A2ᵃ. Poetical Rhapsody (1602), sig. A2ᵃ. Ambassador (1603), STC 13848, sig. A2ᵃ.

11. Chambers, I.6-7. Schoenbaum, Shakespeare: Life, pp. 196, 203.

12. Chambers, I.171, 199-200; III.277-80. D. Taylor, Jr., 'The masque and the lance: the Earl of Pembroke in Jacobean court entertainments', Tulane Studies in English, 8 (1958), pp. 21-53.

13. J. Hughes (ed.), The Complete History of England (London, 1706), II.685. Chambers, III.279.

14. Chambers, III.377.

15. Ibid, III.278. Jonson, Works, VII.178, 218, 317; VIII.67; IX.22.

16. Jonson, Works, I.199-200.

17. Aubrey, Wiltshire, p. 88. Taylor, 'The masque and the lance', p. 45ff.

18. STC 11160. Rowland Whyte remarked in a letter of 20 May 1605: 'The Herberts every cockpit day, /Do carry away /The gold and glory of the day'; quoted in Chambers, I.146.

19. Pembroke's musical interests are possibly reflected in T. Hume, The First Part of Ayres (1605), STC 13958, containing 'the earl of Pembroke's galliard', no. 2; and the dedication to him of T. Tomkins, Songs of 3.4.5. and 6. Parts (1622), STC 24099.

20. The Tragedy of Philotas by Samuel Daniel, ed. L. Michel (New Haven, Conn., 1949), 'To the Prince', ll. 65, 83-6.

21. (1611), STC 6242, sig. E3ᵇ. Civil Wars (1609), STC 6245, rpt. in Works, ed. Grosart, II.5.

22. D. Norbrook, 'The reformation of the masque', in D. Lindley (ed.), The Court Masque (Manchester, 1984), p. 96; and his Poetry and Politics in the English Renaissance (London, 1984), pp. 177-8.

23. Cited in Gurr, p.52.

24. A copy of Bryon in the BL (#C45,b9) contains marginal annotations, reputedly in the hand of Philip Herbert; see, A.H. Tricomi, 'Philip, Earl of Pembroke, and the analogical way of reading political tragedy', JEGP, 85 (1986), pp. 332-45.

25. L.L. Peck, Northampton: Patronage and Policy at the Court of James I (London, 1982), p. 24ff.

26. Letters and Epigrams, ed. McClure, p. 120.

27. Sir Francis Drake His Honourable Life's Commendation (1596), STC 10943, sig. B5^a. Affaniae (1603), sigs. D5^a-6^a.

28. J. Grundy, The Spenserian Poets (London, 1969), pp. 3, 10. Norbrook, Poetry and Politics, pp. 197-200.

29. Jonson, Works, X.465.

30. STC 12582, sig. I2^b.

31. M. Heinemann, Puritanism & Theatre. Thomas Middleton and Opposition Drama Under the Early Stuarts (Cambridge, 1980; rpt. 1982), p. 44.

32. Estienne, A World of Wonders. Tr. R. Carew (1607), STC 10553, sigs. x4^{a-b}.

33. T. de Fougasses, The General History of Venice. Tr. W. Shute (1612), STC 11207. Maurice, Prince of Orange, The Triumphs of Nassau. Tr. W. Shute (1613), STC 17676. T. Charde, The Works of ... G. Babington (1615), STC 1077. C. y Meneses, Geraldo the Unfortunate Spaniard. Tr. L. Digges (1622), STC 4919. W. Sweeper, A Brief Treatise (1622), STC 23526.

34. Aubrey, Brief Lives, p. 225. Clarendon, Rebellion, I.71, 74.

35. Nichols, Progresses of James, I.552-3. M.S. Steele, Plays & Masques at Court (New Haven; Conn., 1926), p. 147.

36. BL Additional MS 34,782. J.H. Bryant, 'John Reynolds of Exeter and his canon', The Library, 5 ser., 15 (1960), pp. 105-17 and 18 (1963), pp. 299-303.

37. STC 13633, rpt. in The Poems of George Chapman, ed. P.B. Bartlett (New York and London, 1941), p. 399.

38. M.A. Shaaber, Check-list of Works of British Authors Printed Abroad, in Languages Other Than English, to 1641 (New York, 1975), G183. Rosenberg, Leicester, p. 286ff.

39. (1609?), STC 12686. R.A. MaCabe, Joseph Hall. A Study in Satire and Meditation (Oxford, 1982), pp.108-9.

40. Revised edition entitled, A President to the Nobility (1612), STC 1234. P.J. Wallis, 'The Library of William Crashawe', TCBS, 2 (1958), pp. 213-28. Dizionario Biografico degli Italiani (Rome, n.d.), pp.336-43.

41. Pembroke's political career is examined in B. O'Farrell, 'Politician, patron, poet: William Herbert, third Earl of Pembroke, 1580-1630', unpublished Ph.D. thesis, University of Los Angeles, 1966.

42. HMC Downshire, II.216. Lodge, Illustrations, III.335. Chamberlain, Letters, I.340.

43. Briley, pp.528-35.

44. CSPD. 1612, p.140. Chamberlain, Letters, I.324.

45. A Panegyric, stanzas 24, 55, 62. Philotas, ed. Michel, p.97.

46. Harleian Miscellany, IV.336; quoted in R. Strong, Henry Prince of Wales and England's Lost Renaissance (London, 1986), p.26.

47. T. Birch, The Life of Henry Prince of Wales (London, 1760), p.97. J. Cleland, The Institution of a Young Noble Man (1607), STC 5393, sig. E2^a.

48. In addition to Strong, Prince Henry, from which the title of this section is borrowed, see E.C. Wilson, Prince Henry and English Literature (Ithaca, N.Y., 1946); J.W. Williamson, The Myth of the Conqueror (New York, 1970); and G. Parry, The Golden Age Restor'd. The Culture of the Stuart Court, 1603-42 (Manchester, 1981), pp.64-94.

49. Parry, Golden Age, pp.71-3. Norbrook, Poetry and Politics, pp.203-5.

50. P. de Mornay, The History of the Papacy. Tr. S. Lennard (1612), STC 18147, sig. x3^b.

51. D.C. Kay, 'The English funeral elegy in the reigns of Elizabeth I and James I, with special reference to poems on the death of Prince Henry (1612)', unpublished Oxford D.Phil. thesis, 1982, pp.171-307.

52. The Works of Thomas Campion, ed. W.R. Davis (London, 1969), pp. 117, 124.

CHAPTER SEVEN

1. Birch, Court and Times, I.191.

2. L.P. Smith, Life and Letters of Sir Henry Wotton (2 vols, Oxford, 1907), II.20.

3. HMC Buccleuch, I.118, 131. HMC Downshire, III.83,

IV.251.

4. Norbrook, Poetry and Politics, pp. 205-6. E. Le Comte, The Notorious Lady Essex (London, 1970), pp. 105-121. (to be used with caution).

5. HMC Mar and Kellie, Suppl. Rpt., pp. 51-2. Peck, Northampton, pp. 30-9.

6. R.E. Ruigh, The Parliament of 1624. Politics and Foreign Policy (Cambr., Mass., 1971), pp. 118, 127-31, 176-7, 192-3. C. Russell, Parliaments and English Politics 1621-1629 (Oxford, 1979), pp. 287-90.

7. Clarendon, Rebellion, I.72-3. Gardiner, History of England, VII.133; quoted in O'Farrell, p.125. DNB article on William Herbert. Chapman, Poems, ed. Bartlett, p.483. Lever, Herberts of Wilton, pp. 74-5. D. Hirst, Authority and Conflict. England, 1603-1658 (London, 1986). p. 142.

8. Pr. in The Dr Farmer Chetham MS. Being a Commonplace Book, ed. A.B. Grosart (2 parts, Chetham Society, Manchester, 1873), II.188.

9. CSPD. 1612, p. 140. Briley, pp. 538-48.

10. STC 11207, 17676. Strong, Prince Henry, pp. 68-9, 72-5.

11. STC 19511, sig. E2^b. Strong, Prince Henry, pp. 49-50, 120.

12. The Divine Weeks and Works of Guillaume de Saluste Sieur du Bartas. Translated by Josuah Sylvester, ed. S. Snyder (2 vols, Oxford, 1979), I.31, 36-7.

13. Homer, The Iliads. Tr. G. Chapman (1611), STC 13634, sonnets to the Earls of Pembroke and Montgomery and the Countess of Montgomery; rpt. in Homer, The Whole Works (1616), STC 13624. In 1619 Donne presented a manuscript copy of one of his sermons to the Countess of Montgomery. An accompanying letter is printed in The Life and Letters of John Donne, ed. E. Gosse (2 vols, London, 1899), II.123.

14. Norbrook, Poetry and Politics, pp. 202-10.

15. Athenae Oxonienses, ed. A.A. Ward (4 vols, London, 1813-20; rpt. New York, 1967), II.366. Browne's Britannia's Pastorals (c. 1616), STC 3915, was dedicated to the Earl.

16. STC 25891, epigram 8; rpt. in Juvenilia (1622), STC 25911.

17. STC 25900, Bk. 4, dedication. C.S. Hensley, The Later Career of George Wither (Hague, 1969), pp. 41-72.

18. Chamberlain, Letters, I.542.

19. W. Scott, Secret History of the Court of James the First (2 vols, London, 1811), II. 261-2.

20. Jonson, Works, X.553.

21. R. Lockyer, Buckingham. The Life and Political Career of George Villiers, First Duke of Buckingham 1592-1628 (London, 1981), pp. 12-22.

22. Lodge, Illustrations, II.281.

23. A Select Second Husband for Sir T. Overbury's Wife (1616), STC 6342. Heinemann, Puritanism & Theatre, pp. 107-14.

24. J.L. Sanderson, 'Poems on an affair of state - the marriage of Somerset and Lady Essex', RES, ns 17 (1966), pp. 57-61. Le Comte, Lady Essex, pp. 68, 149, 154, 178-85. Norbrook, Poetry and Politics, pp. 213-14.

25. Chambers, I.34-40. G. Aylmer, The King's Servants. The Civil Service of Charles I. 1625-1642 (London, 1961), p. 473. O'Farrell, pp. 89-91.

26. A Divine Herbal (1616), STC 111. Three Sermons (1625), STC 130. The Works (1629), STC 104. DNB article on Adams.

27. Sheldon, A Survey of the Miracles of the Church of Rome (1616), STC 22399. Hitchcock, A Sanctuary for Honest Men (1617), STC 13530. Dickenson, The King's Right (1619), STC 6821. Bruen, The Pilgrim's Practice (1621), STC 3930.3. Chaloner, Six Sermons (1623), STC 4936.

28. Bodley MS North E.41, ff. 141-51.

29. J.A. Gotch, Inigo Jones (London, 1928), pp. 169-70. J. Lees-Milne, The Age of Inigo Jones (London, 1953), p. 132. Taylor, 'The Masque and the Lance', pp. 31-2.

30. Stone-Heng (1655), Wing J954, pp. 1-2. J. Webb, Stone-Henge Restored (1655). Wing W1203.

31. Chambers, I.36, 209.

32. J.Q. Adams, The Dramatic Records of Sir Henry Herbert Master of the Revels, 1623-1673 (New Haven, Conn., 1917), p.52.

33. Epistolary Curiosities ... Letters of the Herbert Family, ed. R. Warner (London, 1818), p. 3n.

34. G.E. Bentley, The Jacobean and Caroline Stage (7 vols, Oxford, 1941-6), I.7, 178-9. R. Davies, The Greatest House of Chelsey (London, 1914), pp. 150-1.

35. Bentley, I.6. Chamberlain, Letters, II.501. Gurr, p. 82.

36. E.K. Chambers, William Shakespeare. A Study of Facts and Problems (2 vols, Oxford, 1930), I.178-9.

37. Hotman, The Ambassador. Ed. J. Shawe (1603), STC 13848. Ducci, The Courtier's Art. Ed. E. Blount (1607), STC 7274.

38. S. Lee, 'An Elizabethan bookseller', Bibliographica, 4 (1905), pp. 474-98.

39. L. Rostenberg, 'Thomas Thorpe, publisher of "Shake-Speares Sonnets" ', PBSA, 54 (1960), pp. 16-37. K. Duncan-Jones, 'Was the 1609 Shake-Speares Sonnets really unauthorized', RES, ns 34 (1983), pp. 151-71.

40. Shakespeare, Works, ed. R.G. White (Boston, 1865), I.152; quoted in Shakespeare, The Sonnets, New Variorum Edition, ed. H.E. Rollins (2 vols, Philadelphia and London, 1944), II.166.

41. The Best Bargain (1623), STC 12646. Hall dedicated to the Earl of Montgomery, A Recollection (1621), STC 12708, and Contemplations, the Sixth Volume (1622), STC 12657a; and to Pembroke and Montgomery jointly, The Works (1625), STC 12635.

42. STC 13394a, sig. x3^b.

43. STC 11496. The identity of its author as H[enry] G[oodere] was first suggested by W.C. Hazlitt.

44. M.R. Smith, 'The Apologia and emblems of Ludovico Petrucci', Bodleian Library Record, 8 (1967), pp. 40-7.

45. Anton, The Philosopher's Satires (1616), STC 686. Browne, Britannia's Pastorals (c. 1616), STC 3915. Davies, Wit's Bedlam (1617), STC 6343.

46. Pr. in The Plays and Poems of Philip Massinger, ed. P. Edwards and C. Gibson (5 vols, Oxford, 1976), IV.389-91.

47. Epictetus (1616), STC 10426, sig. A2^b. Bacon, Advancement, Bk. I, A.3.ix.

48. STC 23779, sig. D3^a. Taylor dedicated to Pembroke and Montgomery jointly, The Book of Martyrs (1616), STC 23731.3 and Works (1630), STC 23725. In The Needle's Excellency (10th edn., 1634), STC 23776, no.5, he commemorates Mary, Dowager Countess of Pembroke (d. 1621).

49. The Muses' Sacrifice (1612), STC 6228, dedication to Countess of Bedford, Dowager Countess of Pembroke and Lady Elizabeth Carey.

50. The Scourge of Folly (1611), STC 6341. Fletcher, Christ's Bloody Sweat (1613), STC 11076. Wither, Abuses (1613), STC 25891. Sylvester, Parliament of Virtues Real (1615), STC 23582, sig. A6^a. Taylor, Abuses (1614), STC 23779, sig. D3^a. Anton, Philosopher's Satires (1616). Browne, Britannia's Pastorals (c. 1616). Fennor's Descriptions (1616), STC 10784. Adams, A Divine Herbal (1616), STC 111.

51. E. Partridge, 'Jonson's Epigrammes: the named and the nameless', SLI, 6 (1973), pp. 155, 184.

52. R. Krueger, 'The poems of William Herbert, third Earl of Pembroke', unpublished B. Litt. thesis, University of Oxford (1961), p. xxix. G.E. Onderwyzer, Poems ... by ... William Earl of Pembroke (Los Angeles, 1959).

53. Ben Jonson. Poems, ed. I. Donaldson (Oxford, 1975), p. 99. Pembroke's interest in classical verse may be indicated by the dedication of John Ansley's translation of Ovid, Ars Amatoria, Bk. III (c. 1620), Folger MS V.a.465.

54. Poetical Works of William Drummond of Hawthornden, ed. L.E. Kastner (2 vols, Edinburgh, 1913), II.187-8, 380 (this attribution is not conclusive).

55. Leech, Epigrammata (1620/1), STC 15366; Pembroke is addressed in an epistle to Eroticon and in an epigram in Epigrammatum. Bald, Life, p. 351. Donne. Poetical Works, ed. H.J.C. Grierson (Oxford, 1929; rpt. 1971), pp. 389-90, 394.

56. Buxton, Sidney, p. 242.

57. Amorum Emblemata (1608), STC 24627a.8. Minerva Brittana (1612), STC 19511, sig. E2b. D. Taylor, Jr., 'The third Earl of Pembroke as a patron of poetry', Tulane Studies in English, 5 (1955), pp. 61-2.

58. R. Strong, The Elizabethan Image (London, 1969), p. 86. J. Murdoch, et al., The English Miniature (New Haven and London, 1981), p. 61.

59. Documents Illustrative of the History of the Slave Trade to America, Vol. I, 1441-1700, ed. E. Donnon (Washington, D.C., 1930), p. 47n. DNB article on William Herbert. S.M. Kingsbury, The Records of the Virginia Company of London, Vol. 3, 1607-1622 (Washington, D.C., 1933), p.86.

60. Heinemann, Puritanism & Theatre, pp. 269-70.

61. Thornton, Bodley MS Ashmole 749, item 2. Other works of colonisation interest addressed to Pembroke include: Anon tr., H. de Feynes, An Exact and Curious Survey of All the East Indies (1615), STC 10840. J. Rolfe, 'True relation of the state of Virginia', noted in Buxton, Sidney, p. 242.

62. Heinemann, Puritanism & Theatre, p. 268.

63. STC 24603, sigs. D4a-E2a, F4b, I2a-4a, Q2a, S4b.

64. D. Taylor, Jr., 'Clarendon and Ben Jonson as witnesses for the Earl of Pembroke's character', in J.W. Bennett, et al., (eds), Studies in the English Renaissance Drama (London, 1961), p. 325ff. Aubrey, Brief Lives, p. 225. Clarendon, Rebellion, I.71-2.

CHAPTER EIGHT

1. Shute (1613), <u>STC</u> 17676, sig. x2ª. <u>Balbani</u>. Tr. Crashaw (1612), <u>STC</u> 1234, sig. A2ª.
2. Described in J. Ford, <u>Honour Triumphant</u> (1606), <u>STC</u> 11160, addressed to the Countesses of Pembroke and Montgomery.
3. <u>Rebellion</u>, I.69, 71.
4. <u>STC</u> 917. K. Sharpe, 'The Earl of Arundel, his circle and the opposition to the Duke of Buckingham, 1618-1628', in K. Sharpe (ed.), <u>Faction and Parliament</u> (Oxford, 1978), pp. 212, 239-42.
5. A.M. Charles, <u>A Life of George Herbert</u> (Ithaca and London, 1977), pp. 56, 121. Bald, <u>Life</u>, p. 183. J.H. Summers, <u>George Herbert. His Religion and Art</u> (London, 1954), pp. 31, 39.
6. Taylor, 'The third Earl of Pembroke as a patron of poetry', pp. 62-3. Walton sometimes spiced up his accounts with fictional dialogue.
7. <u>Summers</u>, pp. 34-5, 208-9. <u>Charles</u>, pp. 121, 145-7, 171.
8. <u>O'Farrell</u>, pp. 131-2. V.A. Rowe, 'The influence of the Earls of Pembroke on parliamentary elections, 1625-41', <u>EHR</u>, 50 (1935), pp. 242-56. See my 'William, third Earl of Pembroke, and the MPs for Wilton, 1621-1628', <u>Wiltshire Archaeological Magazine</u>, 78 (1983), pp. 70-3.
9. <u>Epigrammatum Libri Quatuor</u> (1607), <u>STC</u> 23354, epigrams 127 and 172. 'A politic discourse', National Library of Wales MS 5666D.
10. <u>Liber Famelicus of Sir James Whitelocke</u>, ed. J. Bruce, Camden Society, 70 (London, 1858), p. 61. <u>Collins</u>, I.79. Aylmer, <u>King's Servants</u>, p. 354. <u>Memoirs of Sir Benjamin Rudyerd</u>, ed. J.A. Manning (London, 1841), p. 44. <u>Return. Members of Parliament 1213-1702</u> (London, 1878), pp. 472, 478.
11. S.L. Adams, 'The Protestant cause: religious alliance with the west European Calvinist communities as a political issue in England, 1585-1630', unpublished D.Phil. thesis, University of Oxford, 1972, p. 177ff.
12. <u>Briley</u>, p. 606.
13. Clarendon, <u>Rebellion</u>, I.72.
14. <u>The Poems English and Latin of Edward Lord Herbert of Cherbury</u>, ed. G.C. Moore Smith (Oxford, 1923), p. 42. Pembroke's illegitimate children are recorded in Sir Thomas Herbert, 'Herbertorum Prosapia', Cardiff Central

Library Phillipps MS 5.7, a family history (c. 1633). An earlier version of this MS is in Wilton House Archive Room.

15. The Poems of Lady Mary Wroth, ed. J.A. Roberts (Louisiana and London, 1983), pp. 24-5.

16. She also received jointly with her husband the dedication of vol. 2 of T. Milles, The Treasury of Ancient and Modern Times (1619), STC 17936.5.

17. Bald, Life, p. 341. William Browne's elegy on the Countess (d. 1629) is pr. in The Poems of William Browne of Tavistock, ed. G. Goodwin (2 vols, London, 1894), II.294.

18. See my 'The literary patronage of the Herbert family, Earls of Pembroke, 1550-1640', unpublished D.Phil. thesis, 1982, University of Oxford, p. 188ff. Young, Mary Sidney, p. 108. Aubrey, Brief Lives, p. 220.

19. Thomas Heywood made brief references to the Dowager Countess in Troia Britanica (1609), STC 13366, p. 359, and Nine Books of Various History, Concerning Women (1624), STC 13326, p. 398.

20. Spenser, Complaints (1591; rpt. 1611-17); Morley, Canzonets (1593; rpt. 1602, 1606); Babington, Works (1615), STC 1077. Davison (1602), STC 6373.

21. Browne, Works, ed. Goodwin, II.248-55, 294.

22. Budge (1615), STC 12775, sig. A2ª. Campion, Epigrammatum Libri II (1619), STC 4541, Liber Primus, epigram 211. Pembroke was also commended in J. Dunbar, Epigrammaton (1616), STC 7346, p. 38, and R. Bruch, Epigrammatum Hecatontades Duae (1627), STC 3926, epigram 97.

23. Brief Lives, p. 226.

24. Chamberlain, Letters, II.52. Athenae Oxonienses, II.482.

25. Rosenberg, Leicester, pp. 119-38, 295-300. C.E. Mallett, A History of the University of Oxford, vol. 2, The Sixteenth and Seventeenth Centuries (Oxford, 1924), pp. 115-19. M.E. Curtis, Oxford and Cambridge in Transition 1558-1642 (Oxford, 1959), pp. 28, 172-5.

26. STC 19025. The History and Antiquities of the University of Oxford. In Two Books. By Anthony à Wood, ed. J. Gutch (2 vols, London, 1792-6), II.334.

27. Carpenter, Geography Delineated Forth (1625), STC 4676, with separate dedications to Pembroke and Montgomery. Godwin, Moses and Aaron (1625), STC 11951. Whear, De Ratione et Methodo Legendi Historias Dissertatio (1625), STC 25326. Degori Wheari Prael. Hist. Camdeniani (1628), STC 25326.5, includes letters to Pembroke, dating

from February 1621 to April 1628. James (ed.), G. Witzell, Methodus Concordiae Ecclesiasticae (1625), STC 25935. Prideaux, Orationes Novem Inaugurales (1626), STC 20358.

28. Six Sermons (1623), STC 4936. Credo Ecclesiam Sanctam Catholicam (1625), STC 4934.

29. Mallett, p. 199.

30. Athenae Oxonienses, III.329-31, 974. Jonson, Works, I.83.

31. 'Birthday celebrations of Pembroke College Oxford 1624', a Latin address; rpt. in The Works of Sir Thomas Browne, ed. G. Keynes (4 vols, London, 1964). III.148-50. D. Macleane, University of Oxford. College Histories. Pembroke College (Oxford, 1900), pp. 72-5.

32. Bodleian Summary Catalogue, I, nos. 1-244 and MS Laud Misc. 423, 630, 640. W.D. Macray, Annals of the Bodleian Library (Oxford, 1868), p. 68.

33. Wood, History, II.331. Mallett, p. 243.

34. Magdalen College, Oxford MS 281, f. 17.

35. Rowe, 'Influence of the Earls of Pembroke', p. 250. M.B. Rex, University Representation in England 1604-1690 (London, 1954), pp. 76, 114-15.

36. Curtis, p. 171.

37. Wood, History, II.324-6.

38. Arch. Univ. Oxon. W.P.α60(3). In CSP Ven. 1616, p. 245, Pembroke is described by the Venetian Ambassador as 'head of the Puritans' in England.

39. Bodley MS Tanner 74, f. 182.

40. See, for example, W. Dickenson, The King's Right (1619), STC 6821. A. Taylor, Divine Epistles (1623), STC 23720, addresses to Pembroke and the Countess of Montgomery. F. Quarles, Sion's Elegies (1624), STC 2782. G. Goodwin, Babel's Balm. Tr. J. Vicars (1624), STC 12030. A.L., Spiritual Alms (1625), STC 15103. W. Walker, A Sermon ... Nov. 28 1628 (1629), STC 14965. R. Aldsworth, 'Six letters and one oration of the Cardinal D'Ossat ... translated' (c. 1630), Bodley MS Ashmole 768, pp. 272-4. J. Dowle, The True Friend (1630), STC 7101. S. Brooke, 'De auxilio divinae gratiae exercitatus theologica, nimirum', (n.d.), Cambridge University Library MS Add. 44 (xvi).

41. Wood, History, II.344. Mallett, p. 246.

42. Sweeper (1622), STC 23526. Carpenter (1625), STC 4676. D. Featley (1630), STC 10733.

43. Russell, Crisis, pp. 214-15. Heinemann, Puritanism & Theatre, p. 277. Curtis, pp. 212, 224-6.

44. Wood, History, II. 326, 336.

45. Ibid, II.360, 364. Curtis, p.44.

46. James (1625), STC 25935. Statuta Antiqua Universitatis Oxoniensis, ed. S. Gibson (Oxford, 1931), pp. lviii-lix.

47. Works (1629), STC 104, sig. A2ª. Featley (1630), STC 10733, sig. A3ᵇ.

48. Lockyer, Buckingham, p. 9.

49. Quoted in D. Willson, King James VI and I (London, 1956), p. 411.

50. L.B. Wright, 'Propaganda against James I's "Appeasement" of Spain', HLQ, 2 (1943), pp. 149-72.

51. Heinemann, Puritanism & Theatre, pp. 153, 156-9.

52. Listed in Sotheby's Historical Manuscripts Catalogue, 28 March 1983, lot 46. I am grateful to Dr Paul Hopkins for an abstract of this MS. S.L. Adams, 'Captain Thomas Gainsford, the "Vox Spiritus" and the Vox Populi', BIHR, 49-50 (1976-7), p. 141.

53. CSPD. 1621, vol. 108, p. 33. O'Farrell, pp. 97-100, 144.

54. Lockyer, Buckingham, p. 66.

55. Bacon, Works, ed. Spedding, VII.248, 268, 299n; quoted in Briley, p. 669.

56. Heinemann, Puritanism & Theatre, p. 154. APC, July 1621-May 1623, pp. 199-200.

57. Lockyer, Buckingham, pp. 144-54.

58. CSPD. 1623, vols. 139-47, pp. 516, 536, 543-4, 578, 612; cited in Briley, p. 687. Chamberlain, Letters, II.501. Nichols. Progresses of James, IV.883-4.

59. Lockyer, Buckingham, p. 172.

60. S.L. Adams, 'Foreign policy and the parliaments of 1621 and 1624', in Sharpe (ed.), Faction and Parliament, p. 156. Ruigh, Parliament of 1624, pp. 41, 263.

61. CSP Ven. 1624, p. 216, 16 February 1624.

62. Lockyer, Buckingham, pp. 181, 209.

63. See STC 19838.5.

64. National Library of Wales MS 5666D.

65. A Preparation to Suffer for the Gospel of Jesus Christ (1623), STC 7336.

66. Sheldon had dedicated to Pembroke A Survey of the Miracles of the Church of Rome (1616), STC 22399.

67. Heinemann, Puritanism & Theatre, pp. 2, 155, 166, 168.

68. Ruigh, Parliament of 1624, pp. 127, 131.

CHAPTER NINE

1. S.R. Gardiner, History of England ... 1603-1642 (10 vols, London, 1883), V.314.
2. CSPD. 1625, vol. 1, pp. 7, 10.
3. Lockyer, Buckingham, pp. 236-42.
4. HMC Mar & Kellie, Suppl. Rpt., p.233.
5. Gardiner, History, VI.30.
6. Russell, Crisis, p. 303. Hirst, Authority and Conflict, pp. 144-5. R. Tuck, 'The ancient law of freedom: John Selden and the Civil War', in J. Morrill (ed.), Reactions to the English Civil War 1642-1649 (London, 1982), pp. 141, 239.
7. Lords' Journal, III.596; quoted in Briley, p. 801.
8. T. Birch, The Court and Times of Charles I (2 vols, London, 1848), I.123.
9. Lockyer, Buckingham, p. 333.
10. Chamberlain, Letters, II.628. Aylmer, King's Servants, pp. 30, 111.
11. Birch, Charles I, I.378-9, 450.
12. CSPD. 1628, vol. 114, p. 269, and CSPD. Add. 1628, p.290; quoted in Briley, pp. 834-5.
13. Parliaments and Politics, p. 13.
14. Cobbett's Parliamentary History, II.336; quoted in O'Farrell, p. 170.
15. Russell, Parliament and Politics, pp. 13-14.
16. These debates are detailed in O'Farrell, pp. 174ff.
17. STC 10733, sig. A3^a. The Oxford Dictionary of the Christian Church, ed. F.L. Cross (Oxford, 1957), pp. 87-8, 1040, 1239.
18. Jenney, A Catholic Conference (1626), STC 14497. Burges, The Fire of the Sanctuary (1625), STC 4111. Leslie, A Sermon Preached Before His Majesty at Wokin (1627), STC 15495, dedicated to Montgomery. Jackson, A Treatise of the Divine Essence and Attributes (1628), STC 14318. Udny, The Voice of the Crier (1628), STC 24513.
19. STC 25721. Williams also dedicated to Philip Herbert, The Resolution of Pilate (1614), STC 25717, and Seven Golden Candlesticks (1624), STC 25719.
20. The Last Will and Testament of Jesus Christ (1630), STC 24037, sig. A2^a.
21. Earle's elegy is in Bodley MS Rawl. Poet. 172, f. 35. Other elegies are in Bodley MS Rawl. Poet. 147, f. 151 and BL Sloane MS 542, f. 14.
22. The Just Man's Memorial. A Sermon (1630), STC 4931, p. 34.

23. Birch, Charles I, II.73-4.

24. 'Herbertorum Prosapia', Cardiff Central Library Phillipps MS 5.7. HMC 7th Report, pp. 434-5.

25. Chaffinge (1630), Sig. A2ᵇ.

26. 'A sermon preached ... 5th Jan. 1633', Bodley MS Rawl. E.149.

27. Wood, History, II.368. Mallett, p. 303. H. Trevor-Roper, Archbishop Laud 1573-1645 (London, 1940), p. 116.

28. C. Hill, Society & Puritanism in Pre-Revolutionary England (London, 1964; rpt. 1966), p. 108.

29. H. Jeanes, A Treatise Concerning ... Evil (1640), STC 14480.

30. Brief Lives, p. 225.

31. Sutcliffe, Meditations of Man's Mortality (1634), STC 23447, sig. A2ᵃ. Fage, Fame's Roule (1637), STC 10667, p. 23. Preston, The Saint's Qualification. Ed. R. Sibbes and J. Davenport (1633), STC 20262. Read, A Treatise of ... Chirurgery (1638), STC 20786.

32. A.G. Chester, Thomas May: Man of Letters 1595-1650 (Philadelphia, 1932), pp. 49-50, 54, 142.

33. Browne, Poems, ed. Goodwin, I.xxv. The 'Monckton Milnes Manuscript', a verse miscellany (c. 1624-33), bears the note: 'Will. Browne serviens Com. Pembrock'; see Sotheby's Sale Catalogue, 21-22 July 1980, lot no. 585.

34. G.C. Williamson, Lady Anne Clifford ... Her Life, Letters and Work (Kendal, 1922; rpt. 1967), pp. 83, 105, 173. Charles, Herbert, pp. 171-2.

35. The portraits of the first Earl of Pembroke and King Edward VI may predate the 1647 fire.

36. Parry, Golden Age, p. 217.

37. P.W. Thomas, 'Charles I of England. The tragedy of absolutism', in A.G. Dickens (ed.), The Courts of Europe (London, 1977), p. 201. I am grateful to Sir O. Millar for informing me of the present location of this picture.

38. B.S. Long, British Miniaturists Working Between 1520 and 1860 (London, 1929), p. 123. Murdoch, English Miniature, pp. 84, 132-3, 136. J. Murdoch and V.J. Murrell, 'The monogramist D.G.: Dwarf Gibson and his patrons', The Burlington Magazine, 123 (May 1981), pp. 282-9. Aubrey, Wiltshire, p. 91.

39. Aubrey, Wiltshire, p. 88.

40. Ibid., pp. 83-4. Solomon left England in 1613. Aubrey presumably meant Isaac, his son or nephew.

41. Relation of a Short Survey of the Western Counties in 1635, ed. L.G. Wickham Legg, Camden Miscellany, 16

(London, 1936), pp. 66-8. A.A. Tait, 'Isaac de Caus and the south front of Wilton House', The Burlington Magazine, 106 (February 1964), p. 74.

42. 'The south front of Wilton House', The Archaeological Journal, 111 (1955), pp. 181-90, 186. I. de Caus, Wilton Garden (c. 1645), Wing C1530.

43. Hill and Cornforth, English Country Houses, p. 78. J. Harris and A.A. Tait, Catalogue of the Drawings by Inigo Jones, John Webb and Isaac de Caus at Worcester College Oxford (Oxford, 1979), plate 92.

44. Hill and Cornforth, English Country Houses, p. 86. O. Millar, Van Dyck in England (London, 1982), p. 28.

45. Jonson, Works, VII.735-6; X.676-7.

46. The Poems of Thomas Carew, ed. R. Dunlap (Oxford, 1949), pp. xxxv, 59-62, 127-8, 244.

47. P. Edwards, et al., (eds), The Revels History of Drama in English, vol. IV, 1613-1660 (London and New York, 1981), p. 25.

48. Ibid., pp. 57-8, 97-8. Records, ed. Adams, pp. 39, 42, 46-7.

49. Records, ed. Adams, pp. 9, 19, 72-3.

50. Ibid., pp. 44, 64, 121. Chambers, Shakespeare, I. 149. Folger Library MS 2068.7, from Whitehall, 12 March 1630/1.

51. I. Smith, Shakespeare's Blackfriars Theatre (New York, 1964), p. 276.

52. The Malone Collections. Pts. IV & V (Oxford, 1911), pp. 391-2.

53. Chambers, Shakespeare, I.136, 149. Records, ed. Adams, p. 66. See J. Finch, A Letter Sent to the Lord Chamberlain (1640), STC 10875.

54. Heinemann, Puritanism & Theatre, p. 233.

55. Wiltshire, p. 91.

56. Printed in Works, ed. Edwards and Gibson, IV.417-20. William Browne's elegy on Charles is pr. in Works, ed. Goodwin, II.256. M. Butler, Theatre and Crisis 1632-1642 (Cambridge, 1984), p. 54.

57. Butler, Theatre and Crisis, pp. 69, 82.

58. Revels History, 1613-1660, p. xlii. Pembroke's squabble with the Duke of Lennox in 1636 over a box at Blackfriars is noted in A. Gurr, Playgoing in Shakespeare's London (Cambridge, 1987), pp. 197, 200, 204.

59. Rebellion, I.73, III.495. Russell, Parliaments and Politics, p. 13.

60. The Revolt of the Provinces (London, 1976), pp.43-4.

61. Rebellion, I.495. DNB article on Philip Herbert.

62. Catalogue of the Thomason Tracts, 1640-1661 (1908; rpt. 4 vols, Anne Arbor, 1977), I.119, E.150(24); I.176, E121(18); I.177, E121(18); I.188, E126(3); I.187, E124(32); I.188, E126(3). Morrill, Revolt, pp. 36, 42, 102. A. Fletcher, The Outbreak of the English Civil War (London, 1981), p. 277.

63. Clarendon, Rebellion, III.494. Fletcher, Outbreak, p. 399.

64. Bentley, I.34. L. Hotson, The Commonwealth and Restoration Stage (1928), pp. 25, 46, 78.

65. Colvin, 'The south front of Wilton House', p. 189. Hill and Cornforth, English Country Houses, p. 80.

66. The Life and Letters of John Donne, ed. Gosse, II.318.

67. To ... Philip Earl of Pembroke ... Upon His ... Election (1641), Wing C715.

68. H. Ellis (ed), Original Letters Illustrative of English History 2nd ser. (4 vols, London, 1827), III.300-1.

69. See, for example, those listed in Thomason Tracts, I.608-11, 627.

70. Mallett, pp. 352, 357, 376-7.

71. Thomason Tracts, I.675.

72. N.E. MacKenzie, 'Sir Thomas Herbert of Tintern. A Parliamentary "Royalist" ', BIHR, 29 (1956), pp. 32-86.

73. Thomason Tracts, I.738, 743, 757. B. Worden, The Rump Parliament (Cambridge, 1974), pp. 26-8, 73, 178, 180, 192-3.

74. Thomason Tracts, I.783, 785-6.

75. Russell, Crisis, p. 310. Morrill, Revolt, p. 43. Lever, Herberts of Wilton, p. 76. Williamson, Clifford, p. 160.

76. Aubrey, Brief Lives, p. 226. Williamson, Clifford, p. 183.

77. L. Stone, The Crisis of the Aristocracy 1558-1641 (Oxford, 1965), pp. 720, 779, 785. Thomason Tracts, II.64, 'Of the internal and external nature of man in Christ' (1654), bears a note: 'Written by the Earle of Pembrok'.

POSTSCRIPT

1. Williamson, Clifford, pp. 200-3.

2. Churchyard, A Spark of Friendship (1585), STC 5257, sig. A3^b; quoted in Sheavyn, Literary Profession, pp. 33, 35. The Works of John Marston, ed. A.H. Bullen (2 vols, London, 1887), I.5.

3. The Truth of Our Times (1638), STC 19517, pp. 32-4.

Index